Something's Happening Here...
Do You Know What It Is?

A gathering of middle-class men and women who strip naked, throw food at each other, and freely express their desires . . . an outdoor hippie wedding where the bride and groom are forgotten in days of orgiastic celebration . . . a "hate lab" in which a human being's ego is torn to pieces by his fellows . . . a terrifying, illuminating night and day in a universe revealed by LSD . . . agonizing yet exhilarating hours in the lotus position in a Zen monastery . . .

Here is an extraordinary, intensely engrossing report on America's new psychic frontiers—by a young woman who set out to write a story and found herself taking a trip to the unexplored reaches of her consciousness.

"Her book often reads like a novel. But she is presenting the facts."
Louisville Courier-Journal

Other SIGNET Titles of Special Interest

Turning On

by Rasa Gustaitis

A SIGNET BOOK from

NEW AMERICAN LIBRARY

TIMES MIRROR

Library of Congress Catalog Card Number: 68-31278

This is an authorized reprint of a hardcover edition published by
The Macmillan Company.

 SIGNET TRADEMARK REG. U.S. PAT. OFF. AND FOREIGN COUNTRIES
REGISTERED TRADEMARK—MARCA REGISTRADA
HECHO EN CHICAGO, U.S.A.

SIGNET, SIGNET CLASSIC, MENTOR AND PLUME BOOKS
are published by The New American Library, Inc.,
1301 Avenue of the Americas, New York, New York 10019

FIRST PRINTING, MAY, 1970

PRINTED IN THE UNITED STATES OF AMERICA

Contents

Foreword

IT HAD always seemed to me that most people spend the greater part of their lives waiting for something. Until recently, that was certainly true of me. Not that I sat around doing nothing. Quite the contrary. I led an active and varied life as a newspaper reporter and later as a free-lance writer in New York. Self-examiners and Answer-seekers bored me. I had been a Catholic until the dogmas ceased to have meaning for me at age nineteen. Once, for three months, I went to a psychiatrist when I was unable to make an important decision. But that kind of searching did not interest me much. For me, the only way to live fully was by getting outside of myself and acting.

But though I was hardly aware of it, a sense of waiting was always there as an undercurrent to my existence. Most of my work and my adventures seemed, somehow, a preparation or substitute for something else that was, somehow, going to happen. Something was missing in my life. I hadn't the vaguest notion what that was, but it was so important that I tried to keep myself ready for all possibilities. I never made a commitment I could not break and was always prepared to shift direction.

Occasionally, this subterranean current would surface in an irrational sort of urgency. I'd be reading a book, for example, and a vague thought-shadow would press in from the edge of my consciousness, just perceptible enough to divert my attention. Before long I would find that my eyes had run over an entire page but I had not read a word. Or I'd be at a party, or in the middle of some conversation, or enjoying a quiet evening at home and suddenly I'd be seized by a desire to be off and away for there was action elsewhere and I was missing it. Life was passing me by.

The urgency came in cycles. It would grow until everything would go dead, or rather, until I'd go dead to everything. Then

I would break out into something new—new people, new scenes, a trip somewhere. Once I went to Greece, another time to Mexico, a couple of times to the Virgin Islands. With nobody but myself to support, I had a lot of freedom.

I would tell myself that once I was away from my daily rounds I would have the time to lie down on some beach and get everything figured out and under control. For I suspected that I was, somehow, on the wrong track. But when I got to the beach, such thinking became a bore, it only led round and round familiar mazes. So I would let my mind go blank, listen to the wind and the surf and return refreshed. Eventually the urgency and then the deadness would return.

In the spring of 1967 it was time for another trip. So I looked for a writing assignment that would take me out of New York and to some scenic spot for a couple of the hot months. Nothing interesting came to mind until I heard of Esalen Institute in California, where experiments were being conducted in consciousness expansion without the use of drugs. Indirectly, I heard about Esalen through Clay Felker, editor of *New York Magazine,* who sent me to do a story on a weekend encounter group run by Dr. William C. Schutz. It was the first time I ever heard of either Schutz or encounter groups. At this time, twelve people were to meet in a Bronx mansion and spend two days together being entirely honest with each other in context of that time and place. I went with an extremely negative attitude. For Schutz was a psychologist and I expected to find a lot of dull, neurotic people talking about anxiety, penis envy and their mothers, wallowing in self-pity for two interminable days.

But the weekend turned out to be a mind-bender. I got so involved with that group of strangers (all normal neurotics like me), I felt so strongly about them by Sunday, that it seemed we had been shut up together not two days but two years.

The people I met were mostly professionals—businessmen, teachers, social workers, psychologists. Yet all of us behaved in a most uncivilized manner. One woman broke two toes attacking another; a successful financier cowered on the floor and begged people to touch him; I cried, got into a rage, was extremely affectionate, totally lonely, and for the first time in my life physically fought another woman.

For several days after that house party I was shaky. But I also discovered that I was seeing differently. On Monday I went to talk with an editor who wanted to discuss an idea for a book. As he sat behind his desk telling me what he had in mind, I observed that he wasn't talking with me at all—he was talking at me. He was performing with words. It was almost as if he were making faces at himself in a mirror—a one-way mirror that had a little hole in it through which he could pellet words in my direction. Many other scenes, people and relationships also now had a new clarity.

Bill Schutz was then about to leave for Esalen Institute, where his workshops were to be offered as one means of expanding awareness. Some people, he told me, compared the effects of the groups to LSD trips. They were set-breakers: they shook people out of their habits and attitudes and showed them new ways of perceiving themselves and the world.

Esalen sounded worth exploring, particularly since it was situated on the beautiful, rocky coast of Big Sur. I called my friend Alan Rinzler at Macmillan who thought a book called "Turning On Without Drugs" could be just fine. And so, in July, I headed for the West Coast to write something about techniques for getting high, wide and deep without LSD (which I had never taken).

But the subject soon turned out to be larger than I had expected. At Big Sur I was inundated by a flood of entirely new experiences. I flipped—freaked out—forgot about the deadline for the book and found out what it was I had been missing by discovering the turned-on point of view. Before coming to Esalen, I thought "turning on" referred to turn-ons such as marijuana, LSD, or encountering sessions. But out there I saw that it was developing into a whole *Weltanschauung* that was spreading through the middle class of the West Coast and, from there, reaching toward the rest of the country.

In essence, the turn-on message is: clean your perception and you will see that your childhood dream is true. The only obstacle is your own blindness. We have bolloxed ourselves in so that we miss the obvious. Aren't all great discoveries obvious later? Well, turn on—take what is yours. The way is clear and simple. Dig! Life is art. Thou art God. God enjoys being God.

To be turned-on is to be with it, into it, right there; to be fully present at whatever one is in at a particular moment and ready to accept the next moment, whatever it might bring. It is not a matter of performing well but of fully being; not a question of developing a mature attitude toward adult responsibilities but of experiencing anger, love, grief and joy, perceiving subtle inner and outer events and relationships and responding to them clearly and directly.

Nobody is turned on all the time all the way, except perhaps some master gurus and saints. But to the extent that an uptight person turns on, his anxiety becomes excitement. Energy that went toward holding him together radiates outward. Mind, body and senses are freed to reach toward the limits of the possible.

The turned-on person recognizes that continuous change is

the nature of the universe. Everything is part of a constantly flowing pattern of particles. Nothing stands still or is ever repeated. All systems are temporary. There is nothing to cling to. We, as part of it all, change and shift, move and evolve, level beyond level.

So, he says, groove with it. The only way of life that makes sense builds on acceptance of change. We have forgotten this and have built, with our intellects, an illusion of fixed forms and dualities. These, not being natural, have cut us off from life's rhythm and the source of our existence. We have become deformed and are blocked in our growth; the intellect has turned tyrannical and cut us off from our senses, the major vehicles of experience. Perception is dulled and distorted by an endless world-chatter. Our emotions embarrass us and we take tranquilizers to quiet them. We become afraid of risk and fail to realize that to stop is to die.

Now someone who builds his life on acceptance of change cannot rely on the usual props—family, friends, status, property. Nor can he live by a scheme, system or philosophy, on plans for the future or memories of the past. His sense of security must come from within, through a transcendence of self and the capacity to go with changes. This is basic to the turned-on view of life. LSD, Zen, the Maharishi Mahesh Yogi, the Esalen experiences, all lead to this.

Turned-on people tend to think less of risk and security than of "going through changes." and "getting hung up" as alternatives. A man who moves is alive, so motion and change have intrinsic value. Any experience that takes one "far out" is valuable. ("Far out" and "out of sight" is high praise in the hip idiom.) But you cannot stay far out or that too becomes a hangup.

It is not enough—or even necessary—to move physically. The movement is within perception and experience. There are many ways to travel there. Drugs are one, mediation another; encounter groups, fasting, sensory awareness practice, music and dancing, sex and sensuality are still others. Anything that will "blow your mind," blast you out of your frame of reference and into direct contact with the nature of your being and the world around you is a trip. Looking at a flower may do it under the right conditions. So might a sexual orgy. The important thing is to break through mind-sets.

Out of this new attitude there may be emerging a Western *sadhana*, in the view of Michael Murphy, the founder and president of Esalen Institute. Murphy is super-turned-on. He is boyish, charming, enthusiastic, meditates daily, runs a million-dollar-a-year institution without being frantic, and has great hopes for the future of Western man. In the fifties he spent eighteen months meditating at the Sri Aurobindo Ashram in Pondicherry, India, and returned with a new vision of man as a creature emerging through levels of consciousness. He founded Esalen (named after a local Indian tribe) as a forum for exploring that idea. Since then he has become one of the spokesmen for the new life style.

The West lacks a concept of *sadhana,* which is a Sanskrit word that may be roughly translated as "the way." Almost every other culture has some growth discipline to guide man in his unconscious groping toward ecstasy, knowledge and meaning, he says. The West, without one, has been spiritually impoverished. But now he sees the emergence of a new *sadhana* that could become the greatest ever developed because of the enormous resources available to Western man.

Most sadhanas have been ascetic and stressed the development of inner states. One got one's life and affairs in order and proceeded to concentrate on the spirit. The new Western *sadhana,* as Murphy sees it emerging, involves three things: the inner state, sensory and kinesthetic development, and human relationships as something mysterious and ecstatic.

He suggests that in other cultures asceticism was a necessity because there was no other way to overcome the problem of hunger, poverty and physical suffering. But in the affluent society, the struggle for that kind of survival is largely over. In other cultures, barriers to the senses were needed because sensual involvement meant children and serious limits to a man's freedom. Now this too is no longer a problem. So, says Murphy, the Western *sadhana* can be rich and subtle, joyous and expansive.

Huston Smith, professor of philosophy at the Massachusetts Institute of Technology, advances a related view. There is now emerging, he says, a new world culture that draws from the strengths of the Chinese, Indian and Western cultures. The Chinese developed social stability, the Indians developed spiritual growth as ways to survive in the midst of a hostile and overwhelming nature. The West has won man's struggle for survival against nature and also developed a concept of individual liberty. Now all three are learning and adapting from the others and a new great world civilization may be coming.

All this is grand and speculative. But to many Americans, the turned-on attitude is extremely frightening. It threatens values that are held dear, even though many of them no longer make sense in the present context. Hard work, material prosperity, duty, marital stability and sexual constancy are all up for reexamination. The turned-on person will point out that perhaps man's ultimate evolution will bring him to a state where he will no longer work, only play. There is no work, after all, in the Western idea of heaven.

The turned-on life style grows directly out of the psychedelic experience, which has led to new forms of art and music, a new interest in Eastern philosophy and religion, to the hippies and other evolving life-styles. But, particularly on the West Coast, many people outside of artistic and bohemian circles—psychologists, physicians, journalists, businessmen, teachers—also took LSD, began to smoke grass regularly, and found themselves veering in new directions. They became aware that our culture emphasizes action but does not train us adequately to watch, listen, and allow things to happen. The forward-thrusting individual, they found, has lost touch with his context. He feels isolated because he no longer senses how he is part of the whole flow of life.

Through LSD, these people became interested in meditation, in subtler sensory awareness, in expanding the power and energies of the mind, body and spirit. They gathered around yogis and gurus who had been working quietly for years in isolated corners and who until now many had viewed as quacks, if they had heard of them at all. And so the new life-style took shape and spread far beyond the psychedelic drug scene. Now people who would never think of trying LSD or even grass are turning on.

But though drugs were the direct catalyst for the new world view, it caught on because the time was ripe for it. In the 1960s, almost all prophets and wise men agreed, something was dreadfully wrong with the state of the nation.

A sense of wholeness, which healthy men and healthy societies have, was missing in urban America. Everything—man and his world—was fractured, compartmentalized and contradictory: the country had never been so rich, yet poverty was an ever more stubborn and divisive condition. Never had so much material comfort been available to so many, yet millions found life too hard to bear without daily tranquilizers or stimulants. Civil liberties were expanding, yet imaginative and intelligent people complained that their chance to contribute to society creatively was shrinking. The more life was compartmentalized, the more did people write, talk and study the subject of creativity. Corporations even had departments of creativity. And the more the preoccupation with creativity grew, the less did many people feel it as part of the daily flow of their lives.

The spiritual hunger was aggravated, in the mid-1960s, by a growing awareness that the entire social-political structure was somehow out of control.

Hans J. Morgenthau, the author of *Politics of Power*, wrote in the *New Republic* of October 28, 1967, "It is the distinctive and ominous mark of the present crisis that it has produced no remedy consonant with the ideals of America. It could not have produced one, for the inability to do so is an element of the crisis itself. The democratic state is in a blind alley, and so is American democracy."

The basic safeguard to the people's interest in democratic states has always been their power to overthrow the government, Morgenthau pointed out. This is no longer possible now when the government has a monopoly of most destructive weapons and can take over control of most effective transportation and communication facilities at an instant, he argued. The people's recourse now is voting.

But the vote has lost much of its meaning because most important government decisions are now enormously complex. "Thus the great national decisions of life and death are rendered by technological elites, and both the Congress and the people at large retain little more than the illusion of making the decisions which the theory of democracy supposes them to make."

The citizen feels powerless. He is also ambivalent toward his government, knowing that, should it make a serious error in its peacekeeping operations, it would cease to be his protector and become his destroyer.

In the United States, Morgenthau wrote, this general crisis of democracy was further aggravated by a widening racial conflict and the war in Vietnam.

Morgenthau's view of the future was gloomy. He saw a trend toward violence and repression rather than toward democratic solutions. By the time the gravity of the situation becomes clear to the powers that make decisions, he suggested, it may be too late for democratic solutions.

In recent years, many social reformers lost faith in the possibility of change through the political process and sought them through demonstrations, civil disobedience and the disruption of government machinery. But as the Vietnam war and racial guerrilla warfare in the cities continued to grow, even direct action of this sort began to seem futile.

And so people—especially young people—who, under other circumstances, might have become political leaders, now withdrew completely from the political process and began to look for areas where individual effort and dedication would yield creative satisfaction. They turned their energies to themselves and their immediate surroundings. Travelers on the turn-on circuit tend to be apolitical but interested in social experiments such as communes, tribal and extended families. They talk a lot about building world peace through the search for personal peace.

The hippies popularized the turned-on attitudes. But over-exposure in the press led to a pollution of hippie scenes, like the Haight-Asbury. By the end of the summer of 1967, the name "hippie" had acquired such ugly connotations that the true hippies, the ones who knew what the turned-on life-style was, made a public announcement that the hippie was dead. Most left the Haight and the East Village of New York to pursue their lives in less exposed communities and left their old haunts to lost and delinquent adolescents who wore bells and beads.

The early appeal of the hippies to many middle-class squares was evidence, however, that they spoke to general hungers and needs. Together with the hippie movement, new social institutions, frequented by squares more than hippies, began to appear. One of them was the drug-free turn-on center.

Esalen is the biggest, oldest and most influential of these. During its first year of operation, in 1962, it was the site only of summer weekend seminars. Alan Watts, the Zen interpreter, Charlotte Selver, the sensory awakener, Paul Tillich, the existential Protestant theologian and Abraham Maslow, author of *Toward a Psychology of Being,* were among the first to conduct these. By 1967, Esalen was a million-dollar-a-year operation with several workshops going at the same time year-round, in San Francisco as well as on Big Sur. It had a year-round program for resident fellows who spent an academic year at Esalen learning from the various resident and visiting gurus and who later went out to spread their new knowledge.

The emphasis at Esalen was more psychological and sensual than mystical. It was a center for the group of existential and humanistic psychologists whom Maslow has called "The Third Force." Psychoanalysis and behaviorism are still the twin mainstream in American psychology, but the third force is gaining ground. It emphasizes growth, the development of potential and "self-actualization," rather than dwelling on neuroses and seeking cures for them. The Third Force people, together with some therapists and teachers concerned with sensory education, are sometimes referred to as the Human Potentialities Movement. Most of its key people pass through Esalen at one time or another.

Seminars listed in the spring 1968 catalog included a discussion of the state of the nation in the year 2000 as foreseen by Watts, Herman Kahn, author of *On Thermonuclear War,* and Carl Rogers, the originator of nondirective therapy and now one of the most well-known encounter group leaders. There was also a seminar on hypnosis, brain-wave conditioning, meditation and psychedelic drugs, and a weekend on "the possibilities of creating a radically open society in which self-disclosure leads people toward solidarity, adventure and unexpected joy," by Sidney Jourard, author of *The Transparent Self*.

Several centers modeled after Esalen sprang up in other parts of the country. They included Kairos in Rancho Santa Fe, near San Diego, California, and Aureon in New York.

The Zen Mountain Center in Tassajara Springs, California, is another kind of center. Here, though the aims are similar to Esalen's, the approach is very different. Hard work and discipline are the rule and there is no time or interest in freakouts and emotional explosions. Many people go there after LSD experiences.

Tassajara is also, in another way, an experimental community for turned-on people. It offers lessons in a style of life that many who come there for training later continue elsewhere. In that way it is similar to the Morningstar Ranch of summer 1967, which on the surface, was as different from Tassajara as a group of children during class recess is from cadets at military review. Where at Tassajara a meal was a silent and elaborately simple ceremony, at Morningstar that summer, very properly raised young people ate stew out of tin lids and paper cups with their fingers. Yet both communities aimed, in their way, to tune into natural rhythms.

Another turn-on institution, the encounter group (I will here call it truth lab) emerged as a type of emotional gymnasium and instant village. Here people gather to limber up emotionally the way they go to the more traditional kind of gym to get into condition physically. They also find the intimacy that is often missing in their daily lives. Techniques used in these groups vary considerably from the hostile attacks used in Synanon games to a more gentle approach practiced by Dr. Carl Rogers.

As the turned-on life-style spread, turn-on gurus emerged from cultish obscurity to the covers of popular magazines. They come in three basic types: mystical, physical and drug-oriented. Among the mystics, Maharishi Mahesh Yogi enjoyed a sudden, though brief, popularity in 1967-68 However, the followings of others also gained significantly in number. Vedantists, yogis and swamis flourished. Among the drug-oriented gurus, Timothy Leary enjoyed the greatest renown. Many others, however, worked with less publicity, sometimes even with great secrecy. For the sale of LSD was illegal.

The physical turn-on gurus worked through movement, manipulation of the body and concentration on proprioceptive sensations and changes, including brain-wave control. Research on the various turn-on techniques and games was being conducted in several universities and at the Western Behavioral Sciences Institute in La Jolla, which is a think tank of turned-on people.

During the summer and fall of 1967 and into the winter, I visited many of these places and people. I got to know psychologists, mystics, hippies, Zen practitioners and individuals who belonged to no group at all but practiced the new style of life in their own fashion. Everywhere I heard of other names and places that were relevant to the general theme but it was impossible to visit all of them. Almost everywhere I participated rather than just observing. Much of what I experienced I found impossible to describe in words because we have an inadequate vocabulary for experiences in consciousness. In Zen, words and the intellect are understood to be like a finger pointing to the moon. Only a fool takes the finger for the moon.

If we take eternity to mean not infinite temporal duration but timelessness, the eternal life belongs to those who live in the present.

LUDWIG WITTGENSTEIN

Turning On

Chapter ONE

Huh?

THIS MUST be the world's scariest airport, as befits Los Angeles. They should put up banners everywhere: "Welcome to the world's first anti-city." They should, really. For the last two hours they've had me trapped here in a glass cage. They? Yes, *They*. L.A. is run by *Them*, you know, the people behind all those plots. I'm getting paranoid. But two hours of sitting in that terminal behind glass, staring out at planes gliding by on a desert of patched cement—that can get to you. The chairs were extremely comfortable, of course. But I knew that the only way out was by some kind of vehicle. You can fly, you can ride, but *walking is strictly forbidden*.

Yes, I'm glad to be in this plane at last with the doors shut, the steps being wheeled away. But even here the scene fails to regain reality. Outside someone has forgotten a chrome and blue canvas wheelchair. The jet blast catches it, whips it backward, it careens and crashes against a ramp railing. Not a human being is in sight anymore, just this fragile wheelchair with its blue canvas fluttering wildly in the cement landscape. I hear the sound of air escaping. Nobody comes to get the chair. It still flaps as we rumble away. Good-bye, good-bye, happy retirement someone.

I'm en route to Monterey, where I'm to be met by a car from Esalen Institute and driven out to Big Sur. Whatever Esalen turns out to be, at least I can't miss on the scenery. The very name, Big Sur, calls forth visions of Henry Miller glowering from atop a rock into the foaming sea, of beats clambering up mountainsides toward mystical picnics, of Edward Weston's photographs of gnarled tree stumps and water-splashed rocks. I peer down through the little round window. Below is a vast, forested mountain range. This too, like the airport, is out of scale with man, but it isn't frightening, it's grand. The earth's wrinkled skin lies there—the Los Padres National Forest, two hundred miles long, stretching some thirty miles inland. Somewhere down there is San Luis Obispo and farther on is Monterey. Between the two, the eighty-mile stretch of Pacific Ocean edge is Big Sur. Back home in New York my friends are now leaving offices, dressing for dinner, crowding past subway turnstiles. And here I am, at the other rim of the continent, up in space in the midst of clear air on a sunny afternoon, headed for—who cares?—headed somewhere.

The pilot points out Carmel Valley slightly toward the right. We half circle it, wheel seaward and swoop down to land at a nondescript little airport. Here I collect my two suitcases, typewriter and tape-recorder and sit down to wait. Whoever is coming to get me apparently has not yet arrived.

Before long, the door at the other end of the waiting room is flung open and an odd sort of person enters and approaches the ticket counter. He looks like Heidi's grandpa as a young man. The sunburned face is young but the thin shaggy beard and pulled-back long hair are graying. He has on a faded blue workshirt, gray corduroy pants, brown unpolished boots, and a necklace of blue beads strung on a strip of leather. At the ticket counter he pulls a slip of paper from his shirt pocket, stares at it a moment and says something to the ticket girl. She bends toward a microphone and calls my name. I get up. Heidi's grandpa comes toward me. His name, let's say, is Nils. His eyes are pale blue and alert.

"This all your stuff?" he asks.

"Yes."

He tucks the typewriter and tape-recorder under his arms, picks up the two suitcases and walks out the way he came, with a bouncing gait. I follow. Just out the door he suddenly stops and stares out into the field where a small propeller plane is just about to take off. He is transfixed—completely motionless, holding the two suitcases, the typewriter and the tape-recorder, he stands there for quite a while, maybe three or five minutes. Then he laughs. It's a sudden laugh that explodes and ends abruptly. "That's a Stinson," he says, thrusting his chin toward the disappearing plane. "You hardly ever see them anymore." And he bounces toward a black sedan with "Esalen Institute" printed on its side.

After he has loaded my gear into the trunk and we've started up the road he is silent a few moments, then starts talking quickly, excitedly. "Ha! I don't read newspapers, I forget about the war, then I come down here one day and the place is full of the army. Wow! I thought it had happened—

22

we really were in it. Eighty million dollars worth of equipment they blew up last week."

"Who?"

"The Vietnamese. With a missile. They must have wheeled it up a hill by hand and pow! Eighty million dollars worth of our machinery gone. Ha!" He slaps his right thigh and again laughs in that sudden way, delighted, it seems, at the weirdness of that picture in his mind of gigantic machinery exploding because some small barefoot men wheeled a missile up a hill.

"Most of the time I don't even know there's a war on, though," he adds, in a calm voice now but with satisfaction. Apparently he thinks that's good, not knowing about it. I study him covertly. He isn't really like Heidi's grandpa, he's more like someone who grew up running around with wild animals in the woods, eating roots and berries. That way of sudden movement and sudden stillness is more typical of deer, foxes and rabbits than of people I know. I guess he's a hippie, with that hair and beard—the beard is completely untrimmed and some hairs are much longer than others—though that workshirt, tidy and worn by many washings, is more a farmer's.

"I have to stop at Carmel to pick up a woman and I'd also like to get some ice cream," he says.

"Fine, I'm in no hurry."

Carmel is a pretty gift shop of a town filled with whitehaired old ladies in expensive simple linen dresses and boys and girls who probably attend some country day school. Geraniums stand in the window boxes of cheerful frame hotels; the square in the center of town is daintily landscaped with trees and flowers. We park and walk toward the ice-cream place outside of which the woman Nils is to pick up is already waiting. When I see her, standing on the corner clutching a paper bag with two cartons of Pall Malls protruding, I feel a stab of anxiety about the nature of Esalen. For here is the typical spa frequenter: fading belle with varicose veins and Red Cross shoes, lips painted just a little too crimson and a little too pouting; face well-creamed and patted for years, brown hair hanging down to the middle of her back littlegirl-style; a drip-dry pastel print cotton dress and the type of floppy blue straw hat that is sold on St. Thomas. Her voice and manner suggest the aging actress.

"Well, there you are at last," she says to Nils. "Hello, there, I hear we're both from New York. My name is Penelope Twillig." (I've changed her name.)

I introduce myself. It develops that she lives in a modest

23

but respectable hotel in Manhattan, is a free-lance writer—vague, though, about recent work—and travels a lot. She came here especially for Dr. Frederick Perls' month-long workshop and regrets she won't be able to stay on to see a little more of California. But there is the matter of the thirty-day excursion air fare. So, instead, she will be going to Europe in September.

I wonder how typical Penelope is of the people I'm about to meet. But the view soon puts all thoughts out of my mind. This is the coastline I've been looking forward to, the cliffs on the abrupt edge of the continent. At the first sight of the Sur, Penelope, who is in the back seat, gasps theatrically. Nils says nothing but his eyes sparkle and there is just a slight twitch of a smile on his lips. After a while he swerves to the shoulder and stops. "Come look," he says, getting out. "Sea otters."

We peer down a cliff of perhaps a hundred feet toward a tiny rocky beach. Through the surf sound comes barking. Dozens of sleek brown animals are sunning on the rocks or bobbing in the water. Suddenly I blink and am lightheaded. This must be the way prisoners feel during the first moments after their release. I think of Manhattan only hours away and the roar of the subway in my ears. There is too much fresh air, too much brightness all at once. Below me is the near-perpendicular cliff, the ocean and otters barking; behind me is the thin strip of road and the cliff continuing its rise toward meadows of burnt gold. The road is just a thin ledge cut into the mountainside. Some of the peaks just above are two thousand feet high.

Nils hands me a small yellow flower. We climb back into the car and continue on for about an hour. He keeps pointing out things along the way—down there in a gully a place perfect for picnics, up there a dark green canyon filled with red-woods, farther on a small A-frame house built halfway out over a cliff. Is he being the tour guide, doing his duty by pointing out sights to the tourists?

"Have you been at Esalen long?" I ask him.

"A year and a half. I came for a seminar and stayed to work. But now I hardly ever go to the seminars anymore. For me that's not where the action is. See, there are three parts to Esalen—there are the seminars, that's how they make their money. There's the people that work there, and the heads in the hills, the drug scene. The heads come around but Esalen has nothing to do with that. Neither do I. I don't even smoke. If you don't get fresh air or if you smoke you're

24

partly dead. You just can't experience a lot of what's around you. I used to live in Los Angeles. Man!"

Well, if Nils is a hippie he's an unusual one. He's the healthiest-looking hippie I've ever seen and his attitude toward drugs is unusual. But then, what I know of hippies is almost all secondhand.

We stop once more, to look at a waterfall that drops into the ocean from some rocks on a peninsula below the road. Nils squats in the grass, chin in right hand, and again becomes immobile, like a wood creature listening. I decide he isn't being the tour guide.

Continuing along the winding highway we eventually come to a carved wooden sign reading: "Esalen. By reservation only." Nils turns sharply to the right and drives slowly down the steep access road into what its catalog describes as "a center to explore those trends in religion, philosophy and the behavioral sciences which emphasize the potentialities of human existence."

From the top of the road it looks like a motel set in a valley that swoops down and then, leveling, slides gently toward the cliffs that plunge into the ocean. A long, low redwood building—the lodge—faces a well-kept broad lawn that runs to the cliff's top, interrupted on its southerly end by an irregularly shaped swimming pool. Above the lodge three rows of redwood cabins stand in terraces. Another row, of more recent construction, veers south, following the curve of the shore inwards. There is a bay to the south of the valley, creating a particularly grand view of the mountain-shoreline farther south.

At the bottom of the access road a huge man with a mustache, wearing a leather vest but no shirt, steps out from under a big tree and waves us on. "That's Robot, the gate man," Nils says. He looks tough enough to be a bodyguard to the King of Saudi Arabia.

Nils pulls into the big parking lot at the northern end of the lodge and we get out. From this perspective the place loses its standard motel appearance. First of all there are the cars in this lot. Many of them are doubling as houses, although not one is a trailer. There's a Volkswagen bus with bright curtains in all the back windows, a pickup truck with a homemade plywood top and, inside it, a mattress covered with an Indian print; a blue panel truck decorated in blazing Day-Glo and undulating script: "Earthquake Evader." Another truck, an old one, is equipped with a small bottled gas stove. This is a gypsy camp.

Now I notice there are quite a few make-shift shelters in this valley. Up the hill, near the highway, there is a small geodesic dome, a trailer and a semicircular house. A few more trailers stand north of the parking lot. The lawn on the north apparently leads to a canyon.

"The office is right here, the first door," Nils says, pointing toward the lodge. "You get your key there."

Following him, I glimpse a girl in a long cotton dress made of the same Indian cotton print that covered the mattress in one of those trucks. She is sitting on some wooden steps behind the lodge. Her shoulders are hunched forward, her long brown hair hangs like a curtain around her knees. She is eating from a plate furtively, with her fingers. Again I think of gypsies. They used to come around to the house when I was a child in Lithuania. The women wore full-skirted long dresses and lots of jangling silver jewelry. They ate in our kitchen and were foreign and magic. I was both afraid and fascinated by them.

A dozen or more of these local gypsies are drooping in the sunshine outside the office door. A thin, Beatle-haired lad in blue jeans and a marching-band jacket trimmed with red is leaning against a rail that separates the cement passageway from the lawn. Sitting next to him on the rail is a tall, bearded fellow in a multi-colored poncho. Several more are lying or sitting limply on the lawn. Most of the boys and men are bearded, a couple of the girls are in long dresses and barefoot. I see that, as Nils said, the seminars are not the whole scene here. The Hot Springs, as this place is called by Big Sur residents, is also a gathering place for mountain people and a meeting ground for mountain and city-hip gypsies. But of that I am to learn only later.

Nils leaves me at the office where I get the key to my cabin and meet Michael Murphy, the founder and president of Esalen. I recognize him right away from a photograph in *Look* in which he was pictured with arms spread and face turned upward against a background of rocks and sea—a handsome dark-haired young man in an ecstatic attitude. Now he's on the phone, beaming as he talks. The intonation suggests an upper-class upbringing. The blue jacket and light slacks are smart but neither hip nor especially stylish.

When he puts down the receiver I introduce myself. "Hello, yes! You made it. That's marvelous." His hand goes out, he's overwhelmingly friendly. "Why don't you drop your things and come down for a drink. I'll meet you out on the deck, that's on the other end of the lodge."

"Great. I'll be right there."

My room, on the second terrace above the lodge, is an ordinary motel room. I'm sharing it with another woman who isn't here yet. But the view from the deck, where I go as soon as I've changed into slacks and sweater, is something else. The deck itself is like a landlocked ship's deck, with wooden floor and wrought-iron railing. To the west is the lawn and the ocean. To the south, where the coast swoops inland and out again around the bay, I see surf rushing at the rocky foot of a mountain. There is no sign of a beach anywhere. The ocean is yards away, yet inaccessible because of the cliffs.

Several people are standing around or sitting on the deck's benches. They are of varying ages, with neat haircuts and quite ordinary clothes—plaid shirts, madras bermuda shorts, jeans and sweaters. There is not a single gypsy among them. I recall that on that other porch, the little one by the office, I did not see anyone who did *not* look like one.

Murphy is waiting by the western railing. "What'll you have?" he asks. "Beer? Sherry?" I'd like a scotch, but none is proffered. The bar, I find out later, serves no hard liquor. "A sherry, thanks."

He disappears into the building and emerges with one glass of sherry, which he hands me. I transfer my cigarette to my left hand to take it. Suddenly I'm aware of my New York pallor and the smoke in my lungs. Murphy doesn't smoke, he doesn't drink; he's charming and enthusiastic and unbearably wholesome.

"So tell me about this book of yours," he says. "What's it about?"

"I'm not sure yet, completely. Tell me about Esalen."

"Well, it's growing. I'm not here much now because I'm pretty involved with the center we're starting in San Francisco. It's going to be in the basement of Grace Cathedral, right there under the Gothic arches. That's good. One thing we're trying to do here is to jump the gap between religious concerns and experience and work in the behavioral sciences. We're dealing with what Aldous Huxley has called the nonverbal humanities." Huxley talked about training in perception and awareness that would help people to realize their potentialities. Others have referred to this kind of education as affective—rather than cognitive—learning.

"This is an immensely important but delicate problem, bringing together the religionists and the scientists," Murphy says. "B. F. Skinner's work has directly to do with what religion people are concerned about."

He notices that everyone has gone inside. "Come, let's get some dinner," he says. "We can talk later."

27

We enter the lodge through glass doors and pass through an empty room. "This is where seminars are held," Murphy says. "Are you in the one this weekend?"

"Yes."

The weekend has been billed, in the Esalen catalog, as "a marathon group encounter between races" under the direction of George Leonard, the West Coast managing editor of *Look* and vice president of Esalen, and Price Cobbs, a black psychiatrist from San Francisco. "Racial confrontation as transcendental experience" is the seminar's title. I do not see many blacks around but assume they must be inside the dining room.

Beyond the seminar room is a plain rectangular room with large windows to the west, now illuminated by the sun setting over the ocean. At long wooden tables lit by candles, people are eating. Barefoot girls with floor-length cotton dresses and flowers in their long hair serve food behind a buffet table opposite the windows. Soft baroque music filters through the chatter. We take our plates filled with food and look for empty seats. All are filled. Murphy leads the way into the bar, a smaller and darker adjoining room, where we find places at the second of two tables.

The diners in the bar are the gypsies I saw outside the office. The people from the deck are in the other room. In here they speak softly or not at all. From out there comes the roar of loud voices and shrill laughter.

A cheerful, very straight-backed man comes to sit next to us. George Leonard. We talk a bit about the coming weekend. "I just invented a new name for these groups," I tell him. "I like it better than T-group or encounter group or sensitivity training. They're lovelabs or truth labs. But don't spread it around. I want to save it for my book. What do you think?"

"Listen," says George Leonard, "when you've been here awhile you'll stop worrying about somebody stealing your ideas. You'll find there's no idea shortage."

"Yeah, well . . ." I gulp, shamed and instantly angry at him for making me feel ashamed. Mike Murphy says nothing but as he looks at me, amused, I become painfully aware of my tight little ambition. He seems to emanate some attitude that is just the opposite of idea-clutching. I don't feel hostile toward him—only small. And I begin to appreciate there's more to him than bright wholesomeness. Leonard leaves, we finish eating.

Before long, the main room has emptied. "You better go," Mike Murphy says. "I think they're ready to start."

In the next room, I find about forty people sitting in a huge circle on folding chairs. To my dismay, I count only six blacks among them. We introduce ourselves, stating names, occupations and why we're here. Many are social workers, students, psychologists, teachers, or have some personal stake in better race relations. In age they range from people in their twenties to gray-haired men and women.

The scene strikes me as rather depressing. For outside the moon has risen and the night is drawing me out of the room. After many months in New York I'm so starved for the sight and sound of nature that the temptation to get up and leave this smoky room is almost irresistible. But I came here for a purpose and I will persist.

The idea of this seminar is similar to that of Dr. William C. Schutz's encounter group, which I attended in New York. Everyone is to become open and honest and react to each other in a spontaneous manner, whether this turns out to be friendly or hostile. In this way, the hope is that we will rise beyond racial hangups and see each other more clearly.

We are divided into groups of about ten, draw our chairs into small circles and begin to get acquainted. Each group has its own black man. Some have two. It wasn't meant to be that way, but that's the way it turns out. Now, Leonard suggests, it might be a good idea if everyone took a look at everyone else and gave an initial impression of what he perceived.

A very young, very pretty blond girl walks around our circle hugging everyone and telling each either "I like you" or "I hope I'll like you." A slightly older girl—who turns out to be my roommate—sits down in the middle of the circle, pouts, and looks around. She tells the solitary black among us that she finds him sexy. The man shrugs and does not reply. A scraggly-haired, thin woman with uneven teeth and a ravaged face talks a lot, gesturing nervously with her hands, but I can't keep my mind on what she's saying, I only see her grimaces. Next to me sits a morose social worker with a walrus mustache and underarm odor. It's hot in here, we're sweating. I couldn't be less interested in becoming intimately acquainted with these people.

George Leonard and Price Cobbs walk from group to group, eavesdropping. After we've gone on for some time, they suggest we go out onto the deck together. This delights me, except that once we get out there—and the scene is indeed magic with the moon glittering on the water, dark mountains looming beyond, and the coolness—our group gets into a tight circle, linking arms around shoulders, and I'm

29

wedged between the sweaty social worker and a young woman with heavy breasts who wears no bra under her tired sweater. The circle sways back and forth, bodies touching, faces turned upward to the sky. Someone begins to hum and others pick up the sound. What is this I have gotten into? These people are nuts! Locked in there with them, swaying, I remember a young man once telling me, with repulsion, about his cultish mother who, he said, used to flit around on the grass in the morning ecstatically licking the dew. Never mind, now is the time for fortitude. I came here as a reporter. I will not separate myself from this human vise.

Somehow, the evening passes. At eleven o'clock, towels are distributed and everyone walks down the hill to the hot sulphur spring baths. These are not, as I had expected, of tiled Roman-styled vastness. They are more like three-car garages —one for men, one for women—open to the sea and furnished with cinderblock tubs about three feet high and six by six feet horizontally. But they are set on a ledge carved out of the cliff and, leaning on the wooden railing, one has the sea below and all around.

Our whole group, men and women together, have gone into the men's side and there shed all garments, put them on wooden tables near the tubs and, white bodies glowing in the moonlight, piled thigh-to-belly into the tubs. The water is hot and the steam has a faint sulphur smell. There are forty of us for the three tubs, so it's impossible to avoid touching. Again I'm in a human pile, this time a nude one in the moonlight —for there is not even a candle down here. People in our tub are quiet. From the adjoining one come squeals. "We've got twenty-four in here," a woman yells. "Is that a record. We've set a record!"

"Twenty-four! Wow! I'm coming in too!" A man pops out of my tub and runs across to cause more squeals next door. My pouting roommate, who turns up beside me, ducks underwater and lets her hair caress others' legs. "Marvelous, a hair trip!" someone says as she emerges. Too much. This is too much. I can't take any more tonight. I climb out, get dressed, walk back up the path and go straight to bed. My roommate turns up toward early morning. She found a racial confrontation with the black she thought sexy early in the evening.

I wake to a delicious sound—a flute being played somewhere, snatches of tune, then silence, then some more. Pulling aside the curtain by my bed I see only gray mist. The sound approaches, grows distant, disappears. It leaves me glad, for it is like a promise that there is more here than what I've experienced thus far.

The rest of the day turns out to be as unpleasant as the previous night, though there is, thank God, no more clinging and swaying around in humming ecstasy. There are too few black men present for a true racial encounter. Someone says a group from Watts is expected, but it fails to appear. The blacks present provide what confrontation they can manage. A middle-aged professional man does the angry black power part. A lighter-skinned young teacher tells a pretty white girl she's only looking for excitement in her affairs with blacks. The girl starts to cry. But my impression is that this is all some kind of display. The blacks are doing their part, as they would at a chic Manhattan party.

By mid-morning, like a gift from the clouds, a black construction worker from the Monterey vicinity appears among us. It's a mystery how he found his way up here or why he thought it worthwhile to spend $67 for this weekend, but here he is, nonetheless, a true lower-class spade, so authentic that he doesn't even remove his brown felt hat indoors. Immediately he is pounced upon as the spokesman for the oppressed. He becomes the recipient of all white guilt gifts.

I grow ever more weary. That angry black power man was busy with the NAACP and the Urban League when that was the thing for a rising young colored professional to do. Now, however, he has become a black man and, as is now the way, is telling his liberal friends to go to hell. Okay, fine, he meant it then and means it now. But why does it sound so contrived to me? I had an open racial confrontation or two in Harlem during the past couple of years as a reporter. An activist woman who had sent her eight children through school on a maid's wages had shot pure venom at me. "There's no point in talking with you," she had said before I even began to interview her. "You're white, I'm black. Your press twists everything." Those words got to me. But this black power man, saying very similar things, does not touch me. Perhaps it is the setting, this spa we're in.

At mid-afternoon, there is a pleasant interruption. Bernard Gunther, a slim, tall and sunburned man with hair combed in a mild version of early Beatles style, comes in and announces he is about to conduct a sensory awareness session on the deck. Part of the group says they don't want to be interrupted, but about twenty of us go out into the sun.

Sheets are given each of us. We spread them on the floor and lie down on them. Gunther asks questions that direct our attention to different parts of our bodies—"How much space

31

is there between your eyes and the back of your head? What part of your back is touching the floor? Can you feel your toes without moving them?" It's very relaxing.

After a while we stand up and each take a partner. We stand facing each other and look at each other. Then one steps behind the other and quickly, gently, taps him with bent fingers of both hands, loose-wristed, over the head. Then we stop to look at each other again. One keeps his eyes closed, then opens them and we look at each other.

After the head-tapping, we slap each other's shoulders and arms, then begin to move around with our eyes closed, stopping to feel other people's hands and shoulders and trying to gather something about the person they belong to. I am surprised how much one can tell in this way. Opening my eyes to check out my touch impressions, I find no conflict. I only see the person more clearly than I would without the exercise.

The session revives me but it is all too brief. The room, once I return to it, seems even more dreary, the talk and arguments even more tedious. Every once in a while, looking out through the glass doors, I see bearded men in deerskin jackets or blanket vests and girls with quiet faces and long hair. They drift by or stop to sit on the benches of the deck for a while and look out over the water. They look so happy and peaceful. I feel like a schoolgirl forced to do arithmetic while others, just outside the windows, may play. The seminar drags on into the night. A surfeit of words clogs my brain. I shrink into myself and feel more and more hostile and lonely.

On Sunday morning, during the gathering's last hours, there is finally a catharsis. The scraggly-haired woman who grimaced and gestured so much the first evening explodes with the information that she was married to a black and has a son. Then she pauses and, in an anguished voice, says, "Lately, I've been trying to make contact with Negro men because I've given up on white men."

It is a shattering statement. There is a moment of total silence. Then the tall black social worker beside her, who is married to a white woman and was reserved all weekend, leans toward her and embraces her. She falls against his shoulder and begins to sob. This really gets to me. Tears begin to rise to my eyes. To prevent myself from crying, I go out to the deck.

After lunch they all go home. Now, suddenly, it seems as if I've just arrived. Mike Murphy has gone back to San Francisco, all the people I spent the weekend with are gone, I know nobody here—except Nils, whom I have not seen since Friday, and Gia-Fu Feng, a staff member at Esalen who took part in the seminar. I watched Gia-Fu with pleasure during the weekend for, in an Oriental way, he had the same quality of sudden movement and sudden stillness I had seen in Nils. Only Gia-Fu was more graceful. Small, wiry, thin but strong-looking in his khakis and frayed red sweatshirt, he was like a gnarled plum tree that comes to life as a Chinese dancer.

"I am going to take a meditation walk up the mountain," he now says when I meet him on the deck. "Would you like to come? It is a four-hour walk."

"Will there be time before dinner?"

"I do not eat dinner. I take a little yeast before I go to bed."

"I'll come with you part way if that's all right?"

"Three o'clock. I will meet you here."

At precisely three o'clock, I find Gia-Fu striding in circles around the deck and breathing deeply.

"I am preparing for meditation," he says, "I am emptying my mind." With his spread right hand he makes a graceful counterclockwise motion to show the emptying.

We walk up the hill, turn right on the coast road and walk along the highway until we cross a bridge above a canyon. Then we turn left on a dirt road that leads up into the mountains. Gia-Fu walks silently and I am grateful for his company and his silence. All the fuzzy confusion, all the frustration, tension and noise in my head evaporate into the cool afternoon sunshine. The road winds upward, past brown dry grass meadows and clumps of feathery pampas grass, past rocks and wildflowers. Salamanders scurry off as our steps interrupt the stillness.

We climb quickly. Soon Esalen is way down below us and the spaces around us grow vaster. The coast road is a winding line far below, at the foot of the brown-green mountains. The road we walk dips into a canyon and leads us suddenly into a glade of gigantic redwoods swimming in the sun as if under water. Then we rise again to more burnt-gold meadows, to a still vaster view of the Sur. The cold air flows deep into my lungs. It is pure joy to move after the long confinement.

The road forks and we take the branch dipping south. It leads to the sound of water. Again there are redwoods along a brook. Just above the road, where the brook slips under it, is a dark green pool. Gia-Fu stops and smiles at me.

33

"You can sit here and meditate. You have time before dinner. I will go on."

Then he motions that I should follow him along the edge of the pool. A bit upstream, a small waterfall comes into view. We stand silently for a long moment, looking and listening. Then Gia-Fu turns and looks at me. He is shorter than I but now, standing on a clump of moss, he is looking down. He looks steadily into my face. There is a glow in his look, something radiant—kindness? The excitement of the climb? I become extremely uncomfortable. Is he going to make a pass? No, that's not it. I'm ashamed for thinking it. But I cannot bear to let him look at me like that, as if he saw right into me. I turn away, searching for something to say to regain my composure.

"You are a good hiker," he says.

"Thank you. Thank you for bringing me here." The words rush out, nervously. "If you hadn't invited me I probably would not have come here for some time." I am apologizing, trying to wipe out an event. After all, nothing happened. Did it? Gia-Fu chuckles and, without another word, walks away and up the mountain.

I sit down on a rock beside the pool, overcome with confusion. What I just said was said with too many words and it was not what I wanted to say. It was a lovely walk, Gia-Fu showed me something I could not put into words by just letting me walk with him while he meditated. Was there anything embarrassing in that? All weekend a roomful of people screamed and yelled at each other and talked and talked in a huge effort to communicate. And here Gia-Fu, by walking up the mountain with me and looking directly into my eyes and telling me I was a good hiker had reached right into my soul in some weird way. And I had escaped with words because I could not stand it.

I fix my attention on the sound of the waterfall and try to empty my mind, though I'm not sure how that is done. Walking down the mountain a little later, I wonder at how all those people had driven from San Francisco and Los Angeles to sit in a room, shout and talk for two days and nights, then pile into their cars once more. Not one of them had gone up this mountain. Yet what they wanted was surely up here. Gia-Fu gave me my first hint of, as the hippies say, where it is at. I am bringing back from that mountain something I know is the beginning of a discovery.

Refreshed, I am now ready to explore Esalen further. At dinner I see James Johnson, who, I've been told, is working on a research project connected with Esalen. There is a

34

seat next to him at the end of one of the tables and I take it and introduce myself.

"I understand you're doing a project in ways of learning," I say.

"That's right." He doesn't look up from his plate.

"What is it you're studying?"

"I'm sorry, I don't feel like talking about it," he says. That's all. He continues to eat. Another man sits down opposite him and begins to talk about his children, and the other man's children, the baby-sitter who had a nervous breakdown. I'm sitting at the end of the table, between them, but they seem totally unaware of my existence. At first I am paralyzed, then I begin to get angry at their rudeness. Such behavior simply is not civilized. I get up and seek another place to drink my coffee. They don't even look up as I leave.

In the fading light by one of the big western windows I see Dr. Frederick Perls, whom I know from the description I've heard. Long gray hair hangs on the sides of his dome. His beard is white and patriarchal. His face is a landscape of folds and wrinkles with full lips and a big aquiline nose. He's wearing a navy blue terry-cloth jumpsuit that zips up the front and his feet are in moccasins. Perls is the originator of Gestalt therapy, the best-known and most controversial person at Esalen. I have heard him described as a great man and a fraud, a sage and a healer, a guru, a charlatan. Before leaving New York, I skimmed his book *Gestalt Therapy,* written with Paul Goodman and Ralph F. Hefferline. It was, I thought, rather dull but I knew it was written mostly by Goodman. Some people whose opinions I respect think Perls is one of the top minds in psychology today.

Right now he is reading a newspaper in the fading light. I slip into the chair beside him and wait for him to turn toward me. Then I tell him who I am and ask if I may sit in on his workshop, which has been going for two weeks and has two more to run.

He turns slowly and looks at me. His eyes are huge and dark brown. This time I meet the gaze easily. "I will have to ask the group," he says in a cigarette-rough voice and a strong German accent. "They turned down two people last week and accepted one. The two they turned down were visiting psychologists. They accepted the wife of a man in the workshop. I don't know what they will say to you. You can come tonight at nine."

"Thank you."

Perls' house is the semicircular one I noticed up the hill, not far from the highway. The straight wall extends into a balcony above a cliff facing south. The door opens into a hall that leads to two bedrooms at each end of the outer rim and into a semicircular living room where workshops are held. At Perls' request I stand before the group, explain my purpose, and am unanimously admitted on condition that I shall not participate in sessions with Perls. Each morning the group, divided in half, meets for one and a half hours with Perls and for an equal interval with one of his disciples. Afternoons, dance and art therapy are available and, late afternoons, there are encounter groups of eight to ten people each. I decide to watch Perls during both morning sessions and take part in one of the late afternoon groups.

The people here seem, at first glance, more interesting than the ones I met during the weekend. Penelope Twillig is here, but no one among the others resembles her. There are a few professional-looking people, some bearded hip types and some unclassifiable young people. Perls shows a short film of himself working with a patient. I don't get much from it. Then he speaks slowly, deliberately, letting every careful word fall into place, eliciting attention without commanding it:

"The voice never lies," he says. "The contents—yes, the voice—never. If you open your ears you can hear the truth. If you open your computer you'll be poisoned." The computer, I soon learn, is Perlsian for thinking and talking that proceeds out of the intellect only, without touching senses or emotions.

"Most of us are so caught in words that we don't listen," he says. "Now I would like you to have a conversation. But instead of using words, do it in gibberish."

A loud chatter begins. I find myself conversing with a young man of about my age whose face suggests chronic worry. I use a lot of facial expressions, gestures, and a language invented on the spot that sounds like Swedish. His gibberish is more like Arabic. At first there is an impulse to giggle at this foolishness, but soon we are indeed talking, and I'm saying in gibberish, "Hello, you seem like an interesting fellow, but why so intense?"

"Glad you came. Good to see a new face."

"This place is beautiful. I'm excited."

"I want, I am looking, I came here to find out."

When we stop we are acquainted, perhaps better acquainted than we would have been had we used words. For, deprived of words, we began to listen to each other, look at each other and pick up all kinds of cues.

"All right," says Perls. "What did you experience?"

"There's no point in talking," someone says.

"The voice conveys the meaning."

"It's easier in gibberish."

"Now," says Perls, "I want you to have a conversation using only the other person's name. The Evocation Game. Nod when you feel you have made contact. Shake your head when you have not."

This is harder. "Jack." I'm self-conscious, it's so exposed. He shakes his head. "Rasa." It is tentative. I nod. "Jack." A positive statement—too strong. He shakes his head. "Rasa." Too caressing, rings false. No. If we had other words we would talk at a distance. This way we are forced into intimacy.

"Now I want you to think of what is your most effective manipulative behavior," Perls says. "Then think of the opposite and use it in conversation. After every sentence say, 'That is a lie.'" Perls chuckles, his belly shakes.

It occurs to me that, as a reporter, I often could get a person to talk most freely by assuming an attitude of naïve interest. That was effective manipulative behavior. The opposite attitude would be sophisticated boredom. I try to make sophisticated, bored statements to Jack. But when I add "That is a lie," I feel confused about where the truth is. The opposites somehow become the same.

By the time the evening is over, I know that the next two weeks will be an adventure. "Thank you," I say to Perls as I leave. "It was fascinating."

"And that is a lie," he says, chuckling, not unfriendly yet also mocking the cliché politeness.

Others are going down to the baths but I don't, even though I know the unpleasant experience of the first evening would not be repeated with these people. Too much has happened today already. I walk to the edge of the lawn to look out over the ocean and think back over the day—the tearful end of the racial encounter, the walk with Gia-Fu, the rudeness of James Johnson at dinner, Perls' awareness games and his presence. Waves are colliding with mountains below me. Nature allows no easy transitions here and neither, apparently, do people.

Chapter TWO

Fritz Perls—
Prophet of the Now

DR. FREDERICK S. PERLS—Fritz to all at the Hot Springs—is much more like a Zen master than like the standard American psychotherapist. The word therapy does not really describe what he does. He sits against the wall of his semicircular room, evoking mini-satoris. A mini-satori is an "aha experience" or sudden insight. When you have one, he says, "suddenly the world is there, bright and three-dimensional."

Rather than rummage the past for the root of neurosis, he focuses on expanding awareness. When people learn to tune into the moment, he has found, neurosis dissolves. They become free to flow with changes, expand, grow, swing.

Most of us are self-prisoners cut off from our potential being. According to Perls, we don't talk—we produce verbiage. We don't think—we compute. (Our intellect, he says, is an ever-chattering computer that splits us from our senses and intuition.) We don't allow ourselves to feel. Perls' aim, in his workshops, is to stop the cortical chatter and open the flow of existence. "Lose your mind and come to your senses," is his invitation. He seeks to restore the mind's connections with natural rhythms within and without, to loosen the intellect's controlling grasp and free it for discovery. "Don't push the river, it flows by itself," he likes to say; or, "If you try to make semen flow it turns into piss." The key to the secret of being, he says, is understanding the now. ("What does that mean, the now?" I ask one of his disciples. "Did you hear that bird just now?" he replies. I shake my head. "I am listening to you and I hear the bird," he says.)

Perls sits in that bring room, under mobiles that admirers have hung above his head, and he claims, "Where other therapists count in years we count in months. Where psychoanalysts take six weeks for a warm-up, in half an hour I can get right into the center of the personality."

Bunk! an analyst will answer. But as I watch Perls in action, I see again and again how worried, tense faces suddenly light up in a flash of some inner reality. And, in watching them, I myself begin to go through changes. My ears begin to pick up more nuances in what people are saying, my eyes notice more fleeting changes in faces. My mind begins to spin along some unfamiliar loops and sometimes, when I read over notes typed a day or so ago, I find that they no longer make sense for my perspective is now different.

This morning, as usual, Perls is in his plastic armchair against the east wall of that semicircular room, waiting for the group to settle in a circle around him. He surveys the scene, huge brown eyes blinking slowly, patriarchal beard in a cloud of smoke that rises from the growing ash of his cigarette. It's still in the room. The white cotton curtains on the south window-wall—the only straight wall in the room— sway gently in the sea breeze that blows in over the balcony. Perls looks around. Twenty pairs of eyes look back.

The people in this seminar vary in age from eighteen to late middle-age. They come from as far away as New York and as near as the next mountain. Among them are an electronics engineer, a writer, a couple of musicians, a painter, a surgeon, two psychologists, a psychiatrist, some professors and students and a few women, married and divorced, of no particular profession who can spend $600 a month for therapy or self-games at Esalen. All of them are now ready. I'm sitting next to Todd Bryant and his videotape camera. All the chairs except the red one at Perls' left are filled. That red chair is known as the hot seat. Gestalt therapy, as practiced by its originator, involves an encounter with one person at a time in the context of a group. Afterward, each person gets to watch his videotape. The most interesting tape of the day is viewed by the whole group in the evening.

"Who vants to vork?" Perls asks, surveying the faces.

A thin, pale young man with a wisp of new beard comes across the room to take the hot seat. He's Stan, a musician who has his own band. (The names of workshop participants are fictitious.) He looks agitated. He is biting his lower lip and pressing the heels of his hands together. In a hurried, somewhat breathless way, he begins to speak:

"Fritz, I had a dream last night about a turtle. I had this turtle. It kept getting bigger and bigger till it was a giant turtle, it was ten feet high. And that turtle was my meaning. Everywhere I went I was known because of my turtle. I couldn't go anywhere without it. It's frightening, I feel shaky recalling it because it's so clear to me. It's my band. It keeps getting bigger and bigger. I get more and more dependent on it. I don't know what I'd do without it."

"O.K., play that turtle," Perls tells him. Stan stands on the small bench in front of the hot seat, puts his hands on his hips and stares down at the empty chair:

"Well, there you are, you little shit, leading me around day after day, year after year. You used to think you led me around because you started me. But look how big I am. You need me more than I need you. You're nobody without me."

Perls: What are you?

Stan: A turtle.

Perls: What are you like?

Stan: I'm ten feet high. I'm dark green. I'm a friendly turtle. I'm kind of passive, very passive, and I'm getting bigger. (He looks again at the hot seat.) But I couldn't have had any pride in the first place to let *you* lead me around. (He sounds to me like an amateur actor who has rehearsed his lines but can't make them sound natural.)

Perls: What's so special about a turtle? You do a lot of boasting.

Stan (uncertain): I'm special because there's no one else like me. I'm the *biggest* turtle (becoming more certain), I'm the *only* turtle that comes into town. I'm a unique kind of turtle.

Perls: How? You could be the biggest kangaroo or the biggest Empire State Building. What's the uniqueness of a turtle?

Stan: I have a shell.

Perls: Ah! But so does a lobster and an oyster.

Stan: I can withdraw into the shell.

Perls: A snail can do the same.

Stan (more confident): A snail can't move as fast. I'm the only animal that can get this big and withdraw into itself and be a house to itself.

Perls: *Now* play the turtle.

Stan: My house . . . (He is still reciting, standing there rigid, staring down.)

Perls: You're talking, you're not playing.

(Suddenly Stan steps down and crouches on the floor on his hands and knees, hiding his head. There is no bravado in this new pose. He rocks back and forth.)

Perls: (gently) You know something, turtle? I want to take your shell away.

(Stan gets up immediately. Lousy acting, I say to myself. He forgot he would feel pain.)

40

Stan (standing on the floor, facing Perls): I'm naked now and I'm no use to him because everyone can see what's in the shell is not that special.

Perls: Now do this projection. Hurt the turtle. (He hands him a pillow.)

(Stan sits down again. All his movements, I notice, are rigid. When he completes something he seems to freeze, become dead. Now he throws the pillow on the floor and stares at it, his face tense, his eyes glassy.)

Stan: Now I see you. I see you are a naked animal like any other and you can't withdraw now. You can't run away. Now I can tell you what a shithead you are for being led round like that. 'Cause he's *using you*. (Contemptuous. He stands up, faces the chair again.)

Stan: I feel guilty about letting myself be used. Now I have nowhere to go. But I gotta fight for myself, not for him.

Perls: Repeat that.

Stan: I gotta fight for myself, not for you. You gotta make your own fucking music now. I'm not gonna be your bandwagon anymore.

Perls: Say it to the group.

Stan: I gotta fight for myself now. (He sounds a little lost. He sits down.)

Stan: Yeah, I know, fifteen years I've led you around, you led me around. I'm as vulnerable as you now, 'cause you were my shell too.

Perls: Ah! Say this again. (He sounds interested.)

Stan: You were my shell too. (His face takes on an expression of disgust.) Now I see you're not just a band, you're a whole fucking society. You used to direct me. Now I'm gonna direct myself. Kind of feel like I'd like to kick you for letting me think I was directing you. But it's not your fault.

(He stops, turns to Perls. Suddenly he looks desolate. I recognize something in his face. It's that familiar, sickening feeling that rises to the throat and has to be pushed down, that surge of anxiety at which thoughts dissolve and the issues one is trying to consider turn into vague terror.)

Stan (to Perls): Now I feel at an impasse.

Perls: Does this mean anything to you, a kind of pseudo-diagnosis: you don't want to make music, you want to be known as a musician?

Stan: Your suspicion is right. It *was* right for most of my career. But now I want to find my own voice. I know I can. But I keep worrying about it and it keeps me from working. That's why I'm here. I want to fight the monkey on my back that keeps me from making music, that keeps me from reading a book, from focusing on anything.

Perls: Play the It. Play the frustrator.

(Stan gets up on the bench again and stares down at the hot seat.)

Stan: Don't just sit there. You've got thinking to do. You've got worries. Look—you've had fifteen minutes at the piano already. There's the schedule to think about.

Perls: Tell other people what to worry about.

Stan (goes around the circle): John, you better worry about your laziness. Lula, you better worry about getting old. Martha, if you can't find anything to worry about, worry about me.

Perls: Do this to Stan now. But say it not with words but with music. An oboe or a clarinet might be a good instrument. You have to choose.

Stan (stands on the chair and hums a dirge that goes down, down, slowing down until it fades to one heavy note): Worry. Sad, hmmm. Sad, hmmm. Worry hmmm. Hmmm. Hmmm.

(He sits down, looks up to the invisible ten-foot creature on the bench, puts his fist to his mouth and makes a loud fart noise. Then, angrily, he gives the giant the finger. It's a childish defiance of a boy who knows he'll eventually have to yield to his father.)

Perls (belly shaking with laughter): Again the worrier.

Stan (sings slowly, drearily): No, No, nooo. Wor-ry worry. (Sounds like a kid saying nya-nya.) Today is another day. You must worry. Yes, yes. There you are with your sad face. *You dumb skunk.*

Perls: Change sides. Put him there as your equal. (He points to the bench.)

(Stan, in chair, looks at worrier at eye level. For a moment his face becomes cheerful. He begins to whistle a careless tune. But it quickly trails off. His face takes on the expression of a scolded child. He sits on the bench again, facing the chair.)

Stan (again nya-nya voice): No no, you're not working, it's not effective—sad, sad. Down, down. That's the good skunk. (He switches sides again. Sitting in the chair he drums defiance with his fingers on the bench. But again, after a moment, the face sags and becomes hopeless. He looks up, apparently seeing a giant again. Then he changes sides again but after a moment switches back to the chair. Putting his right fist to his mouth he begins to blow. First a baby's wail comes out. His cheeks puff out, his face reddens, there is sweat on his forehead. He puts both hands to his mouth, leans toward the bench and blows an angry banshee wail. Then suddenly he stops, glares at the bench and violently kicks it over.

(Perls leans back, crosses his right leg over his left knee, relaxes. During a long silence Stan stares at the overturned bench. Then he speaks in a surprised voice that has a new resonance).

Stan: I've knocked you down. You're silent. It's my voice that's speaking now. It's my voice and it's gonna grow louder than yours because I'll be free to work more and free to sing more. (There is just a slight trace of uncertainty in the last part of that sentence. He continues to sit in the chair as if in a trance.)

Perls (After a while): Are you ready to come back to us?

Stan: Yes.

Perls: What do you see?

Stan (looks around. Now his eyes sparkle): I see everybody. I see everybody differently. I've changed. Now—for now. (He seems to mistrust it as much as he wants to believe it.) The throbbing inside me is changing into a motor.

Perls: Give me a musical theme for the motor.

(Stan begins to hum a glad, busy tune. He gets up and begins to walk around the circle and elaborate on it, playing a new variation before each person. When he gets to Larry, who plays the guitar, Larry takes his hands and they begin to hum in counterpoint, moving in rhythm. By this time everyone in the room is beaming, the place is bursting with celebration.)

"All right," says Perls. "Time for lunch."

I stand up, exhausted and excited. It was absorbing drama —yet too simple to believe. I ride down the hill to lunch with Perls in his little white Fiat.

"Requiem for a musician," he says. "Beginning of a resurrection."

"It's hard for me to believe," I say. "When you took the shell off he should have felt pain."

"That's your turtle," Perls says. "It's not his. It is a good beginning. You should have seen him two weeks ago, when he came here. He was a dead man."

Later, Stan tells me that had been true. That spring he had fallen into a terrible depression. He had listened to a lot of rock and roll, found it vibrant, and had been overcome by the realization that his own music was lifeless and he himself was dead. For months he felt nothing except once, when his

43

dog was killed by a car. And then, though it was pain he felt, he was almost glad of it for it was at least an emotion.

"I'd look at myself in a mirror and I'd look dead—washed out. There was no color. It was like being white from fear," he tells me.

Despair had been growing in him for a long time and had finally become suffocating. One day he went out into the country, hoping that would help. But he could not bear the beauty of spring and fled immediately. He canceled some concerts and secluded himself with a pile of books. Soon there were books all over his floor, all open—psychology books, yoga books, Somerset Maugham's *The Razor's Edge,* Walter Lippmann's *A Preface to Morals.* Abraham Maslow's *The Psychology of Being* struck something. He called Maslow at Brandeis University, asked about therapists and so came to Perls.

When I see Stan again six months later, he is still enthusiastic about that month with Perls. The workshop in combination with Big Sur had revived him, he tells me. He is making a new record and is in the midst of a busy concert season. Listening to his old records now, he no longer finds them lifeless. "My music needs involvement from the listener," he says. "It doesn't come to you on a platter like rock and roll. You have to have something to bring to it, and if you're dead you can't hear it. I see that now. I did, after coming back from Esalen, have a brief regression into computing and worrying. But this time I was able to catch myself at it, which gave me a tremendous feeling of release."

I have seen a typical example of Perl's dream work. The dream, to him, is an existential message that tells you where you are in relationship to yourself and the world. In entering the dream and acting it out—in effect, in continuing to dream it—under skilled guidance, a person can come upon what he is trying to avoid. All parts of the dream—people, animals and objects—are projections of the alienated parts of the self, Perls explains. The turtle, which to Stan seemed at first so clearly his band, became later "a fucking society" and still later "it" and "the worrier." Actually, they were all part of Stan.

Stan was ready to explode from his despair. He had confronted it. But when he tried to get beyond the realization that he was in a state of paralysis, reasons, explanations and questions whirled like a tornado through his mind, resolving nothing. "I had become a self-junkie," he said.

Perls enabled him to enter and experience his paralysis

44

through the dream and to explore the conflict locked in his deadness through a dialogue between dream figures. No analysis was involved, only experience. The words Stan used in his drama were symbols that worked for him in a certain way but were probably heard differently by others in the room.

When the conflict had been polarized and was clear to Stan, Perls encouraged him to use the means of expression most natural to him—music—to break through his inner deadlock into anger. At that moment Stan experienced what Perls calls a "mini-satori." ("I thought it was a way of speaking, that you saw more clearly that moment," Stan said. "But it's actually, physically true. You *actually* see more clearly and brightly.") This was followed by a feeling of gladness.

Stan's impasse, like most neurosis, had to do with conflict between his authentic self—his own needs, desires and emotions—and a concept of himself derived from the expectations of society. "The critical point during any development, both collectively and individually, is the ability to differentiate between self-actualization and the actualization of a concept," Perls has written in *Explorations in Human Potentialities*, compiled and edited by Herbert A. Otto.

Freud saw a conflict between the superego and the id. Perls sees the superego's opponent not as an id but as an "infraego." He refers to them often as Top Dog and Under Dog. Top Dog, he says, is self-righteous, a bully, a punisher and authoritarian. He keeps commanding, "You should, you better." Under Dog is cunning in evading Top Dog. He replies, "I'm doing my best, I'm trying, I'll do it tomorrow." We all identify with our inner Top Dog and take his righteousness for granted, Perls says. Yet it is the Under Dog who usually wins in a conflict. Perls' aim is to integrate the two by making them listen to each other, so converting energy that goes into conflict into the potential for growth.

"The basic philosophy of Gestalt therapy is that of nature —differentiation and integration. Differentiation by itself leads to polarities. As dualities these polarities will easily fight and paralyze one another. By integrating opposite traits we make the person whole again. For instance, weakness and bullying integrate as silent firmness," he wrote in the article in *Explorations*.

Dream work is one of Perls' most interesting contributions to psychology. But what impressed me most that morning was the way he tuned in on Stan and responded to him. I saw that Perls was a guru, not just a psychiatrist with a lot of interesting ideas. For no matter how fascinating his theories, what he had to teach could never be translated fully into

45

words. It was there to be seen in his response to the uniqueness of the moment.

Throughout the drama with Stan he was completely with him, not missing a cue. When Stan talked distantly, abstractedly, Perls looked bored, so reflecting what Stan was doing. When he became excited, Perls became excited. When he was floundering, Perls knew exactly what kind of prod would set him back on course. Later, with other people, I will see Perls yawn openly, even fall asleep when bored. Sometimes he exaggerates his responses and so brings home to the person in the hot seat something previously unnoticed. But even if they are exaggerated, his responses are always genuine.

The same is true of his behavior outside the seminar room. It is often rude, arrogant, inconsiderate—sometimes even outrageous. But he is always himself. Often he refuses to acknowledge any other encounter than one that is completely natural and direct. This means that some people, including myself, at times freeze into rigid nervous hulks in his presence. But I will remember these dreadful moments later as educational.

That very noon after Stan's mini-enlightenment, I search out Perls in the dining room to ask him some theoretical questions. He seems willing to converse until I begin, "Are dream figures always *alienated* parts of the self? It seems to me that . . ."

Perls lifts his hand in a gesture that stops me in mid-sentence. There is a pause. "Fine spaghetti today," he says pleasantly. But I turn mute. He has shattered my self-confidence. For days afterward I avoid direct meetings with him and when I somehow find myself face to face with him, I invariably burst out with some totally inane remark.

I am furious that I let myself be so demolished. But I also feel challenged. For I saw that others, particularly the hip gypsies, can talk with Perls. Their conversations usually begin with a long silent look—the kind of look Gia-Fu had given me on the mountain. I had exchanged such a gaze with Perls during our first meeting but was later held back by self-consciousness. ("Self-consciousness is the mildest form of paranoia," Perls said one later evening. "We feel persecuted by our environment. When you feel self-conscious, ask yourself what you have disowned. If it's your ears you will talk and talk and not expect anyone to hear you.")

One evening not long after, I resolve to break through my foolish fear of the man. I see him sitting alone by the window at dinner and approach him.

"May I sit with you, Fritz?"

"Yah."

I had something in mind that I wanted to ask. But now, beside him, my mind blanks. He continues to eat silently. Out of pure nervousness, just to break the silence, I begin to tell him some amusing incident that happened in the afternoon. He interrupts, "Please, please! I hate this production of sentences." Again I turn into a rock. My stomach knots, my wrists tense, my fingers go cold. After a while Perls turns to look at me inquiringly.

"You're impossible to communicate with," I say.

"Communicate *what?*"

I have no reply. He offers me a cigarette.

In truth, he had not stopped me in the midst of any communication but only in the midst of nervous chatter, the kind he calls "verbiage" or "production of sentences." I had spewed words in his direction out of panic, losing my self.

According to Perls, verbiage comes in three varieties: chickenshit, bullshit and elephantshit. Day-to-day chatter is chickenshit. Bullshit is role-playing. Elephantshit deals with life and death, meaning, ideals and theories. Perls refers to his lectures as elephantshit. If he had his way, he says, he would permit verbiage only in the form of imperatives, puns and poems.

"But what else is there, then, besides verbiage?" someone asks him.

"There is the I-Thou."

The term is Martin Buber's. He said the two primary words expressing man's twofold nature are I-Thou and I-It. The former is a meeting between two subjects, the latter means use or experience of an object by a subject. The I-Thou unites being to being; the I-It differentiates and separates. A fully aware person swings between the I-Thou and I-It. But many live only the I-It, burying the I-Thou and, with it, the source of life. For an I-Thou meeting is not easy for computerized man:

"The relation to the Thou is direct. No system of ideas, no foreknowledge and no fancy intervene between I and Thou. The memory itself is transformed, as it plunges out of its isolation into the unity of the whole. No aim, no lust, and no anticipation intervene between I and Thou. Desire itself is transformed as it plunges out of its dream into the appearance. Every means is an obstacle. Only when every means has collapsed does the meeting come about," Buber wore in *I and Thou.*

The harsh rebuffs from Perls do not immediately lead to an I-Thou encounter. But they do lead me to understand something about communication. I slowly come to realize that words often block more than they reveal. All too often they are a wall we erect between ourselves and another to prevent a true look. I spoke to Perls because I wanted to hide my nervous condition and lack of self-trust in his presence. Most urgent questions, I realize, do not have to be asked, because the answers are there to be discovered, if only one sharpens hearing and vision.

One evening, after the usual videotape session, Perls plays some rock and roll records and some of us dance. I have a fine time twirling around with the electronics engineer, using a blue Guatemalan shawl to put on a flirting performance. Then I sit down, watch Perls dance with a hip gypsy and see how a dance can be an I-Thou encounter. Perls speaks to the girl with his movements. He does not perform for her, as I did for my partner. Instead of being involved with himself, as I was, he seems to be absorbed in the interplay with the girl and to see her more clearly than himself. I have never seen anyone dance quite so expressively although his movements are simple.

Perls believes that therapy is possible only within an I-Thou relationship. And it is one of his great criticisms of Freud that he would not accept such a meeting with his patients. He made patients lie on couches, Perls says, because he could not bear to meet them face to face. Another major difference with Freud is Perls' rejection of the concept of a conscious and unconscious mind. Perls thinks rather in terms of a constantly shifting awareness. As a disciple of his, James S. Simkin, puts it, the Gestalt therapist sees the human personality not as an onion that must be peeled layer by layer toward a hidden core, but rather as a rubber ball floating and turning in water, partly submerged in its environment, so that only a portion is visible at one time. The Gestalt therapist works with the visible surface—visible within the context of the moment.

"The therapeutic procedure is to integrate awareness and attention," Perls tells me in an interview. "Neurosis is built on avoidance, on a phobic attitude. By deliberately concentrating on what one is avoiding, the phobic resistances are overcome and worked through and an integration takes place. I especially mention this in contrast to what I call the free dissociation theory, Freudianism that runs away and does not concentrate. Free association goes along with the phobic attitude. The Freudian trauma is a lie invented *ad hoc* by the patient who needs it for his self-torture games."

All existence is in the present, therefore neurosis must be

dealt with in the present, Perls holds. It is on this point, "in its absolute and rigorous understanding that nothing exists except the now," that his method differs from all others. "We see and hear what is going on now, we don't see and hear what went on in the past—memory is a projection from the present—nor what will go on in the future. This is a concept that is so obvious and so difficult to understand because it is always translated into a requirement—you *should* live in the now, that is, forget about the past and future. That is not the meaning. Now is a point in eternity in which we are in touch with any ongoing process."

"To understand the word now is like understanding Zen in satori," he says on another occasion. "It will take anything from a couple of months to twenty years. Now is the gramophone needle, life is the record. Where the needle touches the record there is presence." In his book *Ego, Hunger and Aggression* he expanded on this point. "By no means do I deny that everything has its origin in the past and tends to further development, but what I want to bring home is, that past and future take their bearings continuously from the present and have to be related to it. Without the reference to the present they become meaningless."

"Now is what is," he says in a film introducing Gestalt therapy. "What was is a memory or an unfinished situation. . . . What will be we don't know but we carry the future within us in the shape of expectations, hopes, fears, fantasies." Some expectations are anastrophic ("If I run faster I'll find the meaning for my existence") others are catastrophic ("Something terrible will happen if I dare"). Together with our goals, prejudices and computerized minds, they keep us from taking risks and prevent us from growing. "So there is always something missing," says Perls. "We think but are not aware. Many have no eyes—they are looked at, demand attention, but cannot give it. Many have no ears—they talk and talk and cannot hear."

Perls' procedure with patients, therefore, is to concentrate on the experience of the moment to find what is missing. He focuses on the voice, the glance, body sensations, and uses a variety of techniques to act out emotions. In a "microscopic examination of the ongoing process," he has found, "one invariably comes across some awareness that is unpleasant. At this moment the inclination is to escape—to change focus, flee into fantasy, break down in tears or go into a rage. If attention is refocused on the unpleasantness, one soon finds oneself facing an impasse," which is a deadlocked conflict at a point where a step toward growth was not taken.

"Growth and maturation are continued transcendence from environmental support to self-support," Perls says. Neurosis begins when a person, confronted with the need to take a step toward self-support, begins to manipulate his environment instead. In *Demian*, a book Perls recommends to patients, Hermann Hesse talks about the transition from childhood to manhood:

"For the average person, this is the point when the demands of his own life come into the sharpest conflict with his environment, when the way forward has to be sought with the bitterest means at his command. Many people experience the dying and rebirth—which is our fate—only this once during their entire life. Their childhood becomes hollow and gradually collapses, everything they love abandons them and they suddenly feel surrounded by the loneliness and mortal cold of the universe. Very many are caught forever in this impasse, and for the rest of their lives cling painfully to an irrevocable past, the dream of the lost paradise—which is the worst and most ruthless of dreams."

"The therapist must by skillful frustration get the patient to encounter the impasse and get through it, to force him to realize, in other words, that he is not a baby," says Perls.

To avoid facing the petrified neurotic conflict, a person will try to manipulate his environment with every tool he has learned to use for such an avoidance. He will flatter, plead, try to control by submission, act helpless and stupid. The therapist keeps bringing him back to his experience, being careful not to give environmental support. ("I trust you," the man in the hot seat says. "Me—not yourself," Perls says, clarifying the demand for environmental support.) "The therapist must be an antidote to the phobic attitude. The only support I always give is feedback. I try to stay with the person on the hot seat and to see how he is trying to stay deaf or blind. If I'm not frustrating, he has no incentive." Eventually the patient becomes aware of a deadness.

"When we approach the impasse," Perls tells the seminar, "we encounter a layer of implosion—a death layer . . . loneliness, boredom, emptiness of meaning. We are stuck in the deadness of being. At best there are two emotions left here —self-pity and anger. There has to be a transition to an explosion. The explosion is into anger, love, grief or joy. Once this transition occurs, change is self-facilitating. In the death layer tremendous energies are bound in themselves. Once past it we move from a neurotic role-playing level into creative being in the world."

The phobic attitude, according to Perls, "is based on the

50

inability to differentiate between fantasy and reality—the fantasy of insufferable pain, of the catastrophic expectation, of other unpleasantness. If we check those fantasies against reality we see that once we are in those painful moments and open up to the pain, the pain becomes tolerable. And what's more, the moment you are at one with the pain, it begins to dissolve. I'll give you an example. You need to urinate. If you hold back, the more you hold back the more painful it becomes. You let go and the pain disappears. And if you become aware that the pain you suffer is the self-made pain of retaining something, you let go and there is no more pain."

Another way he looks at neurosis is as holes in the personality caused by failure to complete Gestalts. Until the hole is filled, growth is hindered. *Gestalt* is a German word with no precise English equivalent. Roughly, it means configuration, a whole which is more than the sum of its parts. Six lilacs in a vase, for example, would appear to most of us as a bouquet. A bouquet is something more than six lilacs. Each of the lilacs, in the bouquet, looks different than it would separately in a vase.

The nature of the Gestalt differs with its context. Thus, the same lilacs may look bluish against a red background and reddish against a blue background. The context also includes the point of view from which we perceive it. The man buying lilacs from the street vendor sees them in context of a visit to his girl. The seller sees them in context with the price of his dinner.

The principle was examined by Wolfgang Koehler and Max Wertheimer who were the main developers of Gestalt psychology. The basic idea is often illustrated in psychology textbooks by a black and white picture that can be seen either as a vase or as two faces in profile, depending on whether one looks at the white space or the black space as foreground. Usually it is impossible to see both at once and takes some time to switch from one to the other. Yet the picture is both.

What Gestalten we form depends on our dominant needs. Thus, Perls says, a man who wants to mail a letter will notice every mailbox in view. As soon as the letter is disposed of, the mailboxes will cease to be the figure in his awareness and recede into the background. Until he finds that mailbox he will be preoccupied with the need to mail the letter and unable to focus fully on other things. The dynamic of Gestalt formation moves toward completion. "If you have insomnia," Perls says, "you can be sure there's some Gestalt waiting to be completed."

51

Living is a constant formation and completion of Gestalten that leads to a constantly shifting awareness. Trouble begins when something blocks the completion of an important Gestalt. It then becomes a hole in the personality that must be filled if growth is to continue. Constance, for example, was preoccupied by an unresolved conflict regarding her father. She hated him for the harm she felt he had done to her as a child. At the same time, she loved him. She was unable to separate the two emotions and express either of them and so could neither reject him nor forgive him. For years she had been spinning miserably round and round the same ambivalence. The futile self-torture was consuming much of her energy, yet she could not get past it. Perls, starting with a dream, led her to polarize her love and rage. Once the strength of both emotions came fully into her awareness, she burst into anger and then, suddenly free, found she wanted to forgive her father while he was still alive. With that Gestalt complete, she was now presumably liberated from this particular anguish. She did not suddenly cease to be neurotic, of course, but was freed to deal with the next incomplete Gestalt. Sometimes, says Perls, hundreds of impasses must be worked through.

For two weeks I sit every morning in the sunlit semicircular room, watching Perls work. The group plays a part in the process much like the chorus in classical Greek plays. It is the context for the person in the hot seat and mirrors his attitudes and projections. Conversely, each of us sees aspects of himself in what transpires before us. The air is charged with emotional cross-currents and sometimes a surprising notion will strike home as we watch someone failing to grasp it. But we all know that, were we up there in the hot seat, we would be as incredibly blind and deaf as the person there that moment.

Sometimes a man or woman gets up there and nothing at all happens. One has to be ready and willing. But again and again I see how, under Perls' skillful guidance, neurotic conflicts surface quickly. They are invariably obvious to everyone but the person concerned. "The difficulty lies in grasping the obvious and leading a person to understand that the obvious is the essence," Perls says.

Mark is a friendly nearsighted teacher who is always smiling—the same, somewhat frozen smile—and squinting from behind clear-rimmed glasses. He is usually with Kim, a pretty girl with long blond hair who smiles almost as much as he, although with more variation. Occasionally she also pouts.

One morning Mark takes the hot seat and says he wants to work on his myopia. Perls has said that myopia is often caused by tension. Mark makes his statement of purpose and sits there, smiling. Perls is silent. Mark fumbles, unable to speak. Perls tells him to say "Now I produce this sentence" before every sentence, to drive home to Mark that he is out of touch with his words. Mark describes his body sensations and what he sees in the room in a monotonous voice and smiles, smiles unchangingly. We quickly get bored. Some people start whispering, drawing, making signs to one another, playing with Mitzi, Perls' little white cat. Gerry, a handsome, broadly built man who sits two chairs away from Mark, whispers to Kim, who is beside him. Kim moves over to sit in Gerry's lap, slings an arm around his neck and becomes involved in a giggly whisper-conversation with him. Clearly this is intended to get some sort of reaction from Mark.

But Mark goes on monotonously about the paintings in the room, the videotape camera, the cat. His glance passes over Gerry and Kim without a change of expression. Then Perls stops the tedium and asks Todd to replay the videotape for Mark. Mark moves close to the screen to watch it and I watch his face. The smile vanishes and is replaced by blank despair. When he returns to the hot seat he says, "I'm scared," and the words ring true.

Perls: Tell people what you are scared of.

Mark (proceeding around the room, stopping before each person): Gerry, I'm very scared. I'm afraid you'll be disappointed in me. George, I'm scared. I'm afraid I'll lose in some kind of competition. Eloise, I'm scared you won't like me.

Perls: You're afraid to go out and collect the green stamps you need and want. (Green stamps in Perls' lingo of the moment means approval and appreciation.)

Mark (looking puzzled): I'm afraid to collect green stamps.

Perls: So what do you play the good boy for? Go out and get some disapproval. Get some black stamps.

Mark (continuing his rounds): Ivan, your pants are dirty, your face needs shaving." (His tone is apologetic, kidding. His voice pleads that no one should take offense.)

Perls: Speak in imperatives.

Mark (stopping before Gerry, who is now making faces at him—Kim has gone back to her seat): Gerry, stop that. (It's weak. Gerry makes more faces.) Stop that, Gerry. (Gerry is a kid clowning. He's brushing his hair toward Mark and dancing around.) Stop it, Gerry, you'll get dandruff all over everyone. (The joke is again an apology. Mark's back is to me but I know he must be smiling. And I see him as the hopelessly ineffectual teacher before the bad boy who is the leader of his class. His tone would only inspire a boy like that into total outrageousness.)

Perls: I am coming to your rescue—"Go fuck yourself, Gerry."

Mark: Go fuck yourself, Gerry. (It comes out flat. But Gerry sits down and Mark does too. There is a silence.) I feel stuck, Fritz. I feel dizzy and confused. I'm boring.

Perls: Try this one for size. You're not scared, you're just lost and don't know what to do.

(Mark seems to be waiting for more. But suddenly he smiles and it's a genuine smile.)

Mark: I don't need to be rescued. (He sounds amazed.) I can help myself. Jesus! What took me so long?

Perls nods and with his nodding seems to say, there, you see? Simple and obvious.

That evening Perls shows the film of Mark's episode and comments, "You see the impasse. There's a point where the patient becomes extremely anxious, stupid, doesn't understand anything, feels incapable of dealing with the world. If he works through that impasse, continuation is made possible. As soon as the implicit becomes explicit there is a brightening."

Once more I am skeptical. Isn't it possible that Mark merely found a clever way to avoid his neurosis by pretending to have a mini-satori when the pressure got too hot? To me that apparent breakthrough was as incomprehensible as all those Zen stories in which a master twists the student's nose or says some simple phrase and the student finds sudden illumination. (Six months after the end of Perls' workshop, I write to Mark. He replies that he remembers that morning vividly as one of many big and little incidents of liberation.)

Watching Perls is often like watching good theater. After the sessions are over, morning and evening, there are other forms of entertainment, other games to play. These are very much part of the turn-on process at Esalen and are at times as enlightening as the experience with Perls in the seminar room. Perls takes part in some of these games.

One evening I go down to the baths after the videotape showing. Several people from the seminar are already immersed in the steaming water. Perls sits on the rim, arms folded, beard and belly silhouetted in the flickering candlelight. I slip out of my clothes, put them on one of the wooden tables and sink into the big tub. The heat seeps through my body, loosening the muscles, seeming to soften my very bones. Perls sinks down, his beard floats on the water. We talk a little about his writing and mine. A bottle of white wine is passed. The candle flickers, the ocean crashes against rocks below us. Perls' arm slips around me, he pulls me toward him, turns my head toward himself and kisses me —the kiss of a sensuous virile man, not that of a seventy-four-year-old graybeard. I am immersed in well-being.

Then, suddenly, I become aware of others quietly conversing in the same tub and I pull away. Are they laughing? What's going on? I get out of the tub, angry, walk to the cold water hose, pour cold water over myself and then spray it all over everyone in the tub.

"Hey, stop that!" people shout angrily. I put down the hose and return to the tub. Perls has emerged and is getting dressed. A middle-aged woman is now sitting in his place. "You don't know what you were doing," she says, motherly. I laugh for I know perfectly well. Perls approaches the tub and leans over to kiss me again. "Good night," he says. "Good night." I know we understand each other and it's all right.

Later I see that up-tight people are shocked when they see Perls—that old man—kissing and hugging girls in the dining room. Perls (and the girls) delights in both the kisses and the reaction of decent, respectable folk. "I was a wild obnoxious boy," he tells me in an interview, while describing his childhood. "It is a characteristic I still cherish."

Sometimes his behavior jams those ever-clicking mind computers and makes people see themselves and others in a different light. It also alienates a lot of people—which may explain why Perls, so much in the forefront of the new lifestyle, is not better known. "The trouble with American existentialists," he likes to say, for example, "is that they talk but they don't exist, with the exception of Carl Rogers." When Abraham Maslow asked him to submit a paper for a symposium on the language of existentialism, Perls, with his scorn for abstractions, sent in a poem:

> I am not a lady perfuming her farts,
> I am a scoundrel and a lover of arts.
> I am what I am and I screw when I can,
> I'm Popeye the sailor, man.

At Esalen, this sort of thing endears Perls to many. For the atmosphere here is charged with sensuality, intimacy, intensity. People come to be jarred into some new aliveness, to have their minds turned around, and expect to see taboos crumble. Only phony or affected behavior is unacceptable here. Madness, promiscuity, all forms of eccentricity are part of the scene.

Once this fact comes through to people, they usually fall into a frenzy of some kind of wildness, like children who yell, fight and run about in the jubiliation that follows a long day in a rigidly disciplined school. The mixed nude bathing serves to break down a lot of inhibitions. The Esalen games, Big Sur and the gypsies do the rest. Well-heeled weekend seekers from Los Angeles and San Francisco slip and flip, explode—freak out.

It's my fourth day with Perls. The morning was exhausting. A reserved and beautiful woman trembled and cried talking about her loneliness and Seconal. A medical student worked on a dream in which he had to do a cesarian section on his sister but resisted because his gown and instruments were dirty. He ended by slicing, carving and cutting up the sister, then lying on his back on the floor and screaming like a baby. Penelope had a gasping and crying fit, which she called a "profound experience." She was furious when Perls told her it was almost totally phony. I've gotten to like Penelope, but she seems to have been overexposed to therapy. She knows all the formulas and they don't work for her anymore.

In the afternoon I wake from a nap and hear rock and roll music. So I go down to the lodge to see what is going on. In the door to the main seminar room, I stop. A mad scene is before me. People are flinging themselves about in time with the music, half naked and covered from hair to toenails to every inch of their clothing in multicolored paints. They writhe, gyrate and roll around on the paint-covered floor. They're people from Perls' workshop. Have they flipped?

As I continue watching I begin to feel the urge to join in. Stan the musician, his face black and green, whirls up to me, grabs my wrists and pulls me inside. I don't resist. He dabs purple on my cheek. Another man, mostly blue, puts a blue hand on the back of my sweatshirt. A painted statue rises from a chair to smear yellow on my nose. Stan and someone else grab my arms and legs and begin to swing me. Wild! I let my head fall back, my hair brushes the multicolored floor while others dab and pour colors on my midriff, which is bare under the pulled-up sweatshirt. Are my breasts showing? I've stopped wearing a bra up here. What does it matter? We've all been to the baths together. We whirl about, smear on more and more colors and it's mad, so what? Someone has pulled the lawn sprinkler onto the deck. We dance out, dance over it. Colors stream down, the deck turns into a pattern of painted footprints. We dance down to the swimming pool, dive in and float, suddenly quiet in the coolness. My sweatshirt balloons like a lifejacket. I have had my first freakout.

Perls has games to teach also, between his dramatic productions. They are designed to shake you loose from the mind computing and bring you into contact with your senses.

"I want to start with the understanding of a most difficult word," he says this morning. "The word I. I want to replace it with the word here. What has to be brought home is that I does not exist. It's a fantasy."

Penelope: Here is a body in a chair, here is standing, here are senses, here is excitement, searching, joy.

Perls: Now the opposite.

Penelope: Here is my excitement, there is your excitement.

Perls: No. A projection. Here is talking, there is silence. The I does not exist. It is a symbol of stating an identification with a certain process. When we talk about the I we don't know anything except that at the moment we identify with a certain part of ourselves. In rare cases, the I and the self identify and then we have a real person. When the I and the role identify, we have game play. Now, how, I. These are our tools. (Why is a dirty word in Gestalt therapy. Perls deals only with process, never with causes.)

Donna: Now is a beautiful morning.

Perls: I would call that a prejudice.

Donna: Now I experience curiosity.

Perls: How? (She is silent.) What do you experience after that?

Donna: I don't really know. (She's near tears. Everyone is at a high emotional pitch toward the end of the third week of the workshop. It takes little now to trigger an explosion of emotion.)

George: Now there is a deep breath, now there's excitement. Now here's a tightness around the mouth.

Perls: Take responsibility for the tightness.

George: I hold my mouth tight.

Perls (turning back to Donna): Let's play the withdrawal game. Close your eyes and go away. Where would you go?

Donna: I would sit on a rock and look at the ocean.

Perls: What do you experience there?

Donna: Freedom to cry.

Perls: Open your eyes. How do you experience this room?

Donna: As a place where I am not free to do anything. I want to yell for help.

Perls: Yell.

(Donna shouts "Help!" but her voice is timid and unconvincing.)

Donna: It isn't even me.

Perls: Who needs your help?

Donna: I.

She gets up and walks to the hot seat, where she is soon deep in a dream in which a tiger and a horse are locked in conflict, rolling down a hillside as she watches. With the withdrawal game, Perls has prepared her to enter her conflict.

"With the withdrawal game you either get more into focus what is uncomfortable in a situation or you go to a situation of support and bring the support back with you," Perls explains later. "If you keep on shuttling, you eventually will feel an integration taking place. It's a one-minute holiday when you are under stress and is especially important when you are bored. Boredom is very important if you investigate what real interest you are blocking. I often withdraw and get an image that becomes a clue to the situation with the patient."

He uses the game again a few days later. He is working with a mathematics professor who sounds so lifeless he bores everyone within minutes. Perls tells us all to close our eyes, withdraw somewhere, return and compare the experience. We are to shuttle several times without opening our eyes. I go out to a beach and return to feel stone-wall rigidity in the room; withdraw to a sunny meadow and return to sense all air being sucked out of the room. I can barely breathe.

"I went into my tiredness," Perls says when we open our eyes. "I felt tired and I felt like crying and screaming with despair so that I could wake up. Apparently your ability to paralyze is so powerful for me I'm driven to despair."

Cruel words? A challenge. Before long I hear a flicker of life in the professor's voice. It is only a flicker—but it is something.

Later, Perls shows us varieties of the game: "Take a time machine. You are here. Go into your childhood and shuttle between now and then to see if it has changed. The whole memory crap is distorted. What we call memories are certain impressions or abstractions that are unfinished. So-called memories are projections of the here and now."

The shuttling idea, and his technique of polarizing and then integrating conflict, grows out of Perls' adaptation of the system of differential thinking developed by Salomo Friedlander in his book *Schoepferische Indifferenz* (*Creative Indifference*). Friedlander saw every event as related to a zero-point from which differentiation into opposites begins. The opposites have a great affinity in their specific context. If we can stand at the center, we can see them together.

Usually, differentiation develops equally on two or more sides. In pouring wine from a bottle into a glass, one empties the bottle while filling the glass by the same amount of liquid. The single motion leads to interdependent polarities. Perls points out that by seeking the opposite of something we can learn about its source. Thus, in the case of disappointment, if one looks not for the cause but for its opposite, one finds it to be expectation. The greater the expectation, the greater the disappointment. Thus, a man who knows how to live without expectation will be able to accept whatever the moment brings him without disappointment. This is the attitude Perls seeks to develop. It is very much the attitude taught by Zen.

If differentiation proceeds beyond a maximum point of extension, the opposites suddenly fuse or reverse: pleasure turns to pain, love to hate, food to poison. It is as if a pendulum swung out so far it flipped over.

Perls demonstrated the closeness of opposites on that first night I attended his seminar, when he had us think of our most effective manipulative behavior, use its opposite in conversation, and say "That is a lie" after every sentence. Later I see that thinking in paired opposites is very much a part of the turned-on style of life.

We learn other Gestalt games, other ways of turning our realities around in our minds. Jack Downing, a well-known West Coast psychiatrist who is learning from Perls, shows a group of us several. In the mirror game two people face each other. One tries to imitate the other, without speaking. The other tries to imitate the first imitating him. Soon their identies are confused.

In the I-You game, two converse using only the two words, I and you. The communication assumes a clarity that frightens me. All subterfuge becomes transparent.

In the awareness guru game one person talks of what he is aware of. The guru may direct him with questions (Are you aware that you are tensing your ankle?) and later tells him what he, the guru, was aware of in the other.

Another Gestalt game is watching another person as one would a kitten—observing without self-consciousness or expectation, allowing him to be what he is. This, like the other games, requires listening, looking and full attendance to the moment; that is, one must be in the now. It is practice for awareness. If one is fully aware, Perls says, one has no anxiety. For anxiety is the vague product of catastrophic expectations and awareness precludes expectations. One can have hopes, plans, paths in mind, without expectations.

We play the games on the lawn, in the dining room, on rocks that overlook the ocean, in the baths. It's hard to get over the self-consciousness—I feel vulnerable. But looking at someone and listening to him in a game like that, I know that I will never forget his voice or features.

Perls is particularly adept with couples. One night I watch him during an evening session with another group, married couples who have been meeting for several days with two family counselors. They have come to learn how to be "close yet free within marriage," in the words of the Esalen catalog. Perls becomes a magician-impresario with them. His acts are brief—five to ten minutes—but pithy.

He asks the couples to take turns coming to sit in the two chairs at his left. What transpires is videotaped and, as they sit there, they can watch themselves on the TV set as in a mirror. First to move up are a middle-aged pair, Mike and May.

Perls (to Mike): What I'd like you to do is to introduce your spouse to me. Then talk to her and tell her how you feel about her.

Mike: Fritz, this is my wife May and at this moment I feel she . . .

Perls: Please do not gossip about her. Say her name. (Talking *about* something or someone is strictly forbidden in Gestalt therapy. All speech must be direct.)

Mike: May. (It is a simple statement.)

Perls: Did you get that, May? (She nods.)

Mike: May, I feel closer to you than I have all during the day. It was a growing experience for us and I hope that . . .

Perls: Are you aware that you are sermonizing?

Mike (automatically): I am aware. (Continues in the same tone as before) May, I feel closer . . . (He catches himself, turns to Perls) Am I aware of what? (Others in the room laugh. Ah! Perls is right about people not listening.)

Perls: Sermonizing. You're giving a lecture. Just say the name—May. (In the evocation game, which consists of using only the name, Mike would show his response to his wife without hiding it in words. But he can't do that.)

Mike: May, it was a good experience.

Perls: May, talk to him.

May: (uncertainly) It was a good experience.

Perls: Can you switch to the now? Not the stale stuff of this morning.

(They look at each other.)

Mike: May. (This time it sounds caressing. Her face lights up.)

May: Mike. (It is firm, warm. They reach for each other's hands.)

Perls: Next couple.

Barry and Martha are next. They both are a little dour.

Barry: Fritz, this is my wife Martha.

Perls: Repeat "Martha" until you reach her.

Barry: Martha. (Martha shakes her head.)

Perls: Your voice gets to about here. (He puts his hand midway between them. To Martha:) Do you see that guy?

Martha: That's Barry.

Perls: What do you see?

Martha: I see smile lines that I like. I see eyes that I feel comfortable looking into.

Perls: Talk to him.

Martha: I am. Am I not, Barry? (It's a cold question with an edge of threat in it.)

Barry: That went right through me.

Martha (impatiently): Then I don't see you.

Perls: You are sitting a bit too smug for making such a important communication. (She's slumped back in her chair, crosslegged.)

Martha: I don't know that I want to get closer.

Perls: Repeat that. (She is silent.)

Perls: Say, "I won't come to you, you've got to come to me." (He's translating what she said with the tone of her voice.)

Martha: I won't come to you, you've got to come to me. (It rings true.)

Perls (to Barry): What do you feel about this?

Barry (ineffectual voice): Hurt.

Perls: Is this your marriage?

Martha: I don't think it is, but then I'm only half of it. (Again the note of threat is in her voice.)

Barry: I don't think so either, but when she said that I felt all tense as if I were opening an old room. I don't know where it comes from but it really hit.

Perls (to Barry): Do me a favor. Lean forward. "I'm willing to meet you halfway."

Barry: No, let her come partway.

Martha (haughty): I don't feel I have any choice.

Perls: Right now you have no choice. It might be phony, it might be real but I want to try out an experiment. (She leans forward.)

61

Martha: Do you feel it's not me?

Barry (tone uncertain): No.

Martha (dismissing the whole thing with annoyance): I feel it's not me.

Perls: Say "I'm stuck."

Martha (yelling): I'm stuck. Damn it, I'm stuck!

Perls: Stay with the feeling of being stuck.

Next come two middle-aged toothy people, whom I'd expect to be members of a weekend hiking group. They both have on bermuda shorts and checkered flannel shirts and suggest the YM-YWCA. As soon as they sit down they flow into each other.

He: Dee-dee! (Soulful.)

She: Yes. (They're both grinning. Their arms intertwine.)

He: Dee-dee, I love thee.

She: I'm glad of that. (The voices suggest they've played this game before. His is automatic, hers has an undercurrent of wariness.)

Perls has them extricate their arms and look at each other without smiling. Then he asks the man to talk to his image on the TV. The man's tone changes.

He: We gotta stick together buddy, and we shall overcome. They said it was the wrong target and dropped the bombs over there but we knew, didn't we, that the target was over here. Sometimes they'll be right and sometimes we'll be right but we'll stick together and we shall overcome.

Perls: Look at her. This is your wife. Do you see any bombs or targets?

He (slowly coming back): Targets yes; no more bombs. (Distant, looking at his wife.) Strange that I can sometimes get closer with Billy and the bottle than I can with you. (He's smiling).

She (spreading her arms, her face scared): Your smile disturbs me.

Perls: Is Dee-dee her name?

He: It's Marie.

Perls: Say Marie. (He does, several times, not coming through.)

She (anxiously): Does it matter that Marie is not what he calls me?

He: Marie. Dee-dee. Marie. It's harder with Dee-dee than with Marie.

Perls: Next couple.

"Two people can be in such jelly-like oneness that they are either in confluence or in isolation but never in contact,"

Perls once said. "All contact and communication is across a boundary."

The last couple does not come up. The man's legs are stretched arrogantly out into the room and he is stiff and straight diagonally across the chair, with hands folded on a sizable stomach.

He: I don't think I care to, Fritz. Unless, of course, you want to, Sally? You want to? (He's peremptory.)

She: Hm. I don't want that question. It's okay.

Perls: He sounds like a blackmailer. Is he a blackmailer?

She: I don't understand.

Perls: You know what a blackmailer is. A Jewish mother is a blackmailer: "I don't care if you don't come home, do whatever you like." Hm?

She: I don't understand. I feel I'm in the middle of something of my own doing. I love my husband very much.

Perls: Say this to him.

She (leaning toward him): Julius, I love you very much.

He (without looking at her or moving): I love you very much.

Perls: In that position? Look at that posture! What a love posture! Could you by any chance be afraid of your feelings?

He: I don't think so.

Perls: What do you dislike about me?

He: I think you're obnoxious.

Perls: Now we're getting somewhere.

He: You're a dirty sloppy old man.

Perls: Ye-es? (He's enjoying this.)

He: At times I see a spark of some considerable ability in you. But I've watched you behave and you just don't measure up.

The man who did the bomber scene: Hear, hear!

He: I don't think you project yourself. You're too wrapped up in Fritz Perls.

Perls: Tell me what I should be like. (He is definitely enjoying this.)

He: You showed each couple how to project what they feel toward each other. Can you do that for yourself?

Perls: I'm pretty mean to hold myself back?

He: I don't know that you're mean. I just expected more of you.

Perls: Aha! Now we're getting somewhere. I don't live up to your expectations. I should be different than I am. Could this by any chance be the case with your wife too?

He: No, my wife is a very happy-go-lucky kind of person. (The woman beside him looks timid, haggard and tense.)

63

Perls: Say this to her.

(He does, without looking up.)

Perls: Is he right?

She (after a pause): I'm afraid to get angry. (Pause.) But boy, sometimes I do. (There is fury in her voice.)

Perls: Repeat that.

She: When I get mad—boy, sometimes I get mad and I feel good. (Her voice is full of rage.)

Cut. Perls has, in each case, found a strong chord to play in conclusion, leaving it ringing in their minds as: that's where you're at. They came in here already warmed up by a couple of days at Esalen. But Perls had not seen them before. His ability to play them struck me as uncanny. Now he gets up, the ever-present ash long on his cigarette, and walks across the room, pleased with himself. He puts the Mahler symphony on the stereo. The performance is over.

Perls freely admits that he cherishes moments "when I'm a prima donna, when I'm functioning in front of a large audience and can do my thing well. The theater was my first love, that and philosophy and literature." But his Jewish middle-class parents did not approve of a theatrical career for him so, after a spell with the Max Reinhardt Theater in Berlin, where he was born, he decided to study medicine. He thought he might move through Medicine into philosophy.

The First World War began while he was a student at the Friedrich Wilhelm University and he volunteered for the Zeppelin Corps. But because he had already passed his *physikum*, an intermediate medical examination, he was made a junior medical officer and attached to the gas engineers who fought with poison gas along the French-Belgian front. There in the trenches he learned about rats, hunger, gas and anti-Semitism.

"I stood it for a year and a half, then I suddenly got the flu with a high temperature. So they sent me to a hospital," Perls recalls. "As soon as I got there, the temperature dropped from 104 back to 98. Two days afterwards I learned that our medical officer was coming to visit me. Immediately the fever went up again. So the batallion marched off without me." In the rear batallion to which he was next attached, he found himself under "a very cruel anti-Semitic captain."

"I came out of this war dead. But we really believed that this was the war to end all wars and we started rebuilding. There was Die Brueke, the painting movement, and Das Bauhaus, the philosophical movement. It was an exciting time. We met in our Romanische Kafe, I wrote some lovely poems and was involved in literature and theater. But mostly I was involved in medicine and its relationship to psychotherapy. I think I was the first psychotherapist in the Berlin Neurological Clinic.

"Freud at the time was the god and his word was Holy Gospel. I went into psychoanalysis and for seven years suffered from the impression that I was too stupid to understand. I wasted my time for seven years."

He began his analysis with Karen Horney in 1925, then worked with several others. His last analyst was Wilhelm Reich. In 1926, an assistant at the Kurt Goldstein Institute for brain-injured soldiers in Frankfurt-am-Main, he met Laura Posner whom he married in 1930. He also met there a luminous circle of existentialists and Gestaltists, including Martin Buber, Paul Tillich and Kurt Goldstein. But being preoccupied with psychoanalysis, he was not then ready for their ideas.

After the burning of the Reichstag, Perls decided it was time to leave Germany. He took a post as teaching psychoanalyst in South Africa. In 1936 he traveled to Marienbad in Czechoslovakia to read a paper on his theory of oral resistances at a psychoanalytic congress. His thesis was that a baby inhibited in biting will develop a fear of hurting and being hurt. The paper was not well received because most of those present were unwilling to accept the existence of such resistances. Perls sought to see Freud but found him brusque and too busy.

He returned to South Africa and wrote *Ego, Hunger and Aggression*, in which he developed theories that diverged from Freud. It was published first in South Africa in 1942 then in Great Britain in 1946. In 1968 it was reissued in the United States.

In 1947, seeing the beginning of apartheid in South Africa, Perls decided to come to the United States. With the help of Erich Fromm and Clara Thompson of the Washington School, he became established in New York with Laura. He worked with Charlotte Selver, who teaches sensory awareness, and, with Ralph F. Hefferline and Paul Goodman, wrote *Gestalt Therapy*, which first gave a name to the methods and theories he had developed. In 1950, shortly after the book's publication, he moved to Los Angeles. Laura Perls remained to practice Gestalt therapy in New York.

Restless, Perls moved several times: to Miami, then to Columbus, then back to Miami, to New York and again to Los Angeles. In the early 1960s he took LSD several times at Mendecino State Hospital. It made him "really paranoic" at first, he told me, but he continued to take it because "it was something interesting, something that made life still worth experiencing." In the long run it was useful, he came to believe. But his most powerful psychedelic experience, he said, was with Psilocybin, a synthetic of the Mexican "magic mushroom." With that drug he reexperienced a life and death struggle he had survived under anaesthetic when he suffered a stroke after an operation. "I finally understood that I was willing to come back," he recalls. "This made a decisive difference between being condemned to life and blessed with life."

He came to view LSD as "a very dangerous, very deceptive drug" which nevertheless could be useful in showing "that there is another life available beyond the thinking computer level." Every qualified psychiatrist should be permitted to use it at his discretion, he believes.

In 1963, dissatisfied with himself and the meager recognition Gestalt therapy had thus far been accorded, he took a fifteen-month trip around the world. He found two places where he thought of settling: Kyoto in Japan and Elath in Israel. "But then I found Hot Springs and I found here I've got people like in Kyoto, who look at each other, regard each other, live with each other not against each other. I found a similar beauty as in Elath, the landscape beauty," he told Dr. James Simkin, a Los Angeles disciple, "and I found a wonderful opportunity for work."

Now Perls sees signs that Gestalt therapy is coming into its own. A growing disillusionment with psychoanalysis, which has dominated the American scene together with behaviorism, has left the door open to the Third Force people who are mostly existentialists. More and more capable therapists have come to Perls for training. There are more than a hundred Gestalt therapists practicing throughout the country. "The danger is that it might become a cult and be identified with Fritz Perls' uniqueness," he says. "But I would say with Churchill that we are now at the end of the beginning. Something real is happening, I feel it all over the place. People are looking for something that works and Gestalt therapy will fall into that gap."

As I keep watching Perls at work, I gradually begin to grasp what he means when he talks about "living in the now"; when he says that "learning is the discovery that something is possible," and that conflict and listening are polarities. Then the process of discovery speeds up suddenly, for at the end of the first week with Perls, I take an LSD trip.

Chapter THREE

A Trip

ESALEN INSTITUTE has strict rules against drugs on the premises but Big Sur is head country. I intended to take LSD sometime during my stay on the Coast, if the right opportunity arose, but did not plan to do it so soon. I am reluctant to add anything still more intense to my experience of watching Perls. Still, the trip being planned for this weekend is the sort of opportunity I have hoped to find. A man who has done a lot of work with LSD is visiting Big Sur and is to be in charge of a group trip that will include some local residents and a few people from Perls' seminar. We are to go to a house several miles from the Hot Springs on Friday night. As Perls has scheduled no seminar sessions until Sunday night, I have the time. I decide to take part.

On Friday I awake scared. I dreamed of a barren hillside with hawks circling above trenches and bomb shelters. Not a single blade of grass grew on the hill. Not a single human soul had been present. Was this some sign from my innermost mind that I should change plans? Will the dream come along on the trip? Does it mean that I'm at odds with myself and the world and will be one of those trippers who end up in mental hospitals?

The morning session with Perls is not particularly interesting and as the day advances I get more and more nervous. I have been advised to spend some time quietly in preparation, so after lunch I go back to my cabin and lie down. But the dream stays with me. I get up and go up the road for a walk. The sight of the ocean and of flowers and plants along hillsides proves soothing, though the dream's shadow still remains. At midafternoon I return to the lodge. As usual, there are hip gypsies draped over the railing by the office door and scattered on the lawn. Eight boys and girls sit in a circle talking and burning incense. I'd like to join them, find out a little about who they are, but they might make fun of a square like me and I should avoid all unpleasantness now.

Farther down on the large lawn Bernie Gunther has gathered a group of family therapists for a sensory awakening session. This is safer. I join them. We spread bed sheets on the grass and lie down on them, closing our eyes. Gunther's voice takes me through my body: feel in contact with the ground, feel how the head touches, the toes, the fingernails. Without moving, travel through yourself with your mind. My right eyelid is burning in the sun, the left one is cool. My head lies heavy and hard, my body is stiff. But I'm aware of the supple grass beneath the sheet.

Now stand up and tap with fingers, loose-wristed, all over the head. Pleasurable whiteness sinks in under closed eyes. Open the eyes. Slap your forehead, jaw, lips, cheeks, tap softly with fingertips on the closed lids. Feel the face loosen and a tingling sensation spread through the head.

Take a partner, look at him. I see a man with eyelid twitching, mouth stiff in self-consciousness. He arouses my sympathy. I tap his head, then look into his face. He twitches less now. Good. We smile briefly, pass on to new partners.

Gunther, like Perls, aims to tune people in to their senses. His method is adapted mainly from work done by Charlotte Selver, whom I am to visit later in New York. He also uses techniques derived from his study of Gestalt therapy, Zen, yoga and massage.

My next partner is a dumpy little woman with cunning eyes. At the distended neckline of her shapeless jersey, I see a bra strap digging into the flesh of her shoulder. She hasn't been here long enough to stop wearing a bra. Standing behind her, I slap her shoulders briskly, then move simultaneously down both arms, back up and down again. Quickly. Then I step in front of her and look at her face while her eyes are still closed. I see weariness. She opens her eyes, we look at each other: there is warmth here and a flash of vague fear. I see no cunning. We embrace, pass on. We yell, pound our chests—Arrrrrrrhhhhh!—then lie down once again. Now the body is buoyant, almost weightless on the ground and the head lies easy. I hear the ocean and birds. The breeze slides gently over my skin. I open my eyes, glad again.

The encounter group to which I have been assigned is meeting at the baths today for a group massage. Massage is big at Esalen, and group massage is one of the games people play to get rid of inhibitions regarding their bodies and physical contact. We take turns lying on tables in the sunshine. Oil

68

is poured over us and six pairs of slithery hands rub and knead us all at once. Someone runs his thumbs hard across my lips, and tension that I didn't know was still there relaxes.

Afterward we climb into tubs, scrub each other, shampoo each other's hair. In the past I've done this sort of thing with a man before or after making love. But here it's different. Love-making is free and easy at the Hot Springs, but sensuality does not always lead to sex. Group massage and mutual soaping are certainly sensual. But nobody gets all hot and bothered and wants to rush out of the bath into bed. Right now all this at the baths is part of a ritual that prepares me for tonight.

By dinnertime I am completely calm and at ease. After all, if the worst happens and I go crazy on LSD, what better place could I find for that than Esalen? Surely there are enough people here who could help me regain my mental balance.

I eat a light dinner, as instructed. Then I dress for the trip. A sea-green velour blouse and orange pants should be comfortable, and I like the colors. I'm really looking forward to those kaleidoscopes. The death dream is forgotten.

After dinner, I leave in a car with a middle-aged couple from Perls' group. The man is a doctor, seemingly calm and kindly of disposition. The woman is very handsome and voluptuous and tends toward hysteria, I think. They are from one of the most prosperous suburbs of San Francisco and have taken many LSD trips together.

"So you're an acid virgin?" she says. "You'll be fun." She puts me off a little. Am I to be some kind of spectacle?

We drive south on the highway and turn right to descend a dirt road toward a small frame house that stands six feet from the edge of the cliff. A pale, somewhat sickly-looking girl with long blond hair and dark eyes opens the door: Mella, the hostess. (The names of the trippers are fictitious.) We enter a comfortable room with a fireplace, candlelight, Navajo tapestries on the walls, couches and soft chairs. Glass doors lead from the living room to the garden. Manos Hadjidakis' "Lilacs from a Dead Land" is playing softly on the stereo. I'm delighted by the warmth of this launching pad.

Several trippers have already arrived and spread mattresses, blankets and pillows on the rug. The guru looks up to greet us. He is building a fire. He is a tall, slim man in his late thirties with a quick smile and strangely bright eyes— bright but not deep, almost glassy. I watch him gather together logs and kindling and light them. The cut crystal on his necklace catches the reflections of the flames. Do I trust him? His movements are quick and assured. Yes, thank God, I do. It would be terrible if I did not.

Within a few minutes, the rest of the group arrives. We are twelve in all, counting Mella and the guru. But only ten of us are "going up," as it's put. The guru asks us to sit in a circle and stops the record player. This is a structured trip, he says. That means that there are certain rules, which he will explain, that we are to abide by. But first he wants to know if anyone here objects to anyone else's presence. We look at each other. Most of those here are strangers to me. There are two hip gypsies: a young man with gentle eyes, long blond hair and a red beard and, beside him, a nineteen-year-old girl who works at Esalen part-time. I noticed her in the dining room one evening because of her unusual facial expression. It was simultaneously ecstatic and vacant. Her features were somehow dissolved.

There's the doctor and his wife; a young psychologist and his wife, who are both friendly and attractive; a college professor who reminds me, for some reason, of a dancing bear; his very fat but sultry wife, and a tiny green-eyed girl in a long green dress whom I remember from that inter-racial weekend at Esalen. I disliked her then. She struck me as a total phony. Inside a fragile doll with a tinkly voice and sweet smile I sensed suppressed rage. When a man made her angry during one of the sessions she had suddenly risen from her chair, stalked across the room and slapped him. Physical violence was forbidden but how could anyone object to the tiny creature's attack? Beware of the Sugarplum Fairy! Yes, I feel venomous toward her and would have preferred not to see her here, but I don't really mind. There are no objections.

The guru now explains the structure. There are four rules. First, we are not to harm ourselves or anyone else either now or later. Second, if we want to leave the house alone and go beyond the road, we are to ask permission. Third, there is to be no intercourse without permission. Fourth, if he comes up to anyone and says "This is structure," he is to be obeyed. We are not to get upset if we hear people crying. And we are not to resent anyone who might push us away as we approach. For we might go off on very different trips and should all allow the others to choose their own direction. If anyone should want to come down at any time, the proper drug is available. However, in the many trips he has led, this has never proved necessary, our guru says.

He deals out the acid, different quantities to each of us. The professor, who is an old head, takes 400 micrograms. The Sugarplum Fairy wants just a little and is given 75. I get one and a half tablets, 250 micrograms, which is a medium dose. I hold them in my hand and look at them closely. A white tablet with a brown core and half of another. The passport, the ticket—to where? I swallow them and sit down on the couch opposite the fireplace to wait. The guru said it would be fifteen to thirty minutes before we would feel the effect.

I look at the bowl of fruit on the coffee table before me and at the candle beside it. Beyond the fruit and candle is the fire. People are settling down on the mattresses, the other couch and the chairs. "Lilacs from a Dead Land" is again playing.

The guru bends over me. "If you see anything frightening, walk toward it and it will disappear," he tells me. Then he holds his hand, palm down, over my midriff and moves it in a circle, without touching me. I feel a pronounced tingling and look up at him, surprised. He laughs. "A chakra message," he says.

Slowly, something is happening to my head. It begins to feel heavy and balloon-like at the same time and seems to sit loose on my neck, as if the muscles had suddenly gone slack. From the head and the neck, a torpor seeps down my arms, loosening muscle fibers; down to my wrists and to my fingertips. It is a pleasurable sensation.

Now the candle flame before me expands into a halo. The torpor seeps down through my body, down through my belly into my pelvis. I loosen and expand. On the mattress below me, Martin, the psychologist, and his wife, Eloise, are holding up the guru's necklace with the cut-crystal pendant. I noticed that Martin has on a handsome blue silk shirt handpainted with golden patterns of leaves and peacocks. The two of them are swinging the guru's pendant high up between them and laughing in delight. But what is happening to Martin's shirt? It begins to glow. The leaves and the peacocks are moving. I think and shake my head. Yes the design is changing.

"Martin!"

"What?"

"Your shirt, look at your shirt. It's moving!" My voice is not quite my voice. It's a little out of control.

Martin looks down at his shirt, then unbuttons it, takes it off and puts it down on the floor. "Yes, you're right," he says "It is." The shirt turns into a jungle of plants and birds. I can let them move or I can make them stop. They are beautiful but almost—they are almost turning into serpents and monsters. I stop that and they become beautiful birds and leaves,

71

growing a third dimension, glowing in gold and blue. "That's some shirt, Martin," I say, laughing. "Look, there's a valley in this jungle." My voice is unfamiliar. Gradually the flowing shirt loses its shirtishness completely. The blue-gold rises up like water sucked up by a vacuum into a cone that turns to gas when it touches the air. I sink to the floor and go into the jungle with Martin. He is an Oriental potentate. His wife, who comes to sit beside us, is a harem queen with a thick braid of black hair falling over her right shoulder. The guru's necklace around her neck shoots rainbows. But at the same time I also know that the three of us are sitting on the floor holding on to a Chinese shirt.

My watch is too tight. I take it off, and also my ring, and lay them in the fruit bowl on the coffee table. Looking around, I see that others have also changed. The fat girl, the professor's wife, has turned into a presence, magic and mysterious. She is a cat woman glowering wickedly as she sits cross-legged under the grand piano, with unearthly jewels in her black velvet hair and elegant snake-eyebrows arching. The Sugarplum Fairy steps past me, unreal but so pretty, also with jewels by her ears.

Someone is doing something on my belly, I feel a pleasurable scratching around my navel but am not interested. It has nothing to do with me. It's the guru and Martin, they're doing something. The music is growing—a Bach cantata. Everything merges now, there is no more jungle, no more sultan, no more separation between sight and sound and touch, me and the music, the vast music. I am holding the doctor's hands and looking into his face. It has a new clarity. His eyes look at me and we meet in unlimited space. I put my arms around his shoulders. "So much space," says a voice I never heard but know to be mine. "It can be filled," he says, sadly. No, that's not what I meant, the space fills us. "I like the space," I say and touch his cheek with my fingers. The Bach chorale and he and I are one, rising and falling within vast cathedral spaces in great depths of sound. This is God, love, life—joyful pain, painful joy. Is this true? "Is this what we've been looking for then?" I ask the doctor. He is wiser, he must know. "Is it all in this small pill? Just a pill?"

"I know what you're asking," he says, "I have been here before." The words go so deep into me—though he has not answered me—that I fall around his neck and begin to cry. He is a prophet with those deep eyes and the beautiful clear craggy face. He speaks out of centuries of Jewish wisdom. I kiss his neck and stroke his face. I sense he wants gentleness.

Suddenly he says, "Carlotta!" and looks around for his

wife. In a flash I see the room, where we were sitting on the mattress and other people are sitting and walking about. Where is the guru? I must know what is real. He is by the fireplace. Somehow, I get to him.

"Is it all in the pill?"

"The pill only opens the door," he says. "It's here and in you."

His voice is a gift. He is holding me up for I'm on my knees just barely rising from the swirling of unlimited multicolored space. Yes, yes.

"But all those books, all those centuries and prophets—they looked so hard and all the time it was so simple. It was in this pill." It's cruel and wrong. And now, will it vanish?

"Tomorrow, will it look the same as yesterday?"

"No, you will see, it won't be the same."

"Is this it then?"

"What?"

"What I've been trying so long to find out." The flowing is taking me away from him. But not yet. "I want to bring it back to those who aren't here."

"It's here for everyone." He knows, I love him. He has been here.

"But tomorrow I'll only have the same clichés to put on paper. I won't know how."

"This is *now*. This is *now*."

Yes. He has gone. And now I know that life is a constant flowing and we are part of each other. I have read it, thought it, but now I know and am overwhelmed with gratitude. If I can't write it down, it's all right. Someone else will go farther. Wherever I fail, someone else will rise. I feel a rush of liberation. But a moment later I want to test it.

Now I am sitting on the mattress facing Mella. "Will you forgive me for the clichés?" For what I write will be part of her also. "I don't care if you use clichés," she says, almost impatiently, "you're beautiful." The overflowing gratitude—Yes, I accept and am accepted. I will grow. I will ask when I need and give when I'm full. I will hold and let go just as I let go the guru, whom I love, and found Mella.

No, I don't trust this. The guru is wise and outside of all this. I find him by the piano.

"I want to know how it looks to you."

"I'm with you."

"But if it's so simple, why is it so hard and why am I so afraid?"

"What are you afraid of?"

My voice goes out from me independent, without letting

73

me choose its words. "Why do I try to hold on when it's time to let go? Why do I cling so when I see how beautiful it is to flow? I love you but when you leave me it won't hurt. I will find you again or I'll find another."

"That's right, that's right." He is pleased to hear me say this. Oh God, the simplicity, the release, the gift of grace.

"I want others to have it. There are those outside whom I love. I want to give it to them. I want to bring them in. I have so much, I want to spread it around."

"You can give."

It doesn't matter to whom since we're all one. I'm so happy I start to laugh. I remember Carlotta, the doctor's wife. She has sorrow in her eyes. I find her in the bottom of a pit, only the eyes looking up frightened and desolate. "You are beautiful, Carlotta," I tell her and stroke her hair.

"No!" She shakes off my hand. Her face is lucid in its desolation, deep in a pit of the suffering eyes. Suddenly her head shrinks, the rich black hair changes to thin gray stubble. Almost at once it changes back. Well, it's all right, I'll go.

Here is Mella again. "Who are you?" I ask her. "You live all alone in the woods here?" "Yes." "That's beautiful and terrible." "Yes, that's beautiful and terrible." All that matters in our lives is in those words. Nothing more is needed. We know each other.

We lie down beside each other on the mattress. She's so thin and bony she must be cold. I cover her with a blanket. We lie there and laugh at what we see above us. Martin, the psychologist, and his wife are doing their own thing, whatever that is. They are dancing around, Martin is making all kinds of funny motions with his hands and whistling under his breath. And there stands the professor, grinning, slightly slumped—exactly like a huge dancing bear. I go to him. He has bad breath. I step back. "I saw your wife as a Persian sorceress," I tell him. "Go tell her that, please tell her."

I go but she pushes me off, hissing. All right. But suddenly I know there's a cliff. It's darker suddenly. I mustn't go over it. I won't go into the fire or over the cliff because my mother and sisters would suffer. I stand up and shout, "I'm strong!" Like the guru. Where is the guru? I find him in the kitchen and put my arms around his neck. "You and I, we're strong, aren't we?" I say. We're superior to everyone. "Yeah, we're strong," he says. "So let's screw," I say. He laughs. "Can't. That's structure." "O.K., not now. When?" "I don't know." "Next week," I decide and leave him, happy. This is like one enormous orgasm anyway, I don't want anything more now. There's the Sugarplum Fairy sitting looking into the fire.

She's from the ballet so I'll give her to my sister. I go to her and pull at her arm. But to my surprise—for I don't see her as human—she resists and won't come along. She looks angry.

What else is happening? On the couch by the fire the doctor and Carlotta are clinging together. Everyone is clinging to someone and I am shut out. I hate them. (Later I'll forget some of this ugly part and won't remember it until seven months later.) I stand up and begin a monologue about my strength, my good life, my suffering during the war, comparing myself to others. The hippie girl comes to take my hand and look at me from her strangely vacant face. I shout at her, "You bitch, you thought you were superior to me but you're not, you're stupid, your face is stupid." She keeps on looking at me, frightened and uncomprehending. I keep spewing hate.

Then I am crouching by the coffee table, shrunken into nothing. If I asked for help now nobody would come, I think bitterly. Someone once said I was afraid to ask for help. Well, we'll see why—no one will come. I begin to call, "I want some water." Nobody answers. "Someone bring me some water." Maybe Martin would. We had a good time in the jungle. "Martin, water." At last I hear his wife, impatiently, "Bring her some water, for God's sakes Martin, stop that yelling." And Martin brings me a glass of wonderful cold water. As he puts it to my lips I am five years old, in bed, released from the frightening dark by the blessed appearance of my grandmother.

Disembodied conversations. Voices seem to respond to me, but to whom are they talking? Sitting on the mattress now I touch a bearded face. "You," I say, amused, "you look like Christ."

"Sometimes I am," he says in Christ's voice. Forgive me! I bend my head, he takes my hand. We lie down. My other hand goes around his head and becomes entangled in the hair of the hip gypsy girl. Mary Magdalen. We lie together, entwined. Voices are rising and falling as the music—flute and guitar now—rises and falls. It's peace to lie with Jesus and Mary Magdalen.

When I get up again everyone is in couples and Mella has gone off to sleep. I sit on the couch again and look at the fire. It is cold. The candle has gone out, there is only the bleak morning after the party. All are in pairs. I am alone. In the whole world everyone is snug hugging in pairs and I shrink

75

and shrivel alone. They are all strangers, foreigners to me. I am cold.

In the bathroom I look at my face in the mirror and see a woman with loose, slack features and eyes that are all black except for a thin rim of blue. She's a good-looking woman but I have never seen her before.

It is dawn already so I go out to walk up the road. Now something new begins—my own private movie. I stop at the edge of a cliff to look at the fog. Nothing is visible except fog. But as I keep looking, a landscape emerges in the mist. A river is pushing out to sea. It has almost broken through the rock that blocks it. Soon its passage will be totally clear from womb-lake into ocean. Drops of water from the trees fall heavily into me and tears roll down my face. I am dazed and quiet. I pluck a yellow flower and walk up the dirt road past wet bushes set on the brink of the fog. Then I come to another overlook and more landscapes, beautiful fairy-tale cities, scenes that Leonardo da Vinci saw and tried to put into his paintings, painted by the ancient Chinese.

The guru and the gypsy couple are coming up the road. I had hoped someone would come looking. I give Mary Magdalen the yellow flower and embrace her. It seems irrelevant to ask her forgiveness for something I dimly remember. "Have you seen your chakra flower?" the man who is sometimes Christ asks. I don't understand. He tells me to look at my navel. There a yellow daisy has been drawn, the initiation flower for an acid virgin. So that's what the guru and Martin were doing last night. I'm pleased and no longer so alone now.

Later I lie in the bedroom and look out at the trees beyond the glass wall. The movie continues. I see my face in the leaves, made of leaves and just barely emerging. It is covered with something so that only the eyes and forehead are visible. Everything that I, here on the bed, feel, the eyes in the trees show me. They keep changing. I watch. This is a visual way of thinking, very different from the kind Perls calls computing. The pictures emerge instead of the usual words and tell me more than words would. I need only to look. The monsters that I knew could emerge from Martin's shirt last night are now out there. But now, when I'm ready to look at them, they have disguised themselves into toy monsters and carved Oriental dragons. They won't move now.

I try to uncover the bottom half of my face but can't. Then I see that it's not covered at all, that what I thought was the covering is a part of the face. I am a choking, gasping, screaming puppet mask with real eyes. I summon all my energy and try to make the mask be a face but can't. The eyes keep changing. At moments they become others' eyes—those of Stan, the musician in Perls' group, Mary Magdalen's, then again mine.

Carlotta comes to sit next to me. She remembers that something happened between us and wants me to tell her how I remember it. She also asks if I met her husband and how he seemed to me. But I don't want to talk about that. An enormity of things happened during the night and I will not reduce them by talking or even thinking about them right now. I'm still very shaky with a sinking, shrinking feeling, and I want to see more of that movie in the trees. But it is over. The sun is up. I go out into the garden. Clear heavy drops of water fall from the leaves.

The professor is in a sleeping bag on the grass, recovering from a bad night. His fat wife, no longer the sorceress, talks with him softly. The psychologist and his wife are still dancing around playing little private games. They look into each other's eyes and are amazed to see their own reflections. They examine flowers and blades of grass. He's still whistling under his breath. The doctor comes up and I take him to the cliff's edge to look at the pictures in the fog but now the fog is parting and gulls and rocks become visible instead.

In the kitchen, the guru and the Sugarplum Fairy are cooking eggs and brewing coffee. I am ashamed as I see them for during the night they have seen me as I myself am afraid to see myself. I must go away and gather all this somehow.

The man who is sometimes Christ has returned and is now dancing alone in the living room to the Beatles' "Sergeant Pepper and His Lonely Hearts Club Band." He says that dancing is a good way to come down. But the house is getting too close for me. I dance out the door and then walk up the road and along the highway toward the Hot Springs. The long walk is what I want now. The fog has all gone, the sun is bright and though my head is still a heavy balloon, as I cross canyons on highway bridges it gradually begins to lighten. Where have I been? I had only expected to see some interesting visual effects, I had gone into glory and ugliness I did not know existed inside me and had met other people for moments in ways I would not have believed possible. Right now, walking in the sun, it's the glory that returns. The ugliness will reappear later and demand to be accepted. I will accept it.

Now I begin to understand much that had escaped me in Perls' workshop about the constantly shifting Gestalts. I see that all of us walk in different contexts and our conversations are often disembodied, but still we answer each other. We walk as if on ice and delude ourselves believing it is solid ground. Beneath our feet, all the time, is all that I and everyone else there saw last night and this morning: the hate, the fear, the music, the childishness, the unity-separateness and the beauty of the moments when we meet. With the doctor and Mella I met as I-Thou. Nothing I experienced was an illusion. It was, as the guru had said, all in me. It was all familiar once it was recognized. But full recognition of the night's events will take a long time.

In the dining room I see the girl who was Mary Magdalen. We greet each other like long-lost sisters. I've forgotten for the moment how I attacked her. Later, when I remember, I realize that she had seen beyond the hate—she had been frightened by it but she had also recognized it as a sickness. She had looked at me the way a child looks at an ugly and bitter cripple; not blaming, just scared and uncomprehending. Beneath love and hate there exists smething that encompasses them both and is the source of all life. I have seen a glimmer of it and though some of it might fade, I will remember what is possible.

It's Sunday, the second day after the trip, and I'm sitting on the steps of my cabin looking down the hill toward the lodge, the swimming pool and the ocean. There is fog all around and I'm part of the fog, light and heavy and all here, letting everything not of this moment drift off into the fog.

The sound of a flute comes from down the hill by the baths, just a few notes, then silence and the faint sound of the sea over rocks, then a few notes again. The fog rolls in from the sea in front of me. Now someone comes up the path, I hear sandals on gravel. It is one of the hip gypsies in a long cotton dress of Indian print and a flower in her long loose hair. She passes. I close my eyes.

Gerry, from Perls' workshop, comes to invite me to his cabin for a glass of white wine. I go with him but after two sips I put down the glass. It's going to my head fast and I want no interference with what is happening there. Gerry warns me not to talk too much about the trip, especially not to people who haven't taken one, because words might make me lose some of it right now. I understand what he means. Words take slices out of ever-flowing experience and lock them into fixed patterns. It's too early for that. Anyway, I don't want to talk with anyone much except my fellow trippers for we have become a secret brotherhood. Especially, I don't want crowds. Gerry knows this and, when it gets to be lunchtime, brings me some spaghetti from the dining room. He says it's awful but it is the most delicious spaghetti I have ever tasted. All food has a heightened flavor today.

Later, Stan the musician and I ride a Honda up the road and walk up a trail. Stan is talking about a trip to Brazil and about his plans for returning to New York. I would like to tell him a little about this way of traveling that I've just discovered, but not now, now I want to listen and look. Never have I seen water, trees, plants and hills so luminous. The late afternoon sun reflects silvery from the backs of shiny leaves, the purplish feathers of pampas grass are fairy fans waving softly against the pale sky. The peace is absolute.

On Monday I notice how much around here comes from acid. The paintings at the lodge especially—flowers, abstract patterns, acid waves. (They don't glow because they aren't very good, but the vision of the artist was psychedelic.) The Indian prints with their curling designs are acid clothes. The hip gypsies wear acid jewels. There is an acid looseness in the movement of the people who sit on the hip lawn.

At Perls' I see the people in the room as if for the first time. There is a richness of color and texture, a depth of field of vision that clarifies all shapes and at the same time gives them a floating appearance as if the air itself had become visible.

Fellow trippers stand out. Carlotta's ochra velvet blouse and brown corduroy pants are glowing. The purple-black-yellow sweater Martin's wife has on is glowing. Their faces still have some of the lucidity they had on the trip. But other faces are also clearer, character traits and movements are more defined while unimportant things like pimples and wrinkles fade into background. Have cataracts fallen from my eyes?

The woman next to me is wearing deerskin boots. I become absorbed in them. The soft folds slipping down over the ankle are so beautiful I want to paint them. But everything is like that. I look again at the semicircular rug with its three green and three redbrown slices; at the five beams on the ceiling forming six thirty-degree triangles. Below the beams hangs a translucent lamp of enormous plastic insect wings or fish-scales that are loosely attached to each other with threads. Lamps glow through, reflecting along the fibers. I actually feel the roundness of brown wooden rings against the roundness of the wooden pole that holds up luxuriously creamy drapes. Friday these were just sheets hung as curtains to screen out the sun. The boot of the woman beside me was only a boot. Now they are that but so much more richly.

I have seen this way before, after moments of great emotion. Once, exhausted from crying, I remember, I knew how a pigeon's feet feel walking on cobbles and exactly how a truck's tire bears down on the earth as the wheel turns—knew it somewhere between earth and wheel. My acid guru says that children see this way all the time. I know some poets, especially Rainer Maria Rilke, had this kind of awareness.

Tuesday. The boring mathematics professor is working on a dream in which he crashed into a party through a window. Everyone looked at him as if he were diseased. He farted, loud, and was mortified. He knew he didn't belong.

"You project attention and acceptance," Perls tells him. "Can you take it back and give us some?"

The professor tries to say something accepting ("Sally, you have nice hair") to several people in the room but it comes out grudging.

"Can you say 'No' loudly?" Perls asks.

He says it uncertainly. "It usually comes out, 'No but,' " he says with an apologetic smile to Perls.

And now my mind flashes why I so disliked the Sugarplum Fairy. She and I and this professor were self-prisoners in the same way. I hated her because in her I saw myself: someone lonely who would not risk herself because she was afraid to have anyone really see her. We had different shells but they were all confining. Mine was pride in my independence, my adventures, a certain kind of strength, which masked my loneliness, in time, even from myself. Loneliness was something shameful suffered by people who were weaker than I. But all of us, in our way, had these nightmares of being left out of the party. (On the trip, the Sugarplum Fairy saw her skeleton shivering outside in the dark trees.) So we could say neither yes nor no.

How could I have failed to realize something so obvious when there are so many parables for it, starting with the one about Jesus and the loaves and fishes? And yet, from childhood on, even as we are *told* to share and be truthful, most of us are *taught* that such behavior can be stupid, or even immoral or evil. We learn that we must "keep up appearances" and think of what others will think of us. That seems more important than whether our actions are just or true. Later, we learn that members of the opposite sex must be captured rather than met as fellow humans whom we might enjoy or love. We lay out conscious or unconscious strategies: show yourself at your best, don't let it "drag on" before marriage, make sure you know how he feels before you let him know you're attracted. Then spring the marriage trap, for without wedding vows he might flee.

Beneath all that the assumption takes root that if anyone saw you as you really are he would run. You come to assume —without realizing it, usually—that your true self is ugly and worthless and that your survival depends on keeping it hidden. You are taught, also, that you have only so much to share and must beware of exhausting yourself. (There is the phrase "used-up woman," for example.) When you give, you learn, you better make sure you are also going to get.

Turned on people know that there is both beauty and ugliness beneath the walls, the games and the ice, that the story about the loaves and fishes is true, and that uptightness is a form of blindness.

Wednesday. Last night there was music from the trip flooding into my sleep from outside the window, making me blissfully warm. Then—only now I remember—some scarier stuff. Going somewhere. A ramp at the airport. An enormous phallic missile rising, dissolving in a pink stream of fume like a jet blast. I hold onto the ramp, I cling, blown like that blue wheelchair at the Los Angeles airport. Monstrous planes rise and set right over me, balloon-like and at the same time roaring with steel. What is it they rise over? A wall. They land and take off over a cement wall. I can't see them touch ground though I want to, I want to so much. Then I see there's someone here with me, on a platform—a clown putting on a show. His face is painted red, his nose is a purple potato-plum. It's my acid guru. I'll stay and talk with him but, wowalluja, the music is like love, completely engulfing, harplike, guitarlike, singing with voices and instruments I never heard before. It couldn't matter less if all this disappears tomorrow for right now I'm where I always wanted to be.

Thursday. Stan the musician and I slept out by the big tree on the cliff's edge last night. It was lovely to wake up with the tall wet grass leaning over us. This evening we sat down together at a table with some other people and went off into different Gestalts, neither of us minding. There were so many currents and cross-currents across that table, so many bombardments of vibrations and configurations and chakra massages that someone more lucid than I would probably have seen sparks flying. Perls was there, listening, and James Johnson next to him. I still haven't asked Johnson those questions about his research. Why? Perls says when you let someone intimidate you you're handing your power of self-criticism over to the other person. He says you get over it if you criticize the other in your mind. Yeah, James, you rock with slow but not by far, oh no, not by any means stupid little eyes. Rocks don't come to meet you but if they moved at all they'd smile and burp just like James. Okay, so am I scared of burping rocks? Do I let them put novocaine on my tongue and make my lips stiff? No, I'm not. I start talking with James and he turns out to be a perfectly agreeable human this time.

At the next table a deathly pale girl with empty eyes and long orange hair sits motionless. She had a three-months' miscarriage this afternoon. Not speaking, she sits there alone in the candlelight and the baroque music, a woman out of a Brecht play.

We're talking about the FBI scare last night when everyone who had grass hid it somewhere. Someone buried a brownie and couldn't find it this morning, someone else put a pillbox of it under a bank of dirt that slid down during the night. "Good," says Perls. "Every time someone brings some of that in here it helps to bury Esalen." So perhaps the scare was started by the management in an effort to clean out any drugs there might be on the premises. It's a touchy problem, since so many people in California smoke grass. Any staff member caught with it is immediately fired. But what can one do with people who come to seminars except tell them about the hazard drugs pose to the Institute?

Then Perls turns to the table behind him and looks not at the hollow-eyed girl but at Carl Lee, the potter, who sits there relaxed, leaning against the wall. Carl is tall and blond and reminds me of a Viking. Now he meets Perls' look steadily, not changing his facial expression, tensing or speaking. After a long minute he asks: "How did you like the white bread?" He baked the bread we had for dinner. His voice is strong and easy.

"I liked it," says Perls. "It's good with jam. But I like the other one better."

"Good for sandwiches," Carl says.

"Don't mention sandwiches to me," Perls says. Carl smiles. Perls turns back. But this was no chit-chatty bit of nothing, despite the simplicity of subject and words. This was a full meeting between the two men, an I-Thou conversation. The look is what happened and then the words went directly from one man straight to the other. There was nothing superfluous

82

in the moment and nothing was omitted. It was complete. That's the way Gia-Fu looked at me on the mountain and said "You are a good hiker." That's the way we talked and looked at each other on the acid trip.

I had read Martin Buber's *I and Thou* fifteen years ago and been very excited about it. But at that time I did not know there was any difference between mental and experiental knowledge. The first step toward turning on is the recognition of that difference. "The first sign that you are in the now is that you begin to hear," Perls says.

I realize that I have seldom fully looked at anyone in a casual encounter and almost never when I met a stranger. I would start talking first and then sneak a look. A glass pane would go down between me and the other, the glare of eyes blinded me. The talk was a groping that seldom penetrated the pane. It took wine or love or intimacy, found somehow after plowing through mounds of words, before anything like this look was possible. Even then it seldom happened with this steady acceptance. In this place people learn to see and hear one another. That is the beginning of what Perls calls the now.

Chapter FOUR

Esalen's Inner Space Program

To MICHAEL MURPHY, LSD is a crude body blow that shook American man loose and set him moving on a journey that is every bit as exciting as the space program. In fact, he would like to see an inner space race as well as an outer space race. He thinks America has the potential for putting the first man on the psychic moon. What that man might find there has, perhaps, already been foretold by science fiction, as many space discoveries have been.

The book is *Stranger in a Strange Land* by Robert Heinlein. Its hero, Valentine Michael Smith, is the super-turned-on man. He is born on the first space ship to land on Mars and, as the only survivor, is raised by Martians. A second expedition, which sets out in search of the first sometime after World War III, brings him to earth. He is amazed to find people on earth unaware of things that to a Martian are elemental.

Time does not exist for Martians as it does for earthlings. For them "waiting is" and haste is inconceivable. Eternity is their frame of reference. Likewise, they have no religion because it is obvious to them that God is everything. Mike Smith struggles to express this to his friends on earth and finally translates it as "Thou art God." That means, among other things, that each man is responsible for his actions and, in acting wrongly, hurts himself.

On Mars, everyone knows that nothing and no one ever dies. Martians merely discorporate when circumstances require that. Then they either start all over again being born corporate or—if they have grown enough before discorporation—they join the Old Ones who have no bodies and are guides and teachers to less advanced Martians. Therefore, there is no sadness in discorporation. It is part of life.

Earthlings are as baffled by Mike Smith as he is by them. At first they see him as naïve. But it soon turns out that his mental powers are far greater than those of humans raised on earth. He can leave his body (the ability to do this, called astral projection, is reported by some twentieth century humans, particularly acid heads and schizophrenics); he has a photographic memory, reads several volumes of the *Encyclopaedia Britannica* in one sitting, can control his heartbeat, body temperature, breathing and emotions. When things get too rough, he withdraws into a state of suspended animation to gather his strength. He can move objects around with his mind and, when he sees wrongness—as in a man who points a gun at another—he gives the wrongly acting person a gentle twist with his mind that turns him perpendicular to everything else and so makes him disappear into another dimension. (A classic science fiction story exploring existence in multiple dimensions, by the way, is *Flatland*, written in the late nineteenth century by Edward A. Abbott, a Shakespearean scholar and student of higher mathematics. The narrator is a square living in a two-dimensional world. He visits inhabitants of the one-dimensional world and is visited by a sphere.)

Smith knows how to grok, that is, to accept and understand so completely that he becomes one with what he is perceiving. It takes him a while to grok the human condition

84

fully, but when he does, he sets out to turn earthlings on by founding a commune and beginning to teach a kind of Martian yoga. In the commune's inner circle, those who have mastered the discipline live in a state of bliss, sharing everything and working together. Everyone is beautiful because he has his own face. (Smith's concept of beauty is Perls' authentic personality.) All are water brothers. On Mars, sharing water makes you water brothers—as important to each other as you are to yourself. Water brothers grow closer in every way.

On earth, Mike finds a marvelous way to grow closer which on Mars is unavailable because Martians have no sex. When his water brothers learn Martian—a language that can be spoken mind to mind, without sounds—they find they can make love by entering each other's mind as well as the body. It becomes customary that when a new brother is brought into the commune, he grows closer with all his new brothers at once. He joins physically with one while all the others tune their minds into the union.

The water brothers, untroubled by jealousy, make love freely within their commune. But it would be impossible for them to have sexual union with anyone with whom they did not already have a mental and emotional closeness.

By a peculiar twist of the law, Mike Smith turns out to be the richest man on earth. He puts his riches in trust and takes only what he and his water brothers need. Making money is no problem for them anyway, once they've learned to use their minds Martian fashion. There is a money bucket by the commune's door for anyone who needs some.

Naturally, Smith is condemned as a moral menace and destroyed by a mob. He discorporates, in full view of stereo cameras, under a rain of bullets and stones while trying to give the turn-on message to the crowd: Thou art God. But his water brothers are not saddened. They grok Mike as he joins the Old Ones and prepares to come back later, for one more try.

Stranger in a Strange Land, first published by G. P. Putnam in 1961, has become a guidebook for inner space travelers, together with *The Tibetan Book of the Dead,* Hermann Hesse's *Steppenwolf, Siddhartha* and *Demian,* and J.R.R. Tolkien's *Fellowship of the Ring.* When Michael Murphy read it he called Heinlein at his home in the Santa Cruz mountains and asked him to give a seminar at Esalen on his vision of the super-turned-on man. Heinlein wouldn't do it, shrugging the whole thing off as a fantasy. But his admirers grok the story.

Through LSD, many Westerners have become aware of the existence of multidimensional inner space. Michael Murphy (who is seen by some as the super-turned-on man's ancestor) believes LSD is a first step in a technology that will eventually take us to the psychic moon—or psychic Mars.

"I'm sure that in twenty years we're not going to take LSD the way we do now," he told me. "We'll consider it primitive, like some sort of chloroform anaesthetic or something. But it's the direct blow to the solar plexus that woke us up. And because we're so technologically oriented it's ironic that our technology came full circle with a physical invention, LSD, to deliver this body blow. But I think that's just what it is. It's extremely crude. The Zen monks and yogis they've given it to have usually had terrible trips. Aldous Huxley told me that. That's because their experience is somewhere different. I've taken about eight trips—with LSD, morning glory seeds, mescaline and peyote. I was with good company and good sitters and I had good trips until the last two, which were bad. But my meditation is infinitely richer. I'm on the side of meditation. For me, meditation is a daily turn-on. It's also better because it has a sense of progression."

However, Murphy added, he has been meditating for twelve years and so his perspective may be different from that of most Westerners. "When a person is impoverished for this kind of experience, anything looks good. Like when you haven't eaten for a long time, anything tastes good."

In essence, LSD and other psychedelic drugs can have the same effect as Gestalt therapy, truth labs, meditation and other nondrug turn-on games and techniques. They are all set-breakers. If a person is willing to let himself go to them, they blast him out of his mind-sets and frames of references into a broader awareness. The result, Murphy said, is that "a person may come to see that a lot of things he thought were very important are only part of a game—a game you have to play if you want to move in the world—which you should play well—but still only that. He realizes that's not the ultimate reality. Suddenly he sees a lot more options for himself. You know what one of the meanings of nirvana is? 'Out of the net.'

"And then he begins to ask the question: well, what *is* the nature of man? And we can say to ourselves: we are God. God is waking up. God lost himself in matter and is emerging in time. All these mystical statements become more profoundly relevant. And then we begin to say to ourselves: maybe we can bring it off, this fantastic ecstasy this whole thing has been shooting for in the billions of years since the

86

first atom crack. This is what it's all headed for—the millennium. I think this whole idea of the millennium is the basic intuition that man is God."

As the new inner space technology develops, Murphy believes, there may develop a new Western *sadhana* (Sanskrit word meaning "the way")—a path toward enlightenment, bliss and identification with God. He sees signs that it has already begun to develop from the turn-on games, social experiments, spiritual disciplines and drugs many Americans are now exploring. Its form may well be similar to what Heinlein described in his story about the man from Mars. Murphy believes it will emphasize three things—contact with ultimate, unnamable existence; permutation of the senses; and the human relationship as an ecstatic experience. Most *sadhanas* have stressed the first and called for renunciation of the other two.

Esalen can be a catalyst to what is already happening, he says. He sees its mission as one of research and dissemination. "The dissemination is what we're in now—reaching everybody in some light and superficial way with this. That's spreading and marvelous and could transform the culture. The other thing—the research in the sense of discovering ways to push evolution forward in dramatic ways—is what we plan to get into more. Why not have a luminous body? Have people literally transform their bodies through thought processes. It sounds crazy but the physical phenomena of mysticism—stigmata, levitation—indicate the enormous power of mind over matter. There are at least one hundred and fifty registered stigmatics who through their belief in Christ got these wounds. I think there's an enormous thing ahead of us, a dazzling thing in evolution. The methodology and the objectives will evolve together, just as they do in the space program."

Like Mike Smith, the Man from Mars, Michael Murphy sometimes sounds naïve in his wild optimism. But his enthusiasm is infectious. And if one wonders whether Esalen can meet even a fraction of its founder's expectations, it is nevertheless apparent that it is offering something middle-class American society is hungry for.

During 1967, four thousand people came to Esalen for seminars, seven hundred psychologists were trained in Gestalt therapy, sensory awareness, and other techniques developed by Esalen staff members. Twenty-two people—including an engineer, a literature professor, a musician, a dancer and some students—began a nine-month resident fellowship program (cost: $3,000) in Esalen techniques. Twelve thousand attended lectures and seminars in the San Francisco branch of Esalen during its first seven months.

For everyone involved with the place, Esalen means something different. Richard Price, a Stanford University classmate of Mike Murphy's and vice-president of the Institute, helped Mike to found it in the hope it would be "a quiet place where things happened and a therapeutic community," he told me. Edward Maupin, a psychologist on the staff sees it as a place that "crystallizes and makes palpable to middle-class culture what's happening" by bringing together people who would otherwise never be considered together—yogis and psychiatrists, mystics and masseurs. "But the other meaning of this place is a truly religious one," he says. "We are dealing with the mysteries here."

In the view of Stuart Miller, one of the resident fellows, "the official curriculum is the least important experience in this, like in most other schools." Miller, a literature professor, was sent to Esalen by the State University of New York, College of Old Westbury, to see what Esalen had to contribute to the college's experimental curriculum. The important thing at Esalen, he found, is "the relatively unrepressed environment into which have come diverse people who are radically dissatisfied with realities. They encounter each other and what happens is that the rate of normal experience is accelerated to a hundredfold, say, the rate in the suburbs. Encounter groups provide the excuse to be honest and not withdraw. They provide the tone, but no more than the hippies and the Tarot cards. They all say—find yourself, find the world, it's different than you think. It's a very creative environment because people have come to ask the right questions and the setting is right for finding the answers or exhausting alternatives."

To some hip gypsies who work there it is freaksville, and a place of employment. "Sometimes I feel like a steward on a cruise ship of the psyche," one of them told me.

I saw Esalen in different ways during my six weeks there —as a hip spa, as the place where Fritz Perls gives seminars, as an exciting community. But basically I saw it as a place where, instead of doing anything, one allowed things to happen. The Esalen gurus, official and unofficial, help to develop the receptive attitude needed for discoveries. Here one could learn how to be quiet, relinquish control, listen to what is within and without. We are taught to move upward and forward. To move sideways or backwards is generally held to be undesirable. We talk about "getting ahead" and being "left behind." Here one can find out what the race is about by being left ahead, getting behind and sideways, going deep in and far out instead of just forward and up. It is a place where one can begin to turn on.

The turned-on attitude begins with an acceptance of what is and expands toward ever broader and deeper experience. The word "dig" implies this. It is not exactly "enjoy" nor "like" nor "appreciate." It carries a connotation of going deeply into something. Zen masters, when asked about the meaning of Buddhism, tended to point at mountains and dried-up dirt scrapers, thereby telling their questioners to dig what was around them. Grokking is digging in its deepest sense.

Digging implies an emphasis on the positive. In the psychedelic experience, and with some nondrug turn-ons, it becomes clear that every truth has an opposite which is equally true. So the turned-on person seeks the positive perspective, and avoids the "bummer" or "downer." Dwelling on one's misery is a downer, it only pulls you down deeper. "I've noticed that all my downs are the same," a turned-on nursery school teacher told me. "But my ups are always different."

The way to avoid downers, however, is not by seeking euphoria but by living every moment fully—appreciating it for what it is and viewing it in terms of growth and expansion. The turned-on person allows himself to experience and is ready to explore.

The turned-on teacher seeks to excite a child into learning rather than stuffing him with information. The turned-on doctor thinks of creating health and well-being rather than of getting rid of illness and pain. The turned-on psychologist talks about potential for growth rather than about neurosis and traumas. Freudian analysis is a downer. Turned-on psychology is practiced by Carl Rogers, Abraham Maslow, Frederick Perls, William C. Schutz and others in what Maslow named "The Third Force." They focus on the expansion of awareness. In the process, they say, neurosis disappears.

Digging means, in Perlsian, living in the now. And that means that the process becomes more important than the goal. Goals are worth striving for *if* one digs the process. Trying to get rich is all right if you dig the way you make money. Aiming at a law partnership is fine if you dig being a corporation lawyer. It is not turned on if you want it for the money or prestige.

The concept of challenge is alien to the turned-on person because he seeks to experience, not to prove himself. If he goes skydiving, he does so for the feeling of flying through the air, not to show that he is brave. If he walks to work five miles every day, it's because he enjoys walking, not because he wants his friends to know he is not an old man yet.

The turned-on man will work ten hours a day gladly if the work suits him. He values work and production—not because they requite effort and will power but as the spontaneous expression of aliveness. Work, however, is not the *sine qua non* of being turned-on. The basic emphasis is on creative experience which may also be possible through contemplation and play.

The concept of self-improvement is also alien because good and evil are replaced by the Oriental idea of yin and yang, which are balancing opposites and similar to Perls' polarities. Instead of seeking to make himself better, a person who is turned-on tries to tune into himself and his environment and expand. This means sharpening powers of perception, increasing awareness of currents and movements that generally go unobserved, and trying new patterns of being.

Tuning into rhythms within oneself leads to a search for self-style—one's natural way of perceiving, moving, being. Dancing becomes self-expression rather than performance. Dress is individual. It may be sumptuous but it allows free play to the body. Spike heels and girdles, thick make-up and bouffant sprayed hairdos are uptight. Nudity can be turned-on but topless waitresses are an uptight phenomenon because they cater to an uptight view of sex.

Tuning in to the environment requires an attitude of openness and withholding of judgment. This makes intimacy and a great range of relationships possible. There is a sense of respect for people as they are. Charlotte Selver, who teaches sensory awareness in New York, San Francisco, and Esalen, quotes D.T. Suzuki about "bowing to the different other." Perls uses Martin Buber's words and speaks of I-Thou. The hip gypsies talk about people doing their thing. To jam into someone else's thing is the ultimate of unhip. An evangelistic preacher who tries to impress his reality on others is not turned-on. A priest or minister may be.

One of the first insights in turning on is that words often block rather than aid perception and communication. (Again it's a case of paired opposites.) Word concepts can be mistaken for reality; in looking at reality, it is possible to see the word rather than what is before the eyes. So, generally, a turned-on person talks less than an uptight one and listens more. He pays attention to the voice, glance, gesture and timing. A lawyer told me, after a sensory awareness course: "I've become much more aware now of what my wife says to me.

There are times when she says yes with words and her whole body screams no. Before, I would not have noticed."

A turned-on person is also less argumentative because he is aware of the constantly shifting reality and because he has moved in realms of consciousness for which there are as yet no words with agreed-upon meanings. He must invent new words, be a great poet or use imprecise language when he talks about travels in consciousness. Therefore, he is unlikely to try to talk anyone into adopting his point of view. Yet, feeling that his life is richer than the lives of uptight people around him, he wants to pass on his discoveries. To do this he must be a guru.

The Hindu word guru has no Western equivalent. He is a teacher who teaches in three ways, the least important of which is by what he says. The next-important is his example, and the most important his aura—the very force of his presence. He does not set out to be a guru. If he has something to teach, those who can learn from him will seek him out. A man who seems stupid to one may turn out to be the guru of another.

Many of the Esalen turn-on gurus came by their guruhood through LSD. Before trying acid they were like a lot of the Esalen seekers and seminarians: they knew something was missing in their lives, were dimly aware of another way to be, and were looking for something. A good example is Bernard Gunther, the sensory awareness guru.

As a boy growing up in Los Angeles, the son of a grocer, Gunther had an image of what a man was: a husky, athletic cowboy, much like the ones in the movies. He, however, was scrawny and delicate-featured. So he took up weight-lifting and built a muscular body that was about thirty pounds over what he now considers his natural weight. At age seventeen he finished high school—hating it and considering himself rather stupid—and began to work in a Hollywood gym.

"I spent a lot of time working out and lying in the sun," he told me one day as we sat on the Esalen lawn. "Sometimes I'd go out to the beach and just lie there for eight hours. Except underneath all that tan and superficial healthiness there was a great feeling of frustration, like a volcano that wanted to erupt but had no outlet. I was depressed a lot and went to a number of psychiatrists, but that didn't help me.

"When I was twenty-five I got tired of the gym and went back to school to get a degree in physical education. Just before I got it, though, I took LSD and about a week later I switched majors to psychology. Suddenly my grades were really good. In high school I used to get C's and D's, but after LSD I began to get A's and B's at Los Angeles State College. It was strange, particularly since I often found myself more involved in the hair of the girl in front than with what the professor was saying."

This was right after Aldous Huxley wrote *The Doors of Perception* based on his experiences with mescaline. Gunther heard Huxley lecture and volunteered to be a subject in a research project a Los Angeles doctor was about to undertake with LSD.

"Suddenly a whole new world of possibilities opened to me. I had shut myself off in muscular tightness. I felt a physical deadness and also a deadness of sensitivity and emotion. With LSD I realized that life was synonymous with flow and openness, feeling and sensation."

He began to study yoga and Zen while continuing to take LSD for more than three years. After he received his BA he began work on his masters, but became bored with his courses, dropped out, and began to teach yoga instead. Then he met Dr. Perls and Charlotte Selver, who is generally credited with bringing sensory awareness work to this country from Germany.

Gunther studied with Miss Selver for about two years, then began to teach sensory awareness, combining it with what he had picked up of Zen, yoga and Gestalt therapy. (His approach is quite different from Miss Selver's, although he uses many of her methods. Miss Selver insists that she has no techniques, that all she does arises from the moment. Gunther has written a book on techniques. Miss Selver works to refine and expand perception. Gunther puts more stress on nonverbal encounters between people and on sensuality.)

Eventually, Gunther moved to Esalen, became so inventive and found such a receptive audience, that the idea of tuning up the senses and playing with them caught on in many settings. He worked with nurses at the University of California Medical Center to guide them toward greater sensitivity to patients; with teachers and students in several colleges.

One night at the Avalon ballroom he stopped the music, got everyone to look at each other, then asked people to form a circle and sing "Om" together. "Much of the dancing is so alienating, so individual," he said. "This brought people into relationship."

Another evening, during a Berkeley concert by Ali Akhbar Khan, the sarode player, Gunther conducted a sensory awareness session to prepare the audience to listen to the music.

Like most Esalen people, Gunther likes to point out that in American society people are "hypnotized with words. Words become more important than what is happening." He sees his work as a way to dehypnotize by quieting a noisy mind, letting go some of the tension, and moving from mental activity into sensory experience. "If you don't verbalize, you come into contact with direct experience. You feel what things are like, not what they're supposed to be like. By the time you are thinking about an experience, it is already something else," he told me.

Though Gunther's head-tapping, hugging and slapping sessions are unlikely to take anyone to the psychic moon, they are a starter.

Esalen Institute's psychic moon plan, however, did not begin with drugs. The turn-on for Michael Murphy was Eastern philosophy and meditation.

Until his sophomore year in Stanford University, Murphy was a lively lad on his way to the Episcopal ministry or a career in psychiatry. He was born in Salinas in 1930, the elder of two sons of an attorney, grandson of a wealthy physician. In high school he was president of the student body, a golf champion, a dutiful student. He began college as what he describes as "a typical rah-rah Stanford student"—a fraternity boy who took his dates to the Top of the Mark, played golf and campus politics.

Then, in his second year, he took a comparative religion course with Dr. Frederic Spiegelberg and soon changed his entire way of life. He dropped out of his fraternity, stopped playing golf, became celibate, and started to meditate five or six hours a day. With a group of like-minded students, he began to study the writings of Sri Aurobindo, the originator of Integral Yoga. He dropped out of college for a quarter, then returned and, received a BA in psychology, continuing to meditate. He continued even during two years in the Army. In 1956, after trying graduate school and deciding that was not his path, he traveled to India, to Sri Aurobindo's ashram at Pondicherry.

"This was a very interesting experimental community, attempting to combine the ideal of self-realization and technology, drawing upon Eastern spirituality and Western thought. The emphasis was on the transformation of your personal life into the divine nature—in our language, trying to evoke higher spiritual possibilities out of all your life," he said.

The community consisted of some 1,500 men, women and children who had gathered around Sri Aurobindo since 1914. He died in 1950, but they continued to study his writings and live according to his ideas. There was an absolute prohibition on sex, but otherwise everyone created his own discipline.

Sports and dance were emphasized, for Sri Aurobindo believed that one line of evolutionary development would lead to a dynamic transformation of the body.

Murphy stayed for eighteen months, then decided to go home. "I wanted to pursue this idea of the evolution of consciousness, but I was restless for something more," he said. On October 4, 1957, the day the first sputnik went up, he was in Japan, on his way home with a vision of man's vast inner space.

For the next two and a half years Murphy was unsure what to do next. He lived in Palo Alto, meditated, worked as a bellhop and an ice cream maker. Then he moved into Dr. Haridas Chaudhuri's Cultural Integration Fellowship Ashram in San Francisco and there met Richard Price, a Stanford classmate who was now also wandering and seeking.

In 1960, Murphy and Price decided to spend some time in the Big Sur Hot Springs, which Murphy's grandfather had bought in 1910. It was now a rather rundown establishment operated by some ladies of the First Church of God of Prophecy, an evangelical sect. It had among its tenants Joan Baez, the folk singer, and Hunter Thompson, the writer. It was also a gathering place for homosexuals. "Every Saturday night," said Murphy, "there were prayer meetings in the lodge and, at the same time, orgies at the baths.

"We decided, why not take this place and create a center to explore the various interests we had," he said. They consulted Gerald Heard, an evolutionary philosopher, and became excited about Aldous Huxley's idea of education in the "nonverbal humanities"—training in perception, in awareness, in receptivity that would help people to realize their potentialities.

In 1961, Murphy and Price took over the Hot Springs, dislodged its various habitués and tenants, and began the Esalen Institute. The first seminar in fall, 1962, was titled "The Expanding Vision."

Gia-Fu Feng, a friend, came to visit and stayed on. At that time, he told me, he was "a wandering monk like a floating cloud." Born in Shanghai in 1919, a banker's son, he had a master's degree in economics from the Wharton School of Finance and worked for the Bank of China on Wall Street before beginning his wandering. In the 1950s he left business to travel through intentional communities. In 1954 he arrived at Berkeley on his way back to China. But there he met Alan Watts and Sabro Hasagawa, a Zen painter. They revived his interest in the religious search through art and meditation.

He stayed on in San Francisco, teaching and searching. Now he joined in the running of Esalen.

In the beginning, Murphy recalled, "Dick washed the dishes, I waited table, my mother cooked, we all made the beds, and Gia-Fu was the accountant using an abacus and little slips of paper. We ran it that way for about six months till my mother had sort of a mild heart attack. Then, in 1962, I started to put together a comprehensive program."

The Institute prospered and grew. By the end of 1967, some 550 workshops had been held and many thousands of people had passed through Esalen experiences. The program had evolved from one mainly consisting of lectures and discussion into one that was about three-fourths experiential—truth labs, Gestalt therapy, sensory awareness. Staff was added: Edward Maupin, who may be the only psychologist in the country to have done a doctoral dissertation on meditation, Virginia Satir, a family therapist with imaginative methods and an open, experimental attitude, Bernard Gunther, William C. Schutz. Ida Rolf took up part-time residence and developed potentialities by aligning people with gravity. Esalen became a center for the Human Potentialities Movement, an assortment of gurus and healers seeking to expand and refine rather than to cure the human condition.

Then Murphy's interest turned to spreading elsewhere the techniques practiced and developed at Esalen. With the help of a Ford Foundation grant, a catalog of consciousness-expanding techniques was begun. George I. Brown, professor of education at the University of California, Santa Barbara, began to develop ways to move the nonverbal humanities into schools. Esalen people began to run programs at San Francisco State College, Stanford, the basement of Grace Cathedral in San Francisco. George Leonard, Murphy's mentor and his bridge to the East Coast literati who sneer at West Coast "freaks," spread the psychic moon gospel through *Look* Magazine.

"The kinds of things that are emerging from Esalen will form the basis of a new kind of educational system and a new *sadhana*," Murphy says. "What it will be I don't know. People come to Esalen and sample things and go home and weave them into their lives in a thousand different ways. Whatever it is, the Western *sadhana* will have to be a social thing. The world has to do yoga together. It can't be just the guy on the mountaintop or they'll come stomping up from the ghettos and knock him off. I've always thought of the beats as the first wave on the beach. The hippies were the second and now maybe we're getting a third, the sadhaks, who will be more experienced meditators. A lot of people have been done in by drugs, I think. Now that has passed its peak. The interest is here to stay but wisdom is coming."

Chapter FIVE

The Wedding at Gorda

IT DIDN'T take long to realize that two worlds coexisted uneasily at this place. The population of one called it Esalen, the people of the other referred to it as the Hot Springs. Esalen consisted mostly of clean-shaven people in sports clothes who drove in from San Francisco and Los Angeles to bare their souls in encounter groups, revive their senses tapping and slapping with Bernie Gunther, and who paid $60 and up for an Esalen weekend. The Hot Springs was an unofficial society of wild-haired people in colorful garb who sat in circles on the hip lawn, lived in cars and trucks, in canyons or on ridges in the vicinity, or had no homes at all and slept under bridges, in the grass or on other people's floors. Many of them were hip gypsies, but others were older people, artists, mystics, seekers and outlaws who had been on Big Sur for many years. There was little overlapping between Esalen and the Hot Springs although a few people seemed to dwell in both. So far I had been only to Esalen, and had had almost no contact with this other society except on the night of the acid trip.

Nils had been my first contact with it but Nils was pretty much a loner, from what I could see. I never saw him on the lawn but noticed him several times under one of the trees along the edge of the southerly cliff, sitting alone, cross-legged, and looking out over the ocean. He appeared to be an extremely conscientious worker for he was always picking up cigarette butts and scraps of paper that lay in his path. But aside from that, I knew nothing about him. We did not speak more than a few words together after that ride in from Monterey.

One other Hot Springs person I had met was Griffin (a fictitious name), a wide-eyed, friendly young man with long wavy blond hair, paisley pants and striped shirt who appeared in my cabin one afternoon to change the sheets and sat down on the other bed to smoke a cigarette.

"What's your sign?" he asked.

"Sign?"

"What month were you born?"

"May—oh yes, I'm Taurus."

"I'm a Sagittarian."

"How do you do."

Griffin was easy to talk with but I didn't understand much of what he said. It was all about Tarot cards and yoga and astrology. His mother, Mim, read Tarot cards in The Macaroni Factory in Los Angeles, he told me. He had had a good talk once about Tarot with Fritz Perls at the baths. After a while, we began talking about drugs.

"The thing you have to watch for on acid," he advised me, "is your aura. Your senses are way out there"—he spread his arms—"and they're in touch with the cosmic forces. If you break the net you won't be able to feel anymore."

"That sounds pretty dangerous."

"Yes, acid can be a bad trip. The most religious trip I ever had was with mescaline. Which isn't a chemical, it's natural. I met God in the forest."

Griffin's blue eyes seemed to open even wider. His voice was breathless, suggesting that he might somehow fly away any moment, and his gestures had a loose and fluttery quality. "But once I had a vision without anything," he said. "I was walking back home through the canyon and suddenly my head was like a balloon and everything all around me was moving. That's right after I flashed this great thing—that we can all do different things but there's one thing we can all, all of us, do and that's to purify ourselves. I was polluted with nicotine then, my body and senses were polluted and I dug the message. Nicotine is bad for the body and spirit."

Griffin kept smoking that cigarette, so I guess the message didn't stay long. But then, it seemed that Griffin had visions quite often. Once he saw the New Christ who was coming, with arms outspread, head tossed back and mouth open and "really with it." Then he had a dream that someone told him was an Indian oracle. "I was in a forest and I saw swarms of humming birds and a hawk that circled round and then dove down and dug me and split over the hill. Then he came back with six other hawks and they all circled round and came lower and lower and it was really far out."

Then he asked for a piece of paper and a pencil, slipped down to the floor and explained to me what he had found out about the center of the universe. "It's any dot along any one of many many wavy lines," he said. "All the lines and colors intersect at any dot. So no matter where you are, you're at the center of the universe."

I helped him to change the sheets. Then he hurried off. He wanted to take a bath before going to the gathering at Roger's camp in the canyon. It started at sundown and there would be food and music. If I wanted to come I'd be welcome, he said.

I wanted to come. The idea of something starting at sundown rather than at some time shown on a clock was appealing.

But that night I was going to a tape session with Perls, so I couldn't make it. When I saw Griffin again in the lodge that evening, he told me he was now "somewhere else." His manner showed it. He was strangely agitated and not quite present. He kept glancing about and humming little snatches of tune under his breath.

"You had a necklace with three blue beads this afternoon," I said. "Now there's just one bead. What happened?"

Griffin said he and two other people had gotten into meditation at Roger's, and it was so groovy that at the end he gave them each a blue bead from his string.

I had no idea where the canyon was that Griffin was talking about, or anything more about Roger except that he tended bar sometimes. But I gathered that Roger's camp was one of the night gathering places for the people who sat on the hip lawn by day. What Griffin said led to fantasies of gypsies dancing in the firelight under redwoods, acting out rituals to the sound of drums.

Until Perls' workshop was over there was no time to explore the Hot Springs. But on my third Sunday on Big Sur, the month-long seminar ended and most people packed up and left. I saw them go with regret, for during the past couple of weeks some of them had become friends. Stan the musician stayed an extra day which we spent together exploring the mountains on a Honda.

That night he had an appointment with Glenna, one of the masseuses of the Esalen staff, in the massage room between the men's and women's side of the baths. I met him later in the lodge and he was glowing. Wow, what a way to end all this, lying in the candlelight, surrendering to the expert gentle hands of a lovely creature. All her freckles were gone in the soft light, only sweetness smiled down elfin, pale green eyes against the roar of waves beyond the wall. Soft sweetness, fading and returning as his muscles loosened, his nerves let go—bliss. Later, when she was done with him he almost floated into the dark bath and lay there as in embryonic fluid, smiling inwardly in starlight, without a single worry, a single must, ought or should. Glenna slipped into the tub with him. Her eyes were dark now but the greenness was still present, silent, floating and catlike nearby. NOW. Absolute bliss.

And then, said Stan, for Christ's sake, those people, the new ones, piled in like some Kiwanis party, jovial and shouting hi there, howdy, wow! They were all bravado, trying to prove they weren't self-conscious about their nudities and they splashed, white-bellied under the stars, all together into the hot sulphur water. Damnation! The whole magic shattered and Stan's computer started clicking nervously once again—click-click-click—so he shot up and out of the starlit womb and fled to the lodge with Glenna. It was all right now, what a thing, a massage.

Yes, the new people arriving do jar you once you've been here awhile. Their voices may be normal for the city but out here they sound like madmen screeching as, all twitchy and nervous—they shove themselves at each other. I'm signed up for this seminar by a well-known analyst. It began tonight. While Stan was getting his massage I listened to the first lecture and found I absolutely could not sit through anymore. I felt the brainwaves undulating and making patterns—interesting patterns. But how could I sit there listening to that man go on and on when all the waves and loop-de-loops came from such a dead voice? No, I couldn't. I was being carried along by an exciting and unfamiliar Big Sur current and this man, with all his scholarship and ideas, was at the moment irrelevant.

That night Stan and I borrowed sleeping bags again and slept out on a hill. I woke to see a snail sitting, translucent in the sun, on the edge of my sleeping bag a few inches from my eyes.

"Talk to the snail, be the snail," said Stan. "Hello."

"Hello, I am a translucent snail and I have a little black ball in each tentacle. Those are my eyes. Eye-I feel my eye-I and don't worry about you for here's a flower. I may look to you like I'm eating but that's not so, I'm just holding on for a while until I go on to something else. Well, eating some and holding on as I go."

"How do you do it, snail? How do you let go?"

"I just flow away, one big translucent muscle as you see me, eating as I go, not planning meals or trips or anything. I leave you my slime tail that looks like spilled semen."

"Good-bye, Perlsian snail."

After breakfast Stan left, eager to get back to New York and work on new music. I waved to him from the parking lot as he drove off, then turned back toward the lodge. Once more the place had turned suddenly unfamiliar. It was time to explore life among the gypsies. I spotted Roger on the hip lawn, went over and sat down near him. So I crossed the border from Esalen into the Hot Springs.

Sundown on whatever day you left

Dear Stan,

My vibrations or something tell me you haven't quite left here yet, even though you're already in San Francisco. So instead of taking notes today, I'd rather tell you about it. There's going to be a wedding tomorrow at Gorda, a hippy commune up in the mountains, and I wish you could come along for it sounds really wild. The celebration starts tonight and will go on till the day after tomorrow or later. And the bride and groom, I'm told, will be wed in a tree.

After you drove away I sat down on the lawn with the gypsies and started talking with Roger (all the gypsy names are fictitious), who, it turns out, got fired yesterday from his job at the bar. It was some sort of argument about what records were suitable for after dinner, he says. But he says he'll stay on despite everything because he has good vibrations in this place. Serving liquor was kind of heavy karma anyway, he says, and even though the change came down static, he figures it needed to happen.

Did you meet Roger? He's one of the people the younger gypsies look to as a leader, or at least an older brother. He's in his early thirties, I'd guess, and is beginning to go bald. He told me he was a roofer in Los Angeles for seventeen years and studied yoga for a long time. He also spent some time in jail for possession of grass. A couple of years ago he took an acid trip with his sister as a guide, he told me. There was a fire in the room and he merged with the flame so that he didn't know whether he was burning or the fire. After that he couldn't stand it in Los Angeles anymore so he came out to the Sur.

We sat on the lawn while all sorts of people passed by dressed for the wedding. Some of the girls and women had on saris, some of the men had extra-bright shirts with embroidery around the neck. One guy, with shaggy short hair and bad teeth, had no shirt at all but wore a golden eagle's claw around his neck. Robot, the night watchman, played the guitar and sang, then someone else sang. Roger started talking mystical and was quite eloquent. It's so new to me, being with people who sit around and talk this way. "Water lives in a circle,"

100

he said. "It goes from the ground to the clouds and down to the ground again. If water is hep it will run straight down to the sea. But some of it gets lost in puddles and then it evaporates and the cycle has to start over again. You can get on an alcohol trip and see and hear nothing. That's lost, that's your trip and your puddle. But in some other life maybe you'll make it to the sea."

I asked Roger if I could come look at his camp. He took me over. I guess I expected some kind of tent town in the canyon. But it's more like a children's secret playhouse. You know the canyon that's north of the lodge, just past the big meadow? It's right near where we spent our time but I'd never been there. You go down the hill past the meadow and then follow a stream up a little way. You cross the stream on a log and go up the side of the canyon for maybe fifty feet, then swing around a boulder and there it is—a little terrace with a fireplace and a cooking place built against a rock, a roofless house. Roger the roofer lives in a roofless house. Tree branches shelter it from some of the mist and rain, I suppose, but in a storm they would be soaked.

The girl Roger is living with, Diana, was sitting on a blanket by the cooking place weaving another Godseye. You know, those little multicolored thread designs on two crossed sticks are called Godseyes. You put them in your house for good luck. The gypsy girls are always weaving them and giving them to people. Anyway, Diana is a pretty girl whom I hadn't seen around the lodge—long blond hair that sort of bushes out in a mane, soft voice with a well-brought-up-young-lady pronunciation. I intend to find out where she came from, for she certainly wasn't raised in the woods.

While we sat talking and smoking, Diana's five-year-old son came home, climbed a tree and sat up there looking at us and dangling his legs. A lot of other things dangled from the trees too—a mobile made of barbed wire and a dewy spider web; a little bell, another Godseye. Farther up the hill, where a second terrace has been leveled for sleeping, hung a carved redwood mobile like the one at Fritz's. Roger made both of them. While I visited with him he was working on still another one.

"I came out here looking for a teacher and I put the roof on Fritz's house," he said. "We felt each other's vibrations and he couldn't be my teacher. The woods are my teacher. Fritz tears it out of you, the woods give you more time and let the changes come. Fritz has never been up here."

"I wish we could get him to the wedding tomorrow," Diana said.

Roger started to get ready for the wedding. He and Diana were going that night. He put on a pair of white cotton pants (he called them peyote pants) and a blue shirt. Then he rummaged through a paper bag behind a rock and pulled out a piece of paper with acid traces, a bit of pot and a peyote button. He ate the peyote button, put back the acid and rolled some joints that he passed around. Then he played a little

101

bamboo flute that someone at the Hot Springs had made. The sun came through the trees and the brook made a very pleasant noise down below.

"Gorda is a strong place," Diana said. "It was an Indian battle ground once and now the children keep playing war there. When I came out here with my son I slept out for six months just with sleeping bags. Then I consulted the Ching about going to Gorda. It said yes and then the change said I had some personal destiny to work out. I went but I think my personal destiny was set back by it. So I came down here to be with Roger."

It's sort of incredible to me to see grownups playing like children—really like children for they are serious about their game the way adults can't be. Did you have any idea there were these people at Esalen?

When I got back from the canyon Bernie Gunther had a group of people out on the lawn pounding their chests and howling for sensory awareness. Some gypsies sat on the rail by the office, watching the freaks. That's what they call the seminarians—freaks. And you know something? They looked pretty freaky to me. I don't mean to knock what Bernie does, I think it's good, but as I watched those people howling and beating their chests I thought it was such a halfway game for them. They didn't have their souls in it. I sat down on the rail with the gypsies and watched. Tomorrow I'll go to that wedding and never mind the widely published existentialist.

A kiss to you,

Rasa

After breakfast the next morning I look for a ride but it seems that everyone who is going to Gorda has already gone. So I decide to hitchhike. I put on a dress instead of the slacks I usually wear here and buy a bottle of good burgundy at the bar to take as a gift. Then I walk up to the highway.

Three men are sitting by the side of the road on blanket-packs and sleeping bags. They're going to Gorda too, so I join them. One of them, jumpy-eyed, immediately starts asking tedious questions: Where are you from? Why are you here? What are your plans? It's obvious he hasn't been here long because around here that is no way to get acquainted. Here people ask "What's your sign?" rather than "What do you do?" and then go on to talk about magic, astrology and the cosmos. Only when they get to know someone do they get more personal and specific.

Mella, my acid hostess, comes by in a car and picks us all up. She's on her way to Los Angeles to sell some of her belongings. After this trip, she says, she'll have nothing more to sell and then she'll have to find a way to make money. She can easily find work as a social worker, she says, but right now she's not ready to leave Big Sur.

When we get to the Gorda road she turns in. She knows it's bad, she says, but she made it to the top once and will try to make it again. But the car won't cooperate. Metal scrapes on rock and she stops. So the three men and I get out and start walking on the dustiest, bumpiest road I've seen since World War Two in Europe.

We take a shortcut through the woods and pass a black man who's sitting on the front step of a shack eating sunflower seeds. His long hair stands out in all directions in corkscrew curls. He gets up to greet us and shows us his tiny garden. It consists of a few heads of cabbage, some beets, lettuce heads, onions and two sunflowers. "I've been up all night," he says. "Gotta get some Dexedrine or bennies or something."

We go on and soon hear drums in the distance. To our left is another vegetable garden with some rock designs and a piece of broken board with psychedelic curlicues in Day-Glo. The road turns right and the roof of a stone house appears. An artist built it, I was told, convinced that if he could finish it he would find God. But after he was done with it he went berserk, came down the mountain and killed some people on a bus. True or not, the story added to the ominous reputation of Gorda. It seems a weird place for a wedding. But then, this is where the bride and groom live.

We pass a damp pile of sleeping bags under a tree, go on past the stone house and come upon the wedding scene. The wedding scene? It looks like the last morning hours of a drunken party rather than the beginning of a celebration. Around the smouldering campfire about thirty or forty people are lounging and drooping. Some are clearly zonked out of their minds. One sleeping bag, right by the fire, is moving with two shapes inside. Beside it, a grimy-faced child sits wrapped in a blanket, a wisp of blond hair sticking out.

"Rasa," someone calls and I see Rebecca, one of the women in Perls' just-ended seminar. She's the one who had that dream about a horse and a tiger rolling down a hill together. Now I see the pretty, vivacious Rebecca, divorced mother of two, has gone hip. She's snuggled against a gypsy fellow and wrapped in a blanket cloak. She mentioned she might stay on Big Sur, so I shouldn't be surprised to find her here. Harry, a hip sociology teacher who was also in Perls' seminar, has also stayed behind and found his way up here. He passes me a bottle of white wine.

"What a night we had," Rebecca says. "We started out last

103

night but ended up sleeping out by San Simeon. I was terrified. You know it's hunting season and those men with guns just go mad. A woman who lives near here told me she had a bullet hole in her window and a neighbor had a bullet hole in his hat. A couple of dogs got shot too. Those men think this is the wilderness. They have no idea it's full of people."

Across the fire from Rebecca and her young man three zonked-looking boys are beating conga drums but nobody is dancing. Drugged dampness seems to be the prevailing condition. I sit down next to Harry and take in the scene.

We are on a plateau dominated by a looming egg-shaped boulder on the south. A slightly higher plateau rises to the west, like a platform for viewing the sunset over the ocean. To the east, rocky land slopes upward. But the fog is thick up here and the horizon is gray and narrow all around. I see a few shacks here and there, mostly plastered against rocks and boulders. It's easy to understand why the place has a bad name. It is forbidding.

To the north, however, there is a more cheerful sight. Under a huge silver oak I see two tables loaded with corn, bread, meat, tomatoes and potatoes. Some women are busy with the food. I go over and give one of them my bottle of wine. It is immediately opened, passed around and consumed.

A community bathtub gleams on the other side of the tree like a piece of surrealist sculpture. It is useless now because someone has once again cut the waterline to the community, Harry says. Across the access path from the tub is a small split-log cabin where Zeke and Maya, the bride and groom, are in residence.

Harry and I walk south a bit to explore. We come upon an old Union Ice Company truck, a couple of Volkswagen buses and, in the middle of nowhere, a small organ painted blue and decorated with flowers. A young man with a black bowler is trying to play it. We keep climbing upward over rocks and poison oak until we come to a place where there is nothing but jagged stone. We sit down on a crag. The mist is flowing up from the ocean, flowing past us, covering the hills, drifting past us together with the faint sound of drums. I wouldn't be surprised to see an old Indian rise up from behind a rock at any moment. Might be hard to tell whether he's a hip gypsy or an Indian, there are so many people down there with leather headbands and tasseled deerskin clothing. When the drum sound stops I suggest we go down, the ceremony might be beginning. But Harry says he heard the sun has to be out for that.

So we wander down again to the gathering place and sit

down on a rickety wicker couch someone has set near the fire. After a while the bride emerges from the house, carrying a pan full of water. She looks like one of the Edmund Dulac illustrations in my copy of the *Rubaiyat*. She is slim and graceful, with light brown skin and small, delicate features. On her head, covering all her hair, is an ocher scarf that is tucked under in back and hangs down like a veil behind her. Set on top of it, straight across her high forehead, she wears a wreath of the orange nasturtiums that grow wild around here. A sheath of heavy cream-colored cloth falls to the tops of her bare feet. It's sleeveless and under it she has on a raspberry-colored jersey. Around her waist is a tasseled silk print scarf, folded into a triangle with the point coming down over her right hip. A belt of golden coins is around her waist, huge round gold earrings hang nearly to her shoulders, a necklace of nasturtiums is around her neck. Her arm bracelets jangle as she walks toward the fire with the water pot and sets it on a grill. Then she turns, without looking at anyone or saying a word, and goes back into her house.

Still there is no sign that the wedding is about to begin. I keep looking around for promises of sunshine, until my attention is drawn by the more excited beat of the conga drums. Now a couple is dancing. The man, shirtless, blond and beardless, moves jerkily. The woman, black-haired, in slacks and sweater, slithers and undulates, her arms high and her hands pressed against his palms. She is a stoned snake-woman. The rhythm quickens. A flute player joins in. Someone picks up an autoharp and starts strumming. The girl's eyes are glassy, her mouth is open as if in orgasm, she moves faster, wilder, with her breasts, waist, belly, knees.

Then the drums slow down and the dancers stop. They stand for a moment staring at one another and then sit down on the grass together. A few minutes later they stand up again, kiss passionately and walk off together. When they return they start dancing again, but more peacefully. The drummers are now no longer interested.

"That should do it," says a bony old man sitting near me. "Now watch the sun come out."

Suddenly the air lightens. The drummers begin to beat a steady, intense rhythm, an incantation. As they beat faster the clouds thin and the lightness spreads. The sun bursts through the fog. They stop. Amazing coincidence. Now, at last, for the wedding.

But nothing happens. Neither bride nor groom appears. Grass and wine are passed around. I should have brought a gallon of cheap wine, I see, rather than that one expensive bottle. No need to have worn a dress, either, slacks would have been better. When I got up from the wicker couch someone took my place and now, sitting on rocks and aware of all the poison oak around, I'm really uncomfortable in my miniskirt. But surely the ceremony will soon begin. It's way past noon.

Up against one of the boulders on the edge of the crowd a woman with long white hair sits like some kind of high priestess. She is dressed in a long brown gown hand-painted with triangles and diamonds, and wears a white feather in her beaded headband. She's strumming lethargically on an autoharp. I go over to talk with her and she tells me she's the landlady in this place. She had read some letters in the papers that criticized the beatniks, she says, so she invited any beats who wanted a place to stay on Big Sur to settle in Gorda. They didn't take her up on the invitation, she says, but the hippies did. For a while this was a lovely community but now a lot of people are gone and it's more transient. There's been too much harassment by the health department, the police and neighbors. She'd like to see it turn into a quiet community of artists but this is how things are now, as I see them. What can anyone do when the waterline keeps getting cut?

Still nothing is happening. I see the bride is now standing against a tree, looking a bit unhappy. The groom is cutting a small naked child's hair and she's watching. He looks like a ruddy French provincial with that maroon beret and gallant mustache, the boots and red and black checked hunter's jacket. When he finishes with the child he starts to trim the nape of a tall man. What is going on? He's moving about his daily business and completely ignoring his bride. She's trying to look serene but the nasturtiums are wilting and so are her spirits. Roger comes to sit beside me. "She must want it pretty bad to wait for him like that," he says.

"So what's this all about?"

"He's too busy to marry her now, he's busy cutting hair," Rober says. "Maybe they won't have the wedding here anyway, they might just go off somewhere and have it by themselves. He said it had to be Sunday and the sun had to shine. I don't know. There's a lot of food and a lot of strong people here today. Nobody's in a hurry. Maybe people will stay up here a day or two, till the food's all gone. I might stay, tune in, feel the thing, dance. Then for days you feel loose and clear."

What's clear to me right now is that this is some sort of wedding game rather than a prearranged ceremony. It's a theatrical performance played without a script. The groom

106

finishes cutting hair and goes off to talk with someone. The bride disappears into her cabin. More people are dancing now, each one or each couple performing some private ritual.

It's late afternoon. The well-published existentialist, apparently through with his seminar-sessions for the day, appears with a buxom schoolteacher who has rented a house for the summer near Gorda and attends some of the Esalen seminars. I spoke with her at the baths one day. "You know that song of Bob Dylan's where he says, something about you don't know what's happening, do you Mr. Jones? Well, I came down here because I want to find out," she told me. "I have a daughter who just dropped out."

When she starts to dance she moves like a chaperone at a high school prom, social pastiming. Meanwhile, under the trees, others are absorbed in their personal dance ceremonies. Again, the contrast is the one I noticed between Roger and Diana's intense game in the woods and the timidity of sensory awareness seeking on the lawn. This is why I'm so drawn to the gypsies. They are living—no matter how imperfectly, foolishly and temporarily—what the squares come to learn at Esalen weekends. So you still don't know, do you, Mrs. Jones?

Dancing and music seem to come as naturally to them as walking and speech comes to me. Everybody plays something, even if it's only a simple bamboo flute. They aren't afraid to pick up an instrument and improvise. When I tried to learn how to play the guitar, I struggled to learn chords that went with particular tunes. But they seldom if ever play anyone else's tune. Neither their dancing nor their music has any fixed pattern.

I remember a businessman in New York who once told me he didn't understand music. "It's just like you don't understand Arabic, right? You hear it but it doesn't mean anything to you? Well, that's what I mean. Music isn't my language," he said.

"But we're born with it," I argued. "Babies know it."

"It's all mathematics," he said. "To understand it one should be able to grasp it in terms of mathematics."

"What rot. Music isn't in terms of anything. It's music."

"I can hear the rhythm and the tones," he said. "But it just doesn't communicate."

"Because you analyze it into rhythm and tone and mathematics and terms of. Why don't you just listen to it?"

"If I don't know if the notes are being played correctly, as they were written, how can I understand it?"

"It doesn't matter about the notes. Forget about understanding it. Why don't you try just listening to the sound."

"To hear music, to reproduce it, one should know about . . ."

We were talking in a restaurant. At the next table a man had been eavesdropping. As he got up to leave he said to my companion, "Sir, you don't need to *understand* music. You only need to *feel* it." Then he turned and walked off, feeling superior, no doubt, to someone whom he considered an insensitive clod. But I happened to know that at the time this businessman was reading books about creativity and that he was a hungry man. Someone had scared him away from music by telling him about "reproducing" it and about things "one should know." I wish he could hear the gypsies.

When Ravi Shankar gave a concert at Esalen, a lot of people from the hills and canyons came to the Hot Springs. Ravi Shankar sat inside the seminar room, facing the people who had paid $67 for the weekend to hear him. But the real audience was outside the glass doors, where the people from the mountains sat in the dark and the cold wind. I sat outside for the first half and inside for the second. There was no question about which audience dug Ravi's sitar sound.

But I'm noticing some action here, some new stir. The groom, with a tall, bleached wood cane, is walking toward the bride. She is again by the door of their house, now talking with a pretty girl in a white muslin dress. He keeps walking toward her but she pretends she doesn't see him. When he is a few feet away he stops, puts his chin on top of the cane and looks at her. She looks back. He turns away again, goes to get a drum, sits down a good distance away from her and, looking at her sideways, starts to beat it. Aha. So this is how they'll do it, I say to myself. She'll now dance to his tune. But I'm wrong. She's back to her conversation with the girl in white. After a while he stops drumming and begins to take off his boots. She comes over, helps him to pull them off, and carries them inside. When she emerges she no longer wears the nasturtium wreath. Well, so it's not going to happen or what? It's nearly sundown.

"Come over here, princess," Roger calls her. "Why don't you go over and hug him and see what happens. I'll watch you and I'll know too." She shakes her head sadly and walks off. A bit later I see that she and the groom are kissing. By this time Roger is deep in his own dance under the tree.

A girl approaches the happy couple, kisses each of them and gives them a package wrapped in pink paper. It's the only present I've seen anyone give them. This was supposed to be a "people energy exchange," Roger told me, not a gift exchange. The bride and groom sit down by the fire and open the package, pull out some scraps of the *Los Angeles Free Press* and then a small Indian chest. But by now few people are watching.

All day the food has been cooking on a fire behind the two tables under the silver oak. Now people form lines in front of the big kettles full of rice and stew. No plates are provided, so each hungry person has scrounged for some container and holds his tin can, lid, cup or whatever. Those who can find no receptacle wait till someone has finished eating and take his. As there is no water readily available, nobody bothers with washing of dishes or eating utensils. I find a used plate, and, being hungry, ignore all thoughts of sanitation. The food is delicious.

Later on I sit down to talk with Virginia, an attractive middle-aged woman who, I'm told, is a priestess of sorts around Big Sur. She's sitting on a field cot with a manila envelope from Greenwich, Connecticut, lying next to her and a poodle sitting on her other side. Her garb must have cost quite a bit at some import shop—it's a Finnish *djellabah* of rich wool woven in a lovely design with brown, tan and black. She doesn't look like a priestess to me but rather like a Greenwich matron in disguise.

I ask her some questions—though I'm aware that's gauche —and she quickly becomes annoyed. Esalen is all wrong, she says, because it's not spiritual. There's too much coming in from the outside world and it's corrupting what's happening. What's happening is here, these people being together, feeling each other, living in trust. Esalen is intellectual and scientific and that's all wrong. It's on psychology and psychology is sick. People who want to find themselves come here, they drop out. The people who come to the seminars would be afraid to come here, they think all this is evil and full of witches. Soon people will have to go off to the hills because the coast is becoming a real Coney Island.

Her attitude is a bit too anti-everything for someone who is so obviously intelligent and prosperous. "And what kind of a life did you come from?" I ask her. "I lived in San Francisco for a while. My husband was on the stock exchange and I had a cosmetic company." She says it impatiently and somehow triumphantly. "And did you leave it all behind?" I ask. "Are you no longer dependent on any of it?"

"Yes. One thing about people around here is that they

109

don't interrogate each other," she tells me, cutting off any urge I might have to pursue the subject. "They make contact and feel each other. Over there"—she points toward a light-skinned Negro with wild hair—"I made contact with him while he was wearing a white robe and for a moment I didn't know whether he was a man or a woman, his face was so soft and serene."

That's all very mystical but I hear it as hostile and domineering. Turned off, I move away. The sun is setting, there has been no wedding ceremony, but people don't seem to mind. Maya takes off the necklace of wilted nasturtiums and dances a sundown dance. She dances beautifully (later I find she studied dancing in San Francisco after she dropped out of college), in a style more Oriental than Western. Her face is serene now, the drawn look of the late afternoon is gone. I watch until she is finished, then leave. No doubt the party will continue all night for more people are coming, more grass is passed, more food is cooked. But I'm ready to go back to the Hot Springs for a long bath. Virginia, who is also leaving with her poodle and two other dogs, gives me and several others a ride down the mountain in her Volkswagen bus.

So it was a fine wedding except that they didn't get married. Yet what an idea—to arrange a celebration during which a marriage might or might not take place, depending on the weather and the moment's vibrations; to let ritual evolve out of the moment so that everyone creates his own. The next day I ask people who stayed the night at Gorda whether the ceremony had taken place later. Nobody is quite sure. For days afterward the word among the gypsies is "Believe in the wedding."

Two weeks later, Zeke and Maya do get married in the presence of a few close friends, but not in a tree. The way I hear it, "They were making it up on the big rock and someone was beating the drums." Then I hear they had still another ceremony. "He just likes to keep marrying her," Pat Cassidy, one of the old-timers in the mountains, explains. "He might keep marrying her for the first fifty-nine weeks. But he's certainly never going to buy her from the state. He'll never go down to any courthouse and ask some cat they don't even know to recognize their existence. That would be an insult to themselves."

I like the idea of marriage as a constant wedding that, every day, might or might not take place. That is typical of the way the gypsies live up on Big Sur. Later, I will hear marriage counselors, psychologists and sociologists talk about "marriage as an open-ended contract," and "keeping communication lines open." But I will continue to prefer the style in which the gypsies said those same things up at Gorda.

Chapter SIX

Freaked Out
with the Gypsies

A PINCH-FACED physicist with close-cropped hair in a red flannel shirt and leather jacket, has slipped into the chair at the end of the table beside full-bearded Judah. He has already eaten his dinner with his fellow seminarians and now seeks a conversation with the hairy local characters. Everyone at this table is either long-haired or full-bearded.

The physicist's back is very straight, his eyes dart around the candlelit table, blinking rapidly behind round clear-rimmed glasses. He is obviously eager for a chat and, equally obviously, nobody here is interested in talking with him because he is so nervous. At last he turns abruptly to Judah. "You work here?" The tone sounds peremptory but that's because he's so very nervous.

"Yes." Judah barely glances up from his plate of macaroni.

"What do you do?"

Judah straightens up, drops his fork and looks across the table at pale, dark Mary with an expression that says "Good God! Did you hear that?" He turns toward the physicist. "I'm a shelf cleaner," he tells him.

"Oh." He is vaguely offended but not silenced. "You get to go to many of the seminars?"

"Well, you see, I'm sort of in a constant seminar." Judah's voice has an impatient edge.

"Oh? There's a group like that?"

"No, it's unofficial. Some of us are just like that here," Judah says but now he seems a bit embarrassed. What he said

111

sounded pretentious. "And what do *you* do?" he asks, conciliatory.

"Right now I'm a bum," says the guy, eagerly, as if he had been waiting for just that question. "I don't have a job. For the past two months I've just been bumming around."

He reminds me of a clean-cut kid out on the lawn yesterday who tried to establish his credentials with the local dropouts by knocking his new college diploma. "It's just a piece of paper, there's nothing behind it but wasted time," he kept saying. This man comes across just as phony.

Judah says nothing. The physicist goes on. "I'm trying to meet the staff because I'd like to be in the residential program next year and I think this is a way to find out a lot about the place." His words fall into silence. A lot of the gypsies flee uptight people because they make *them* uptight. I feel sorry for the physicist but not sorry enough to say anything. Judah gestures across the table. "This is Mary. She's a very interesting person."

"Hello, Mary."

"Hello," she says, shooting daggers with her eyes at Judah.

But now Judah seems suddenly struck with a guilt pang. He looks the guy full in the face and says in full civility, "My name is Judah. This is Mary."

"I'm Jack," the physicist says gratefully.

"You in Bill Schutz's seminar?" Judah asks.

"Yes, I'm also here because I'm writing a book. It's called *Getting There Without Drugs.*"

"Too much!" says Judah's face to Mary. "This uptight little phony!" "Getting *where?*" he asks the physicist.

Deaf to the implications in Judah's voice, the physicist plunges ahead. "There was a man named Korzybski in Poland who was interested in the way the genius mind worked and he could show everyone how to think like a genius. This program at Esalen with just a little expansion and some changes fits right in with Korzybski. And it leads to Zen and meditation. Drugs are just a gimmick, you don't need them."

Perhaps what he says is true. But Judah isn't listening to the words as much as to the way the man comes across—and that is, as a frightened fellow who is trying to talk simply so that these strange people would understand about something he himself doesn't understand. Judah slams shut the door he had opened:

"There's only one way really," he says. The physicist is alert, listening. "Through Jesus," says Judah. The physicist looks bewildered. He stares at Judah trying to find out if he's being had. Judah looks earnest. The freak-a-seminarian game is on.

"Judah," Mary asks, equally earnest. "Do you think Jesus is the Redeemer?"

"Yes I do," replies Judah gravely.

The physicist glances back and forth across the flickering candle. Their faces are solemn—too solemn. He decides he *is* being had. "Jesus saves," he says brightly, wheeling in there to show he wasn't falling for it. I wince, anticipating the rest of that sentence. "Jesus saves green stamps." His eyes dart around for a reaction, his shoulders twitch, his mouth twitches into an uncertain grin. People continue to fork their macaroni as if not a word has been spoken. Then Mary again looks at Judah and her voice is soft and melodious. "Do you *really* believe He is the Redeemer?"

"The son of God."

"But if nothing is lost, what is there to redeem?"

"Green stamps!" the physicist crows.

"Jesus is the Redeemer because He saves green stamps, you heard the man," says Judah in a tone of disgust. He turns to the physicist. "Brother, why do you jest?"

Oh no, now the guy is really lost. Could it be they were *serious?* I'm sure he's remembering this moment that hippies have been compared to early Christians.

"Because . . . because you weren't communicating," he says miserably.

"You see it's . . ." Judah spreads his hands, shrugs and turns the Meeting Look on the physicist. The poor fellow tries to hold the steady gaze but can't. Blink, blink, blink his lids go behind the round glasses. His mouth twitches, his face turns a deep red. He is exposed and pinioned by Judah's eyes.

"You could maybe do something for this place," says Judah, cruel now.

"I won't have time. I have to hurry back."

Hurry back? Just a bum, eh? Judah looks around the table triumphantly.

"Where to?" I ask.

"To Washington. I have to present a paper."

The game is over. A fraud is exposed. Judah and Mary rise and go. The physicist looks helplessly at the empty chairs, makes a stab in my direction. "Do you work here?"

"No," I say, "I'm just here for a while."

"Well, here is better than there," he says inanely, giggles and bolts to the next room where Bill Schutz's More Joy Workshop is meeting.

Esalen—Hot Springs is a laboratory of free behavior, a con-

113

tinuous truth lab. The standard rules of politeness are mostly suspended. What is expected is an authentic response, whatever that might be, short of physical violence. As a result, the atmosphere is intense and encounters can be diverse and subtle—and sometimes hostile. People who walk into this scene unprepared find it hard to take at first and tend to become uptight in it, as I was in the beginning. A truly turned-on person would not play cruel games with them. So, when I reflect on that incident with the physicist, I am reminded that turning on isn't simply moving from one subculture into another.

Right now, though, I am spending time with the gypsies—not because they are wiser or more honest than squares but because they know how to groove in a way most of us middle-class squares have ruled out of our existence.

The gypsies are dropouts, misfits, runaways from the law or society, seekers, mystics, adults playing children. Some of them are half crazy and only half literate, some have spent years in schools. A lot of them smoke grass the way other people smoke cigarettes. Some are so disoriented by too many mind drugs that they walk around blank-eyed and wince at any loud noise. But though it's unofficial, they are part of the Esalen turn-on. Seminar people tend to be both attracted to them and afraid of them, for they live outside the middle-class value and status system—or try to, anyway.

Not long after the wedding at Gorda, I give up my comfortable life in a cabin, for I can no longer afford $16 a day for room and board, and begin to live more like the gypsies. I store my belongings in a friend's place, work there sometimes in the daytime and sleep out in the tall grass. From then on I eat only one meal a day at the lodge and buy the rest of my food from the mailman, who brings bread, cookies, milk, yogurt and cheese every afternoon. Some of the gypsies call dining-room food "plastic" and keep to a macrobiotic diet. They cook in their living wagons or over campfires and get their brown rice, sea salt, sesame seeds and dried fruit from a macrobiotic merchant who comes by with a truck twice a month.

My days flow by in wandering. I spend a lot of time on the hip porch or inside the lodge, just listening and watching. As Mike Murphy says, you never know who will turn out to be your guru.

There's Bill Thompson, who washes dishes and makes musical instruments. He saw himself as an Asian instrument-maker in a previous incarnation during one of his acid trips, realized that was his karma, came to Esalen, found a job and a workshop, and tacked on his door: "Karma Strings." I visit him one evening and find him sitting on a high stool, his pale dark-bearded face bent over a piece of wood he is carving. He shows me an instrument that looks somewhat like a guitar and somewhat like a sitar.

"It's made from six kinds of wood," he says.

"What is it?"

"It's Ben's ax. I made it for Ben. It's out of my head," he says. "I'm going to build eleven more and they'll all be out of my head. We're going to have a band—it's going to be called the Indian Headband. Ger is building an electric harpsichord for it."

Bill is from Monterey. Before he saw his karma, he says he did a lot of different things—drove a truck, built boats and cabins, worked as a farmhand. Then he lived in Gorda for a while but it was too noisy up there with all those Indian ghosts fighting their old battles at night. He saw himself in six previous lives, he tells me. In each he was of royal blood and in each he died violently. Once it was as a samurai in battle.

A lot of gypsies believe in reincarnation and talk about seeing themselves in previous lives. A surprising number were princes or shepherds or something equally romantic—like beautiful Greek slaves in Caesar's palace, or bootleggers during Prohibition. Many of them have discovered that present friends were friends in past lives also. Nico, Bill's "old lady," for instance, was Queen Nefertiti and Bill was her royal lover.

All this puzzled me until I noticed that if you put the past characters together you got a pretty good, if glorified, portrait of the person in his present life. Bill certainly has something dark and violent inside him. A lot of people are afraid of him because of the way his pale eyes glower in his haggard face. One kid, who calls him "Bummer Bill," told me, "I can be sitting with my breakfast and he'll just walk through the dining room on his way to the john and give me one look and I'll be cowering."

But there is also something regal in Bill's bearing and his fierceness. One night I watched him play a conga drum by a fire. His face was still and white, he sat very straight, with the light flickering over him, and he was, indeed, what his friend Ger said he is—Prince of Darkness, Lord of the Lyre and the Edge of Light. The gypsies' self-games are magical. Instead of talking about "self-actualization," they talk of past lives and mystical titles.

The morning after visiting his workshop, I find Bill sitting alone in the lodge, having coffee. I join him and he starts talking about auras. "Most people have blue ones with a lot of red in them," he says. "I learned to see them on acid. Some people have off-color ones."

"What color is mine?" I ask, apprehensive.

"Yours is blue with a little red. I saw it last night. That's all right but it should be white with gold. You'll get there. Mine is black with gold."

"Like your name. Who gave you that name—Prince of Darkness, Lord of the Lyre?"

"I gave Lord of the Lyre to Ger," he says. "But I may take it back. The other's too heavy."

So all right, maybe a grown man talking like this is mad by most people's standards. But does the average normal person have such gifts to offer his friends?

An average normal person from New York sits down next to me. At the first pause he charges in with questions. What's going on here this weekend? He just stopped in because he was driving by. What is this place all about? What's my name? Why am I here? Bill's face turns black, he doesn't hear. I answer but resent the interrogation. Then I go out to the deck.

On the other side of the swimming pool Gia-Fu is walking in circles, which means it is nine-fifteen. Gia-Fu is the closest thing to a clock around here. He's always out by the pool, walking in his concentration circles at precisely nine-fifteen. My watch stopped a week after I got here and there are no clocks anywhere but in the office, which is the border checkpoint of the outside world. I sit down on a bench to watch Gia-Fu lead Tai Chi Chuan exercises with whoever will join him.

A man comes to sit next to me. He is one of the people here for the seminar on marriage and he has just come out of a twenty-four-hour marathon truth lab. Two nights ago, when people arrived for this seminar, they were talkative and noisy. This morning I noticed they were all pretty quiet. Now this man is sitting next to me, silent, and I think how good it is to sit like this, feeling a stranger's presence before a word is said. We look at Gia-Fu as he begins his slow dancing movements. The four people trying to follow him are too large and very clumsy in contrast to him. The fog is already gone, the water glitters behind Gia-Fu and his group. Trees and grass are morning-fresh. Someone is working in the community vegetable garden to our right. When the man beside me speaks his words come as part of the scene.

"Where are you from?"

I answer gladly. A few minutes ago, the New Yorker ran questions at me like a cavalry charge and I gave him only the bare bones of politeness.

116

"This morning," says this man, who is from Eugene, Oregon, "I was looking for some kind of order when they served us at breakfast and then I realized the waitresses were just putting a plate here, one there, just as the spirit moved them, I guess." His voice says he was bewildered but not annoyed. "I'm working on a doctorate in school counseling," he says after a pause. "I know there are a lot of questions I should be asking people. But the longer I stay here, the less important they seem."

"Yes, I'm finding that too," I tell him. "I'm learning here much more by listening and watching than I am by asking questions. Sometimes I wonder how it will be when I try to write it all down."

Learning what? I ask myself. To see, to listen. There used to be times, when I was working as a newspaper reporter, when I'd get down on paper what some man said but couldn't remember, after an interview, how he sounded or what he looked like.

I go down the cliff-side path to the baths and sink into the hot water. A morning soak has become a luxurious ritual for me. Usually I get here much earlier, when no one is here. Today I find a young woman and a girl already here. The woman, here for one of the seminars, is the vivacious wife of an attorney whom she is thinking of divorcing, because, she told me, "we interfere with each other's growth." She has had a busy and diverse social life during her past few days here. Now she is in one of the individual tubs, scrubbing herself energetically but without touching her face, which is made-up with false eyelashes and lipstick. (That's unusual. Most people stop wearing makeup at Esalen.) She is in a hurry to get to her seminar, rinses herself and dresses quickly, gets annoyed when she finds a snag in combing her hair, hurries away.

The girl, a gypsy, is in the other big tub. When the woman has gone she climbs out, pours cold water from the hose over her head and then stands for a while by the railing looking out over the ocean, her blond hair around her shoulders like a cloak. She is very young—no more than sixteen—and very pretty. After a while she begins to get dressed.

The gypsy women preen themselves like cats when they're down at the baths. They soap themselves slowly, caressingly, in the individual tubs, wash off, then soak in the big tubs. Then they sit in the sun inspecting their bodies, combing their hair. Usually they don't talk while grooming themselves. When they do, their voices are soft. Some of them sit cross-legged on the wooden tables, looking at the ocean as they

117

meditate. Quite a few consider the baths holy. I know Gia-Fu also comes here to meditate some mornings. Now I watch this girl as she combs her hair slowly, laces up tall deerskin boots and puts on a purple cotton minidress with a hole under the left armpit. She is lovely to watch because she is digging what she is doing, paying attention to every movement she makes—living the now.

Everything keeps changing among the gypsies though a lot of it never goes beyond someone's head. People are constantly trying new styles, new turn-ons and self-games, new partners. You can go away for a few days, come back and find that someone you thought was a permanent fixture has vanished without a trace, that a couple which seemed mated forever has split and already both the man and the woman have new partners. Sex is so casual among some of the gypsies and nobody lifts an eyebrow even a micro-inch seeing two who are not of a pair together for the evening.

Even names keep changing, for both mystical and practical reasons. With Roger it's both. One morning in the canyon, Roger and Diana offer me crushed wheat cereal, honey and coffee and we sit around talking while Roger whittles a fish sculpture and Diana sews a lilac cotton shirt for him.

Roger is thirty-one and the name he is using is his second. The first one was on the right track but didn't make it, he says. This one will also be short-lived, it's just to go through the changes. The third—he saw it written on a piece of paper that blew across the sidewalk in front of him in Los Angeles —will be his when he's right with himself and respected by everyone.

Before he got deep into drugs and decided to make a spiritual trip to Big Sur, Roger says, he was a journeyman roofer. "At one time I was working for five contractors at once and they all thought I was what they expected a man to be— someone ready to do forty hours a week until he retired. Actually, I just worked when I needed to. I'd call one of them and tell him I had just finished a job and had time for two roofs if he could use me. Then I made sure to get there on time and work hard. They would have thought I wasn't responsible if they knew I only worked part of the time."

Then he suddenly had even more leisure—he was arrested for possession of marijuana and sent to jail for eighteen months. "I read all of Alan Watts' books there," he says, "and I learned self-hypnosis from my cell partner. There was a group studying semantics, I got into that, and an old Russian cat showed me how to read a slide rule and do square roots. Every night I'd meditate when the sun was going down. I wrote my mother that the view of the mountains out my cell window was the most beautiful view I'd ever seen. It was true."

Jail did not stop him from further psychedelic exploration. He took LSD several times until one day he left his house and all his things and came out here with nothing but a hundred dollars. "A man gave me a ride and his truck broke down so I got the message I should walk. I walked along the coast road and after a while I started working on a walking stick. I put a man on top with a pack on his back. Some cat picked me up and admired the stick. It occurred to me I could sell it but maybe I should give it to him. So I gave it to him and when I got off, right away I got a job.

"When I first started taking acid and peyote, I got this power. When people were down I could hold their hands and get them back up. I turned a lot of people on. But I kept taking acid and peyote and I got into this beautiful state where I don't want to bother doing that anymore. That's bad for me. It's all right for an old man."

"So you stopped taking drugs?"

"Not yet. That's still in my head but maybe it's coming."

"We're going to move pretty soon," says Diana. "It's too foggy here. We're going up higher, to Pat Cassidy's."

Diana was a bookkeeper in San Francisco two years ago. She teased her hair into a beehive, wore makeup, high heels. It's hard to visualize, looking at her sitting here in the woods, barefoot, loose-haired, dressed in faded cotton.

As I leave, Roger takes one of his carved redwood mobiles from a tree and gives it to me. "I give these to people," he says awkwardly. I'm overcome. He must have spent days making it. I can think of nothing I can give him in return.

These people I'm meeting seem to be living on the thin edge —between sanity and madness, childhood and adulthood, bliss and despair, religion and superstition, love and hate. But Big Sur itself is a thin edge, and not everyone can survive here. At first it makes you dizzy. Later, if you manage to get back your equilibrium, you begin to notice what else is here—the flowers, the cobwebs, the surf and the sea otters. "The way of excess leads to the palace of wisdom," Blake said. But it is a treacherous way.

Ger Agrey is tending bar, dressed in a smart sports jacket, a relic of four years ago, when he was working in an advertising agency. But he has a paisley shirt with it, to show where he's at. "I met this woman," he says, "who said she had a bad trip on acid. She saw a wheel with herself the hub and all the powers and energies of the world going from it. Man, it was *the* trip, but she was scared. It shook her Protestant ethic."

"America, it's wonderful," says Bill Thompson, who's behind the bar with Ger.

"Yea, it really makes it," says Ger and doubles up laughing.

It's quiet in the bar. Most of the Esalen people are in Bill Schutz's truth lab next door. I can hear them thumping around, encountering physically, from time to time. Most of the gypsies are in Carl Lee the potter's place, for some kind of celebration. Bill Thompson is building a candle from a lot of candle stubs.

"Twelve shitty years I spent studying music and now I listen to Mozart and he's linear and mechanical, where Ravi Shankar can go on and on, with just one instrument, making it all up as he goes," says Ger.

"I've got a plan that would make peace in Vietnam in a month," says Turtle, who came to Big Sur recently from a commune called Strawberry Fields. He got his name way back, when he was a motorcycle rider. "But it might start World War Three."

"Let's do it, man," says Ger.

"You get fifty people," says Turtle, "and you teach them to be. You put ten of them into each branch of the armed forces. Give each man two pounds of acid and let them go."

"That's fine, man," says Bill, putting another candle on a stalk that's about two feet high now. "But the other side won't be turned on so they'll keep shooting." The candle is growing like some freaked-out plant.

"Besides, who'd want the job?" says Ger.

"Must be some of our people in there somewhere to break the chain," says Turtle. "I'd do it if I could get in there."

"America, it's wonderful," says Bill. He's starting a second candle stalk at the roots of the first.

"Yea, it really makes it," says Ger.

Lorna, who's all the young gypsies' Indian mother, comes up. "I wish the *I Ching* were here," she says. Someone walked off with the *I Ching* three weeks ago. It used to be kept behind the bar as a standard reference work, just the way Webster's Unabridged Dictionary was kept at Bleeck's, the bar of the *Herald Tribune* people in New York. Lorna gives me a tiny triangular piece of abalone shell.

"I hear Diana went off to New Mexico," someone says to Lorna.

"It was time for her to go," she says.

"But just yesterday she and Roger were going up the mountain together," I say.

"She's gone," Lorna says.

"I was out on deck," says Turtle. "They were talking violence versus nonviolence. And inside they were actually fighting, two cats going at each other," he says, nodding toward Schutz's workshop.

"Help, I'm a rock!" says Bill Thompson. Ger laughs.

Nico, Bill's "old lady," is standing next to him. "I freaked in the Carmel A & P the other day," she says. "I don't know what happened. There was this voice on the loudspeaker saying 'Only five more minutes to save on our special something or other' and I was standing in an aisle under those fluorescent lamps looking at my list. I didn't know where the frozen peas were and I freaked. I started crying and the manager came running up. All I could tell him was 'I can't find the plastic peas!' I kept saying it over and over. He was very nice. He said it wasn't abnormal at all. Sometimes they move something around and it happens to a lot of people. Some women will stand there and actually hit their heads against the wall. But man, I'm not going into that A & P by myself anymore."

A man walks in and asks for a towel. He doesn't seem to notice Bill's candle, which by now is a twin-stalked burning plant of amazing height. A second man walks in, says, "Some candle," and climbs up on a chair so he can look down on it.

"Reality is a mind deep-freeze," says Ger.

"It's just that most people don't realize they can create their own," says Turtle.

"I have two koans about this place," says Ger. "The first one is, 'How fast do the yin and yang have to spin before you lose consciousness?' You can only ask that if you're unconscious, see? The second is in the answer. 'What goes on here? The answer—I have no idea.' Do you flash on that?"

Chapter SEVEN

The Way of Excess

THIS WEEKEND'S seminar is called Allowing, but to some who came that word must have read Orgy. According to the brochure, it is to consist of "several approaches to the art of letting go, such as sensory approaches; meditation, a game to develop a 'group-mind,' massage and other ways being developed at Esalen." I have signed up for it and am staying in a new cabin, with sliding glass doors that lead to a balcony, for the duration.

"The art of letting go" has a dangerous, alluring sound, like "the art of loving." The anticipation is so palpable in the group that gathers Friday night that Edward Maupin, who is in charge of the seminar with Bernard Gunther, feels called to explain, "An orgy is not particularly the scene."

On Saturday morning we break into groups of five or six and Maupin shows us the "group-mind" game. It's called "Symbo" and was invented at Esalen by him and five other 1966–1967 resident fellows. He tells us to think of the group as one organism and ourselves as part of it. We are to listen to the group's heartbeat instead of our own and to let the organism move as it will, without coercion. We sit on the floor while he directs our attention to tensions, strengths and energies in each of the little groups.

When the resident fellows played this game, they became aware—as in a flowing psychedelic experience—that what happened grew out of the process rather than from individual invention. The game turned into a kind of a group meditation, Maupin says, in which everyone saw his identity in relation to the world he is part of. But the Esalen fellows spent days on the game. The few hours we have for it are barely enough to give a glimpse of its possibilities.

Saturday afternoon there is a group massage session at the

122

baths intended, as Gunther explains, to "explore the area between touching and sensuality. There is a whole range of sensuality that we tend to exclude in our society," he says, "although it can be enormously exciting and pleasurable. There is a feeling that if we have any physical contact it *has* to lead to a sexual situation."

The group has already made progress in this direction by visiting the baths. Now people go a step further by lying on wooden tables in the sunshine and allowing several pairs of hands to rub them all over. All parts of the body may be touched except the genitals. (One girl objected, saying she wanted to feel free to touch genitals if she wanted to, but Gunther said he did not see how sexuality would be avoided that way.) I watch from one of the big tubs as people pour hot and cold water over each other and work each other over. I've been learning how to give the Esalen super-turn-on massage from Molly Day Shackman, a lovely woman who is an artist at it. This is more primitive but for most people it is an entirely new experience to lie there nude, with several people massaging them. They get up from those tables looking blissful.

The high point of the weekend, however, is a "food experience"—a Tom Jones dinner, inspired by the scene in the film *Tom Jones* where two lovers bite sensuously into roast fowl while playing eye games across the table with each other. It is to take place Saturday night in the seminar room, which will be closed from the dining room. The meal is to be eaten without silverware.

I come down a bit late and find the feast already underway. On the long tables stand uncut fried chickens, huge bowls of salad, bowls of salad dressing, rice, squash with sour cream, string beans—beautiful food. But what is happening to it is hardly beautiful. People are tearing off hunks of the meat, shoveling salad into their plates with their hands, dipping fingers into the squash and the dressing, slobbering all over. I'm really hungry and in the mood for a pleasant, peaceful dinner. This scene fails to delight me.

Spotting some coffee-stirring sticks on the table, I take two and use them to get salad onto my plate. But as I'm doing this, a man grabs my wrist and shoves my hand into the bowl. I turn on him with fury. *"Allowing* is the name of this game," I hiss. Down the table a greasy-necked wine bottle is passed. Next to me a tiny grade school teacher is using coffee stirrers as chopsticks. Some people are undoubtedly enjoying themselves.

Suddenly from the other end of the room a paunchy middle-aged man comes running pursued by a laughing young woman. She traps him by the fireplace and smears salad dressing over his face. During the chase, a large painting behind me has been nearly knocked off the wall. I get up to right it. She brushes by on the way back and, still laughing, smears salad dressing across my nose. I'm becoming more and more angry. At the next table, a man shakes a bottle of champagne and sets it squirting toward the ceiling in a wide arc. Goddamn, I don't want my sweater ruined. I take it off and sit on it. Now a man appears from outside—nude. He wraps his arms around a woman, strips off her blouse, smears squash over her mouth and then kisses her. Lumps of food are flying through the air. *Mamita mia,* but this is disgusting, this is horrible! Everything in me rises in revolt. I have been brought up with a reverence for food and still feel guilty when I have to throw bread away. During the war in Europe bread was precious. I remember how once my mother brought an orange home from somewhere. It was a magic fruit. We passed it around, admired it, smelled it. Then mother cut the peel carefully into five petals, turned them back—with all of us watching—and divided the fruit into five sections. *That* was a food experience. We ate it slowly and closed our eyes to taste the juice more fully. No, I will not endure this, this is barbaric, sick! I leave the meal unfinished and flee into the dining room.

Here, as usual, there is quiet talk and soft music. The candles on the tables reflect in the windows, lighting elegant avenues into the sky. I look with envy at a plate of fried chicken and vegetables that a waitress is placing before someone. In the bar I find Bill Thompson and some others and sit down with them.

"Are you going to Gorda?" someone asks.

"Next week maybe."

"No, tonight. To the peyote festival."

"Really? Can I come?"

"No," says a man I don't know. "There aren't any peyote festivals around here."

"You can come with me," says one of my friends.

I've heard a lot of talk about peyote on Big Sur. Right now the heads favor it over acid. They say it's better for you, being organic rather than chemical, and that it gives a religious trip. As we set off, in an old car, I'm full of anticipation. Gorda will be ghostly this bright night. There is no fog. The dark crags will loom above the campfire, we will sense the presence of Indian warriors. Here I'll find a different kind

124

of allowing, an adventure far from cavorting with squash and chicken legs. Perhaps I'll even try a little peyote.

But as it develops, we don't get to Gorda. When we stop at a farmhouse to pick up some people, we learn that the site of the festival has been changed for fear of a raid. The people from Gorda are coming down here. I'm disappointed. This house is a shabby two-room affair, home of a vague number of mountain gypsies and passing travelers. In the living room a dazed-looking girl stares out of a deep chair and a young man is asleep under blankets on a double bed. In the kitchen, two men and a girl I recognize from Gorda are preparing peyote buttons. They take out the fur and seeds of the brownish-green cactus buttons and put the remainder, now a ring, in a pile on newspaper. Some buttons are ground for peyote tea in a meat grinder, others are eaten as they are, with sea salt. I taste one. It is bitter and makes me feel nauseous. No thank you, no more.

People drift in until there are maybe thirty in the house. Someone lights a red candle and places it in the middle of the living room. The drummers sit around, staring into it. A girl in a long dress, carrying a baby wrapped in a Mexican shawl, begins to dance. The bride from Gorda droops over her knees in yoga position then begins to rise slowly, her upper body and her arms moving in a pulsating dance. In the kitchen more buttons are prepared and eaten. Every once in a while someone goes out—peyote makes everyone nauseous —and returns to eat some more. And so it goes on for hours. There is almost no conversation, the drums make the house vibrate and make me somewhat high, but not high enough, I guess, to keep me from getting bored. After a while I'm ready to go back to the Hot Springs but nobody is driving back and it's much too far to walk. Finally I climb into a loft and find my friend there. When I wake it is morning and the drums are still going. There are voices downstairs.

My mouth feels like rough wool and I want to get out of here and into a bath. A couple of other people are lumped under blankets in the loft. I go downstairs, past the kitchen where some people are drinking coffee, past the room where a dazed boy is drumming, and out into the early morning fog. My friend is standing with three others over a fire. "I had the mantle for a long time," he says. "I was inside everything and I could have done anything. Then it passed on." He goes on talking but I don't understand him. He says he ate twenty-eight peyote buttons.

In the cars and on the grass, people are sleeping. Nobody is about to leave, so I set off alone toward the highway, breathing deeply of the fog to clean my lungs of the night's smoke, to clean the mess out of my mind.

So I attended two kinds of orgies and was put uptight by both. The Allowing seminar had turned me off from the start, I realize, as had the nauseous bitterness of peyote. I know that those who were fully into what was happening must have had a different experience. To each man his own excess. Right now the morning is like a gift and every flower, every stalk of grass stands out in complete perfection. I tune my ears to the birds, my eyes to the dewy foliage, my lungs to the damp air.

The highway is empty for it is still very early. But eventually I hear a motor and stick out my thumb. A couple of newlyweds from Los Angeles pick me up. They've been driving all night, ever since they left their wedding party, and have not yet found a decent motel, the man says. I guess they must be feeling the same kind of wool in their mouths by now. The ashtray is full, they look grumpy. Something was wrong with a lot of celebrations last night, it seems.

After breakfast, the Allowing seminar meets to talk about the Tom Jones dinner. One woman says it was possibly the most beautiful experience in her life because there was so much sharing and caring at her table. A man says, "I had to withdraw and watch the strange feast like some weird movie. Some revolted me, others I felt sympathy for."

"Now I feel you're hurting and I want to come over and touch you," a woman tells him.

"Tell me where first," he says, giggling. She embraces him. "Feel better?" he asks, patting her shoulder.

"The primitiveness allowed me to feel a lot of things I hadn't allowed myself to feel for a long time," another woman says.

"I had a mystical experience with the food," says someone else.

Gia-Fu had my reaction. His voice trembles with emotion as he says, "For the first time in many years, I felt like a foreigner."

In the afternoon I lie on my bed and listen to some tape recordings of a seminar held here in spring 1967 by R. D. Laing, a British existential analyst who runs a radical program for schizophrenics in London. His theory is that the schizophrenic experience is a trip—"an auto-initiatory voyage"—that can be therapeutic if completed without interference. To allow this, he has set up communes, called blowout centers, where schizophrenics take care of each other and the household without doctors, nurses, medicines or treatments. "All that has to be provided is a room that would be a genuine sanctuary, a genuine asylum, a genuine place to check out and check into oneself . . . just four walls and other human beings who will be guardians, and someone who might in some respects be a guide," Laing's voice says.

A few weeks ago, at a seminar here, I heard Julian Silverman of the National Institute of Mental Health agree with Laing. He pointed out that in some cultures a schizophrenic break makes a man an honored shaman rather than an outcast in a mental hospital. Richard Price, vice-president of Esalen, who himself had what he calls a "shamanistic experience" after a schizophrenic break, is working with Laing and Silverman to set up a blowout center at Esalen.

"Consider the metaphors that we have for living," Laing's voice now says. "We are concerned with getting on, making progress, going forward, going upwards . . . and this is related to certain fundamental fears of going to pieces, falling and becoming down and out. . . ."

In his blowout centers, people get a chance to try all these feared, taboo things. He tells of a woman who brought her brother, a patient in a mental hospital, to one of the communes and asked if he could stay. People are admitted if they want to come and the group accepts them, not through another's commitment. The brother, it turned out, did not want to stay but the woman who brought him did.

This woman, Laing says, came with "the personality of a regimental sergeant-major." She had a job of some responsibility in a hospital and kept it after moving in. But every night, after returning from work, she would come into her room, lie down on her bed, and stay there until morning. Soon she discarded her clothes, then her mattress, then became incontinent. Still, at five A.M., she got up, took a bath, dressed and went to work.

After a while she took temporary leave from the job and let herself go completely. For three months others bathed her, cleaned and bottle-fed her. Then she refused to eat or defecate. She lay on the floor wrapped in a blanket, silent, a bag of bones with staring eyes and a beatific expression. Finally when she was in danger of pneumonia or starvation, she was told that her guardians would not tube-feed her. She would have to take in food and make her bowels expel waste. The rest would be done for her. She accepted this and continued to lie on the floor in a blanket for two more months.

Then, Laing says, she emerged very quickly. She sat up, talked a little, took some porridge. One night Laing half carried her across a room where people were dancing to soft music in candlelight. She danced a little on the way back. After this she began to draw on the walls with her shit, then asked for paint and went into a fury of painting. Her canvases were powerful and massive, Laing says, and her dancing became wild and free. She had come to the blowout center because she felt she had been living a lie. Now she emerged as herself.

I lie on the bed, listening. It is seductive—the ultimate in letting go, the ultimate orgy for self-game lovers. Madness scares people, as do psychedelic drugs. Why? Perhaps we are afraid we might not want to return from such trips. So we make them taboo. Something is twanging inside my head. The waves beyond the balcony wash through me. Why not let go? What am I holding on to? "The way of excess leads to the palace of wisdom," said Blake. I see hands gripping a dock, letting go and sinking into dark water.

But then I sit up and snap out of my trance. What nonsense am I committing? I'm romanticizing this idea of madness as holiness but I know nothing about it. A schizophrenic breakdown is no pleasant sinking into waves. It is a desperate way for people who can find no other. Suddenly I want to be among people. I wash my face and go down to the lodge.

At the baths one evening soon thereafter, I find Nils collecting dirty towels. I haven't spoken with him since the day he brought me from Monterey airport.

"Ger tells me you've built a beautiful house," I say to him. "I'd love to see it. May I, sometime?"

"I'm about to go home," Nils says. "Come along if you like."

We hitchhike some five miles down the road and then walk. Later when I think back on it all, Nils and his house stand out as symbolic of what Esalen and turning on are all about. Everything about this place is experimental, everything changes constantly, so that no single seminar or person gives an adequate picture. Mike Murphy's willingness to take risks with new ideas is bound to lead to some exciting things and some disasters. Behind all the activity lies the quest for the self and the new *sadhana*. Nils, with his house, is a living statement of that quest.

The house is a tiny, irregularly windowed one-room shack that seems to teeter on the edge of a cliff. It extends eight feet over the edge. Below, surf collides with the mountainside. Inside, I have a sense of being suspended between sea, land and air in a cheerful and lovely—and impermanent—

room. The furniture is a bed, a bench, a bookcase. Some red flowers stand in a bottle on a sill. A small iron bell hangs from the edge of the roof over the ocean.

"This is one of the most beautiful houses I have ever seen," I say and I mean that absolutely.

"It's all put together out of my head," Nils says. "If anyone says 'I love your house,' I tell him, 'you love me, 'cause that house is *me*.'" He taps his chest with his right forefinger and laughs. Again I am struck by something at the same time childlike and ageless about Nils. It's partly that wispy, untrimmed beard with its gray, but mostly it's his way of paying total attention. I could not say anything flip or caustic to Nils. His manner elicits directness.

"It started with needing a place to live," he says. "So there was this shack out here, half the size of this place now—it's a hundred and seventy square feet now—and I moved in. The first nights I was cold and the surf kept me awake. I could have fixed it up for warmth and a bit more space but it was strange, I didn't. I sat here looking at it for a long time until I knew exactly what I wanted."

He found some bridge beams and laid them on cement blocks under the house so they stuck out over the cliff. Soon he could balance himself on the ends and be solid in the middle of nowhere. Several months later, the deck was finished and he could walk with the ocean under his feet. He put in a wooden floor, reinforced the walls with wood that had been ballast on Japanese ships and, discarded, had floated up on the beach in Monterey. He made the roof watertight.

There was no over-all plan, Nils says, and sometimes the house seemed to direct its own growth. One day he began to hammer a frame above the place where the two-burner bottled-gas hotplate now stands. He didn't know what it would be for until one day, wandering around Monterey where they were tearing down some houses for urban renewal, he found exactly the right window for the space.

Basically, the house is now sound but the connections are not too good yet—as is the case with Nils' life. The foundation of his new existence was laid eighteen months ago when he came out here, at age thirty, leaving behind a string of dreary jobs and years of frustration.

"I was bruised and insulted as a child," Nils says. He sucks in a deep breath, his shoulders go up, his eyes narrow in remembered anger. "The principal should always apologize when he hands out diplomas. He should say, 'This is what we've got and maybe it's not what you need, but this is all we've got.'"

He repeated reading and arithmetic twice in grade school and did so poorly in high school he was sent to a school for delinquent children, Nils says. There he learned to swim but not much else. Afterward, he got a job in a post office putting envelopes into slots.

But school was not the beginning of bruises and insults he remembers. There was the time, when he was barely as high as his brother's baby carriage, when he asked his mother why she walked beside the carriage rather than behind it. Instead of answering him, she whammed him; and the time when he watched for the traffic light to change and stepped off the curb when it was right, proud he knew when to walk. She yanked him back and again whammed him. "It's an awful thing to be a child," Nils says. "Funny, my brother doesn't think so, but all he can talk about now is the telephone company."

A couple of years ago he rented a room in Santa Barbara from a woman who used to come to Esalen. He thought of going to night school, for all he did with his spare time was skate once a week and drive around in his car. But when she showed him the Esalen brochure he came out here instead. He came for a seminar on creativity and never left.

He got a job working around the place—cleaning baths, driving people to and from the airport, picking up cigarette butts ("Man, the one time you really aren't aware is when you litter") and slowly he began to change. At first he couldn't stop himself from saying "Hi!" all the time, over and over, as he ran into people. Now he can do it with the eyes. He can talk with people now and gets uncomfortable when someone is just being sociable and saying words.

He practiced accepting things. At the baths he would soak in hot water and then pour cold water over himself until he didn't flinch anymore. He shed a lot of belongings. Now his only clothes are two blue shirts, a jacket, two pairs of pants and two pairs of shoes, all bought at Goodwill Industries. "There's also a seventy-five-dollar suit in that drawer by the wall," he says, pointing. "It's synthetic so the mold won't get it and it's lying there, like, you know the little blue labels on bananas? Sometimes you see a banana peel that's all shriveled and black lying somewhere and on it will be this label, 'Chiquita,' shining like new."

Nils doesn't know what he'll do next, but so far, besides building the house, he has learned to dance. For a year he just watched others without daring to try. Then he was at the Steppenwolf, a place in Berkeley, on the night after the first be-in. He drank three ales very fast—usually he won't drink that many in a month but he thought it might help—and he started to swing a little to the Mamas and the Papas, Donovan, the Jefferson Airplane, the Grateful Dead. He kept time by drumming his flute on a table. His eyes were fixed on a girl who "must have been high on acid for you could see she was into something so big she didn't care what she looked like or what anyone thought," Nils says. "I kept looking at her and keeping time until my flute broke. Then I got up and danced. Now I can move as freaky as the really stoned ones. Drugs aren't for me. For me it's changing attitudes and man, attitudes are like the fog that drifts in here, but they have the resistance of cement."

Nils salts the brown rice, pours out some tea, puts the rice into bowls, builds it into smooth mountains and gives me one, together with chopsticks.

I notice a couple of mosaics in the corner. "I made those out of California wine posters," Nils says. "I painted over the words and put these little stones and glass in the foreground. The background is painted, see, for depth. But I'm not going to do any more of these because the design isn't mine. I'm not going to copy anyone."

"Have you ever read Thoreau's *Walden?*"

"Man, I started reading it one day but I closed the book because, man, that was me, wow! But this house is out of *my* head, so I'll wait to read Thoreau after it's finished. I don't read much now. In the Los Angeles newspapers everything is all flattened out. Once, though, I picked up a paper and it told how an astronaut said, "Hey, look you guys, it's really round!' The rest was just words but this part was it, this was what the guy *said*.

"After you've been here awhile, all this," he swings his arm around to include ocean and mountains, "take the place of newspapers and all that stuff. But when you get here there's first the void. Then you can go back where you came from or you can stay. It's hard at first. You know, I saw a picture in a magazine once of a woman who jumped off the Empire State Building. She landed on a lower floor. Her face was beautiful, it had a beautiful expression on it. She didn't expect the fall to end so soon. She was like that astronaut who got out there and didn't want to obey orders and come back, wow!"

Nils got past the void by building this house, slowly, out of his head. The entire time he only hit himself once with the hammer. He put the nails in along the grain, slipping them in so he wouldn't bruise the wood, and as he worked on it the bruises and insults of his childhood began to heal. He got a double bed and thought of making a closet outside that a woman could use, but he hasn't found a woman yet. And even if he does find someone to do the housekeeping thing with him, it will be a while before he has children. First he wants to watch the kids around here to make sure he knows how not to bruise and insult his own.

Julian Silverman, a psychologist from the National Institute of Mental Health, believes that many capable and talented people end as dropouts on the fringes of the social scene because our educational system and our social sciences fail to recognize certain innate differences. He is now doing research on a theory that humans come in two basic types. The one can maintain a mental set without distraction, solves problems with a clearly observable set of responses, articulates information in a segmented, analytical, structured way. The other is hypersensitive, responds to peripheral cues, is more imaginative and yielding to all kinds of stimulation. The first might become a scientist or executive, the second an artist or mystic.

In Silverman's view, American society provides mainly for the first type. He is trying to correlate perceptual and sensory response data and brainwave patterns to permit recognition of the two types. "I want responses that have certain kinds of numbers attached to them," he told me, "so that we can get mamas who'll say, 'Yeah, we've got a little mystic in the house,' instead of, 'Get a job, you creep!'"

Silverman was once as turned off by the educational system as Nils. He was about to flunk out of college for the third time when a stroke of good luck—an encounter with an understanding person—steered him into a new direction. He went on to get a doctorate in psychology. Perhaps Nils is not as gifted or as lucky. Whatever the reason, the only place he found in society before coming to Esalen was a cramped corner where he was a human machine. Here he found the way to express his sensitive, intuitive nature.

As I leave Nils that evening, it occurs to me that his lovely house is strictly illegal. If a building inspector finds it he will surely push it down that cliff.

It's time for me to leave Esalen. Some of the important turn-on gurus who pass through here have not been present during my six-week stay and I must look them up in San Francisco or New York. Right now, however, I want to go to the Zen monastery within these mountains. After all the chaos of these past weeks, I long for a structure for my discoveries. Frank Lloyd Wright once said that all creation depends on structure. I've met a student here, Chris Miller, who

132

had just come back from a month at Zen Mountain. He had a lot of questions, he said, and the Zen master answered them all by saying two things: "Everything changes" and "Practice zazen." I must meet this Zen master.

Ben Weaver gives me a ride into San Francisco. I intend to stay there a few days before going to Tassajara. Ben is an engineer in his mid-thirties who plans to be a resident fellow at Esalen in the fall. He has been visiting to make arrangements. He drives scrunched down into his shoulders and wears a habitually worried look. His smile is warm but ends just a little too soon in uncertainty or sadness. In his voice I hear a suggestion of dissatisfaction and impatience—perhaps it is the same urgency I knew, that sense of something missing.

The note of complaint disappears when he talks about the weekend he just spent. "Virginia is really an amazing woman," he says. "I don't suppose we've exchanged more than a hundred and fifty words but her nonverbal communication is fantastic. We just looked at each other and she said a thousand things with her eyes."

Aha, the Meeting Look gets another uptight square, I reflect, remembering my own first encounters with it. That it happened for Ben with Virginia surprises me, as my reaction to her was so different. Big Sur and its people are different for everyone.

"Glenna gave me a massage and it was one of the most wonderful experiences in my life," Ben goes on. "I never realized what a thing like that could do. I was so grateful all I could do was kiss her hand."

Ben was a provincial representative for the Agency for International Development in Vietnam until last year, when he resigned dissatisfied with American policy in that country. He has since been a training officer for the Peace Corps at Davis. There he met Mike Murphy, Bernie Gunther and others from Esalen who came to run a truth lab with Peace Corps volunteers.

"I was very put off by them at first," he tells me. "I saw them as pied pipers luring the trainees away from more important things. Then a friend persuaded me to come to Esalen and take part in an encounter group. I did and caught a glimpse of the person I might become. I had always considered myself as a naturally aloof person. People respected and admired and feared me a little. It was a lonely kind of life but it didn't occur to me anything else was possible. Then, in that group, there was this beautiful freedom of being able to

133

respond without hesitation for once in my life, acting without stopping to think."

We drive along the coast road, past houses perched on rocks, toward the city.

"I came back appalled at the way American policy operates overseas and wanted to change that," Ben says. "But then I found that the society that makes the policy is pretty sick. Now I'm intrigued with working here. We do a terrible job of rearing children by programming them to deny their feelings. Nobody really knows who they are." Ben is turning on, there is no doubt about it.

He leaves me at a hotel in downtown San Francisco. I go to sleep early. In the morning I sit up in bed, having slept nude, and begin to study a map of the city. Something makes me look up. From an office across the street, three men are staring at me. With a curse I dart for cover in the bathroom. Ah yes, and then there's the rest of the world.

Chapter EIGHT

Morningstar Ranch— Dirt and Revolution

IN THE morning, I make my way to the San Francisco Zen Center in Japantown. It is in an old building that was once a synagogue. Inside, in a small cluttered office, I find a Japanese man with shaved head and black robe—a priest, I guess —who gives me the home number of Richard Baker, the Center's president, and also a few copies of the Center's bulletin. I call Baker and am invited to his house at noon.

That's a couple of hours away, so I walk to a nearby park and sit down on a bench to look through the literature. Each bulletin contains summaries or texts of lectures by Shunryu Suzuki, Roshi, the Zen master. And, though the idiom is different, what I read sounds much like that I heard from Perls:

"The secret of the entire teaching of Buddhism is how to

134

live in each moment. Moment after moment we have to obtain absolute freedom, and moment after moment we exist interdependent with the past, future and other existences." This is what Perls calls living in the now.

"When we view the world from a boat on the ocean, it looks circular and nothing else. But the ocean is neither round nor square and its features are infinite in variety. It is like a palace. It is like a jewel. For a hungry ghost, the ocean is a pool of blood; for a dragon, the ocean is a palace; for a fish it is his house; for a human being it is water. There must be various understandings. When the ocean is a palace it is a palace. You cannot say it is not a palace. For a dragon it is actually a palace. If you laugh at a fish who says it is a palace, Buddha will laugh at you who say it is two o'clock, three o'clock. It is the same thing.

"If you try to pick up even a small stone you have the whole universe. But if you try to pick up the tail of a comet, you will be crazy. People will sympathize with you."

Suzuki Roshi and Perls are on the same wavelength. I become more and more certain that the discovery which began during the meditation walk with Gia-Fu on Big Sur, continued with Perls and the hip gypsies, leads naturally to Tassajara.

At noon, I go to Dick Baker's house on Fillmore Street and meet him returning, with his wife and small daughter, from a wedding. He wears a black silk yoke around his neck which, he says, is a symbol of Buddhist priesthood. He is a tall, ascetic-looking man with closely cut hair and a quick, energetic manner. We eat lunch sitting on pillows around a low table and he talks a little about Zen. When I tell him I plan to write about Tassajara as one of several turn-on centers, he objects.

"The idea of a turn-on has nothing to do with Zen," he says. "It implies dualistic thinking—its opposite is turn-off. In Zen, there is no on or off, no high or low. The purpose of Zen training is to give you some sense of what it is to perceive your life moment by moment. Satori is knowing what that is like."

Experiments with out-of-focus photographs projected on a screen have shown, he says, that people who see a specific object—a milk bottle, say—before the image is quite defined have trouble seeing it when, brought into focus, it turns out to be something else, like a fire hydrant. Zen seeks to develop an attitude that allows perception without prejudgments. This is an expansion of awareness.

The more Baker talks, the more I am sure that, though the

135

word turn-on is objectionable to him, the Zen attitude is at the very heart of the turned-on attitude. But there will be time later to explore that.

Baker is driving to Tassajara the following week, he says, and I can come along. This afternoon, he and his family are going to visit a friend, Dick Werthimer, who is the Zen Center's attorney. He invites me to join them and I gladly accept. As it turns out, the visit leads to a postponement of my trip to Tassajara.

Richard J. Werthimer is the attorney not only for the Zen Center but also for the Morningstar Ranch, which I have heard of as the most radical among communal living experiments. Just now, it is in the midst of a crisis and, as we sit with cool drinks beside Dick Werthimer's swimming pool, we talk less about Zen than about Morningstar. Its neighbors have united, it seems, to either clean it up or destroy it.

"There are a lot of retired people near Sebastopol and they're upset," Dick Werthimer says. "They say the place is a fire hazard and a health hazard. There are only two toilets for sometimes a hundred and fifty people and they have cooking fires in several spots. We have to go to court Tuesday. Lou Gottlieb is charged with running an organized camp without a license. That's kind of funny, because if there's one thing the place is *not* it's organized. It's the most disorganized place you can imagine. Actually, I think the neighbors are afraid that there are drugs on the ranch, and of the place in general. But it's going to be all right. I've talked with the D.A. and we'll work it out. They're going to give him time to clean it up. Everyone likes Lou Gottlieb."

"Who's Lou Gottlieb?" I ask.

"Oh, you should definitely meet him. He's a fascinating person. Has a doctorate in musicology, I think, and used to be one of the Limeliters—you've heard of them? A folk-singing group. They made a lot of money on a Coca-Cola commercial and he bought the ranch—thirty-one acres—as a real estate investment. Then he got turned on or something and now it's this commune."

"What's it like?"

"We finally went up there last week, Jean and I. They've had trouble with some winos taking over part of the place recently. Lou has this idea that he doesn't really own the land, he holds it in the name of the Great Spirit, so he can't tell anyone to get off it. It's all very mystical. He's got a faith that it's all part of a great plan and everything will work out, that it's an experiment in leisure. They just don't seem to care about things like toilets and garbage."

"It certainly is *not* very clean," says Jean Werthimer. "Somebody handed me a piece of cake but I couldn't eat it. Just handed it to me, without a plate or napkin or anything. They're all awfully nice, but the dirt . . ."

It is pleasant in the garden. The Werthimers' teen-aged children and their friends, the peaches-and-cream-complexioned youngsters who grow in California, wander in and out. In the pool a mechanical waterbug cruises, squirting a beam of water around itself. It sucks up the debris on the surface and washes the sides of the pool. Round and round it goes, cleaning, cleaning. I will think of that water robot later, after meeting Lou and visiting his unsanitary utopia.

"Perhaps I should go up to Morningstar now, instead of to Tassajara," I say. "I've been meaning to go there, and this seems to be the perfect opportunity."

"You can come with me when I go to court Tuesday," Werthimer says. "Then you can go on with Lou."

So it happens that I arrive at Morningstar just in time to witness that summer's spectacular—the first major engagement in the war between Lou Gottlieb, the mystic revolutionary, and the forces of the law.

On Tuesday morning, we find Lou standing in the blank supermarket-modern hallway of the Sonoma County Municipal Court, surrounded by friends, holding a paper cupful of coffee and a newspaper. He is tall, long-haired, with a sensuous mouth, intelligent eyes and a beard so wild and bushy that it seems about to engulf his large nose. His clothes are casual but not unusual—boots, corduroy pants, sports jacket, sport shirt. He's searching the paper for mention of the moment's crisis. Beside him are Sandy, a plain girl in a loose and faded farm-girl dress, her husband, Don, a quiet man with blond hair and beard, and a young barefoot black fellow in an army blanket, named Mystery.

There isn't much time to get acquainted. Lou is called into the judge's chambers for a conference with the D.A. When he emerges, he tells us all is groovy. Two probation officers will be assigned and the charge will not be pressed. All he has to do is plead *nolo contendere* (no contest) to running a camp without a license. It's a mere formality.

We file into a courtroom, he makes the plea, we say goodbye to Dick Werthimer, pile into Lou's brown station wagon and head toward the ranch. Little do we suspect that the day's encounter with the authorities has only begun.

On the way, Lou tells me that Morningstar is "an alternate society for those who can't make it in the straight society and don't want to. It's a community that emphasizes being rather than doing." There are no rules—anyone is welcome, be he cop, tourist or dropout. He can do whatever he wants to, as long as he doesn't commit violence on others. Some people work, others sit around and talk most of the day. There is no organization, no structure.

Later, when I think back on it all, it seems clear that no agreement was possible between Lou and the authorities for they spoke from entirely different frames of reference. For Lou, the laws of society-at-large do not apply to the "alternate society." The confrontation with society-at-large is, to him one grand piece of living theater. He is grooving on it rather than trying to compromise. The probation officers' impending visit is the next exciting scene in the ongoing play.

"We're in a new stage, folks," Lou says, driving along past the apple orchards, "Mr. Taggart and Mr. Hall are going to help us run Morningstar for a year. That's good. Now we've got an anchor to the old world. Everything that's happened is according to plan. What plan, Lou?" He laughs. "Oh, it will be interesting. I asked them—are you the toughest? They didn't say anything so I said, let's get the toughest. Then they straightened up a little. You should see Mr. Hall, he's a sick man, definitely sanpaku. Maybe they'll move in with us. We'll give 'em a little macro, a little yoga. . . ."

He is kidding, but as he keeps up the monologue I gather he also means what he's saying. He actually half expects the probation officers to see his point of view once they get to Morningstar—or he will play that he expects that. He's making freedom from sanitation a matter of civil rights. He thinks we need liberation from our compulsion for cleanliness.

"I can see them now," says this Ph.D. turned hip guru. "'I'm paid by Sonoma County to keep you where it's clean.' But they don't want to be where it's clean. They *like* it where it's dirty. The Lady Macbeth complex again—wash it, wash it. Even our friends. Did you hear Dick, our lawyer? 'Of course you'll clean it up a bit, right Lou?' All the perfumes of Araby. . . ." He's charming and funny and lovable, this strange man. I keep listening for a note of the put-on, a hint of cynicism, but there is none. Nor will I hear any later, in the midst of the coming crisis.

At the entrance to the ranch, opposite some woodland, several living wagons, trucks and cars are in a parking lot. A tall wooden cross is in the middle of the dirt access road for mystical reasons no one quite remembers and to keep out tourist cars. Mobs of curious people have visited Morningstar this past summer and, though everyone was welcomed, all but Lou were expected to leave their vehicles at the foot of the hill. Lou maneuvers past the cross and keeps driving up, past a couple of bends, to a hilltop that once was the center of a chicken farm but is now, more or less, the village square.

We pull into a garage shed and get out. Several people get up from under a nearby tree and approach. Some are dressed, others nude. I do a bit of double-take, even though I've known about the optional nudity here. Mystery, who went ahead of us in the car of some reporters, is now wearing nothing but a gray feather in his woolly hair. Beside him is a blond boy who must be new here for the skin is white where his shorts would normally be.

"Got a cigarette?" the blond nudie asks.

"Sure."

I pull out a nearly full pack. They close in on me and, within ten seconds, the whole pack is gone. One more kid comes up. "Sorry, I have no more," I say.

"Can I have a drag?"

"Sure," I say, numbly. As he takes it, I notice there's a sore on his lower lip. But I think of the anthropologists who force themselves to eat sheep's eye so as not to offend the local people. When he returns the cigarette I take another drag.

Lou is explaining the day's events. "I want you to be polite to the probation officers," he says. "Yes, Mr. Taggart, of course, Mr. Hall. Full courtesy."

I survey the scene. We're on a slight slope. Downhill is what used to be the farmhouse. Uphill is another, smaller house and a chicken shed in which Lou lives and plays his grand piano. Beyond the chicken shed is a vegetable garden and, beyond that, redwood trees. What else there is to the ranch is hidden because the land falls off toward the creek on one side and is covered with trees on another. Before the main house stands a pile of garbage. Between where we are and the chicken shed I see a shingle-roofed well with a cross on top, a green public phone booth (strangely out of place) and an unfinished small building containing one commode which has not yet been connected to any pipes.

"That's the crapper," says Mystery. "It will be a four-seater. Have to make sure Mr. Taggart and Mr. Hall see that."

I notice that nobody's working on this important building.

"Come on," says Mystery, "I'll show you around."

"Let's go."

We go through the vegetable garden where cabbage stands

139

unpicked and aging, past the sheds at its end, a small trailer that appears uninhabited and go down the road to a pond that once had ducks in it. On the other side of the pond we take a path up a hill to the right, through a redwood grove. Here and there I see sleeping bags or leftovers from campfire dinners. Someone has made a home in a hollowed-out stump. Nearby, a tree house is so well hidden by leaves that if Mystery hadn't pointed it out to me I would not have noticed it. It's a five-story house and belongs to a couple right now, he says.

"Most of the houses aren't built by any one person," he says. "Someone will start it, then he'll split, maybe, and someone else will finish it and move in. So nothing really belongs to any one person."

The more I see, the more this looks like another place— like Roger's camp—where adults are playing at being children. We come to the orchard, where gnarled fruit trees stand in a field of tall grass. It's warmer here, and very quiet. We find a couple of A-frame structures and a house that has been built with mud against a hillside and is covered with a roof of twigs. Inside I see a mattress and a couple of dishes. Outside, on the grass, a fellow sits cross-legged, with eyes closed, naked above his waist.

"He meditates all the time," Mystery says. We pass quietly, not to disturb him, and see next a tepee made of saplings and sheets that surely will be blown over by the next strong gust of wind or knocked over by the next gang of children.

Nobody is at home anywhere except for the meditator. Mystery picks up a few green apples from under a tree and feeds them to a couple of horses that stand looking at us from the other side of a fence.

"Where are you from, Mystery?"

"Haight-Ashbury."

"How'd you get your name?"

He tells me a long involved story about a girl he met at a supermarket in Berkeley, and the next day in a supermarket in the Haight, and a week later in a supermarket in Monterey. She started to call him that.

We pick our way down a steep path, through the redwoods, down toward the creek in the ravine. There is a lot of litter along the way and even, here and there, human turds. Some kids are digging up the creek below.

"Hey, what you doing?" yells Mystery. "That'll mess up the drinking water."

"It's all right," one kid yells back, "I'm just making a dam so I can swim in it."

"Don't use any soap in there. It's gotta stay clean," Mystery yells. I make a mental note to avoid water.

From across the creek, a girl calls, "Hey, Mystery, come here."

We cross over, rock to rock, and come to another dwelling, a plywood box that had once been the cover for the back of a truck. On its side is written "Home is where you are." A pretty girl, her dark hair cut and combed neatly, is sitting inside the box.

"Hey, you got a cigarette?"

"No," says Mystery and it's clear he isn't lying. I've got another pack in my bag, but it has to last me today and tomorrow, so I don't offer it.

"Would you like an apple?" the girl asks, and I'm ashamed. But it's too late to offer now, it would be humiliating.

At that moment a weird figure appears from somewhere, a short, graying man dressed in sandals and an Indian bedspread that is folded and wrapped around his waist like a skirt. He is beaming.

"I am Franceesco," he says with a strong Spanish accent. "Saint Francis. You know?"

He steps back and spreads his arms. "Ah, you are beautiful! Both—beautiful! May I kiss your hand? He bends over my hand and bows. Then, before I realize what's happening, his hands are on the sides of my head and he's pulling me forward to plant a kiss on my brow. There are great sores filled with puss atop his eyebrows. I try not to flinch. Two people with sores on their faces within an hour.

"I'm going for a walk," Francisco says. "Will you join me?"

"No, thank you."

He moves off into the trees.

"God, I'm glad to be back," the girls says. "I was kidnapped last week. These two guys wanted to kidnap a hippie girl. They locked me up and took my shoes. I had to climb out the window and get back here without shoes."

"How did they kidnap you?"

"These guys came by here and said they were friends of my husband's in jail and that he told them to come see me, that I had a package for them. If I had a package I wouldn't be here. Well, I would, but I wouldn't be out of cigarettes. So I said, no, I didn't have a package, and they said my husband said I should go with them, so of course I did. But they were lying, I'm sure of it."

She goes on with the bizarre story and I cannot make up

my mind whether she's telling the truth or living a fantasy. She looks bright and alert and, really, like a healthy Midwestern coed. Mystery seems bored.

"Come on, let's see if the probation officers are here," he says. When we're out of the girl's hearing distance he grumbles, "She's always got some rap like that, somebody's done something to her. I don't believe she was even off the place."

We're walking up the main road when the officers drive up behind us and stop. "We're looking for Mr. Gottlieb," says the driver, a man with a blond crew cut and a policeman's face.

"Would you please leave your car in the parking lot," Mystery replies, politely.

"We're looking for Mr. Gottlieb," the man repeats.

"He may be up there, but all the cars have to stay down in the lot," says Mystery.

"Yes, we know you've got your rules, here, but we'd just as soon talk with Mr. Gottlieb," the man said in a cop's move-a-long voice. And he pulls away, leaving Mystery's dark body covered with dust.

"Wow, those guys sure respect order," says Mystery. He bends to pick an orange lily from the roadside and gives it to me. We walk faster toward the hilltop. By the time we get there, Lou is escorting the two probation officers toward the chicken shed. The driver, it turns out, was just along for the sights. Lou closes the door and I sit down on a table just outside to listen. I sure would love a cigarette now, but Mystery is nearby, so if I produce one, he'd know I had some when the girl by the creek wanted one.

"What are those other structures?" asks a voice inside.

"They're crash pads," says Lou's voice.

"How many people are using them?"

"Last night maybe five or six, next week maybe zero, it changes all the time."

"But you gotta regulate it somehow."

"No, that's the only thing that's new about this place—we don't."

"How do you feel about the meeting this morning?"

"Let's see what happens," says Lou. "There has been pilfering from the orchards, that's bad. Maybe you can help us run Morningstar. May I read you something from George Kateb?"

He launches into one of his favorite quotations, from Kateb's essay "Utopia and the Good Life," in *Utopias and Utopian Thought:*

In the modern age, it would seem appropriate that two conditions be assumed as the basis of any seriously projected utopian society: (1) leisure resulting from the greatly diminished need for materially productive labor and (2) abundance. . . . In confronting new possibilities, the proper aim would not be to offer a blueprint. . . . The combination of abundance and leisure is inherently dynamic and hence is at war with the traditional utopian fondness of fixed patterns of perfection. . . . The "design of cultures" must proceed in a tentative spirit.

When he finishes there is a pause. "Are we ready for you yet, Mr. Gottlieb?" one of the officers asks. The voice carries more bewilderment than irony.

Lou laughs, flings open the door, and the three men emerge. "Gentlemen, make yourselves at home," he says. "Go anywhere, ask questions, look around. I myself have to practice now."

He steps back into the egg shed, closes the door again. Moments later there's the sound of a Bach fugue on the piano. Marvelous! Here are these two flustered officials, pale and soft-bottomed from desk work, headed toward the garbage, the turds, the dirt of Morningstar, and there is Lou, pursuing them on a grand piano in an egg shed with Johann Sebastian Bach.

I follow the officers toward the big house. But they have barely begun their inspection when the sound of another car coming up the hill makes me turn. After it comes another, and another, and another. Within moments the place is full of the forces of the law. Juvenile officers, public health officers, parole officers, the sheriff, the judge, reporters from the local paper—about thirty people come out of the automobiles.

Later, officials will claim they can't remember just how it was that everyone showed up that afternoon. They will also maintain that Dick Werthimer and Lou Gottlieb misunderstood what the conference with the assistant D.A. was. They will disclaim any promises of time to clean up the place and point out that a plea of *nolo contendere* is much like a plea of guilty.

Right now, Lou does not yet realize the snare he's caught in. He comes out of the egg shed, a look of faint surprise on his face. There is a quality about him, a certain slightly comical awkwardness combined with innocence and dash that suggests Don Quixote. "Welcome to Morningstar, everyone," he shouts. "Gentlemen, welcome! Here where you're so well-protected. . . ."

Pretty soon everyone is having a good time. A policeman is taking pictures of Mystery, the bare blond boy and a couple of other nudies. "Hey, that's obscene," someone yells.

"No, no, it's art," the cop replies, laughing.

"Hey, you got a cigarette? Someone got a cigarette?"

Officers hand out cigarettes, Lou hands out welcomes, Francisco runs about, gesturing, exclaiming. The juvenile officers spread out to look for runaway kids, the health officers scatter to nail "condemned" signs to shacks and buildings. Four undercover police, conspicuously cops in their near-identical outfits of white shirts, and jeans, parade up the hill, wave at everyone, grin, and descend the back way. Everyone is grinning, making cracks, grooving. It's the big confrontation spectacular.

In the midst of all this, Mr. Taggart and Mr. Hall are trying to be probation officers.

"Could you say," asks Mr. Taggart, "that after a certain number of days permission to stay here is revoked?"

"I can't do that," says Lou. "I hold this land the way the American Indians held it, in the name of the Great Spirit. I have never denied access to anyone and never will. It's a different form of land tenure known as let go. I feel that this country is too tight. Let go, gentlemen, it's for your health!"

"*We* could do it," persists Mr. Taggart. "*We* could revoke permission."

"It's your duty," Lou says gravely.

"That garbage pile," continues Mr. Taggart.

"Yes, I know," says Lou. "If we'd only clean up we wouldn't be dirty. You see, there are different standards of cleanliness. I feel that America has something like a Lady Macbeth complex. . . ."

The officers don't seem to understand the Lady Macbeth complex, just as they missed the relevance of George Kateb and the Bach fugue to the question of garbage. They do, however, know the pertinence of reports of "the obnoxious aroma and the deposit of human feces along the fence of some adjoining landowners," of complaints about bonfires, nudity, pilfering, gunshot sounds, runaway juveniles, and buildings that don't conform to the building code.

If Lou's land were somewhere in a wilderness, none of this might have mattered so much. But it is in the midst of a staid, comfortable community of old people, many of whom worked many years through endless tedium to retire here. Their idea of leisure clashes violently with Lou Gottlieb's "alternate society." Weird-looking strangers have intruded into their lives. Angry and frightened, they complained to the authorities. Now the authorities are not receptive to Lou when he tells them, "It requires a little sympathy. You'll have to stretch a few regulations or we'll have to close."

As suddenly as they have appeared, the officials depart, taking with them a couple of kids suspected of being runaways, and leaving behind signs that read: "Danger. This property is deemed unsafe for human occupancy."

And now Lou realizes that he's confused about just what has happened. Some cop told him, in pulling away, that if everyone wasn't gone in twenty-four hours, everyone would be arrested for trespassing. This doesn't make sense—Lou, the owner, hasn't complained. But none of it makes sense to Lou. He calls a meeting.

About forty people and one goat gather in front of the chicken shed. (The goat is a communal pet. She eats cabbages but nobody will tie her up or build a fence around the garden. After all, eating cabbages is normal goatish behavior, so who is to jam into her thing?) Some people look rather uncomfortable with bare buttocks on the gravel, but they sit still as Lou tells about the twenty-four-hour ultimatum. What should they do now, he asks.

"If they throw us in jail," says a black man with bad teeth, "the first thing they'll do is cut your hair and put you in solitary."

"Can they take the children from us?" asks a girl with a baby.

"They might," says Lou. "The mothers and children better split. Also anyone else who thinks he might have trouble."

"Why don't we draw up a letter and send it to all the neighbors telling them what's happening so they'll be personally responsible?" suggests a man. The trouble is, nobody *knows* what's happening.

"All I have is what I have on," says a blond fellow who would look like a typical law student if he weren't sitting there with only a blanket around him. Besides the blanket, he has horn-rimmed glasses and, on a chain around his neck, his draft card, a health insurance card, and a picture of his little daughter, who is with his ex-wife somewhere in the Midwest. "I absolve my claim to anything except what I have to have and I don't have very much. If anyone sees me sitting by a tent, it's not mine. I absolve my right even to my guitar."

I'm puzzled as to how giving up his belongings will help in the present communal crisis, but one thing I do see is that everyone is digging this scene. The enemy is at the door—

something is happening! And I wonder what Morningstar would be like without police and tourists for panhandling and entertainment.

"Maybe we should have five minutes of silence and see if we can call a little information from the higher forces," Lou suggests. Yea. People close their eyes. After a while, a girl speaks up:

"Lou, how does this sound? Maybe we should have a picnic tomorrow and invite four hundred, five hundred people."

"Yeah!" "Yeah, man!" "Far-out!" "Someone call Haight-Ashbury."

"We ought to have a be-in or a love-in," Lou says. "The Last Day Love-in."

And so it is decided. Messengers are dispatched to the Haight. Lou goes to the phone and begins to call newspapers and radio stations. Meanwhile, the pile of garbage, which so bothered the officers, remains untouched. Nobody moves to finish the toilet building. It stands there, in its preposterously prominent place, like some kind of monument.

It is a monument—to Lou's discovery of the last remaining American sin, the one thing that will still outrage people, the one thing nobody until now has dreamed of defending—dirt. "Dirty" is the worst epithet in the language—dirty Commie, dirty old man, dirty hippie. "The trouble with hippies," I heard over and over, "is that they're dirty." Invariably someone would counter, "They're not—you're just prejudiced." And now here is Lou, not denying it, he's defending it. So what's wrong with a bit of dirt, a few cozy beasties? he's saying. Had he chosen to fight for the right to live in tree houses or walk around nude, he might have gotten all kinds of support from civil libertarians. But nobody will stand up for dirt.

It's dusk now and I go down to Don and Sandy's, where I left my sleeping bag and sweater. Don is putting up a real house, not a playhouse. It has two rooms, a kitchen and a loft. Only half the roof is up, but they're already living in it. When I get there, I find Sandy cooking rice and beans on a hot plate. Of course everything is impeccably clean all around.

"Would you like a cigarette?" I offer.

"Thanks." She takes one and I put the pack near her, glad to be rid of it.

"We'll be eating in a minute," she says. "You're welcome to stay."

"Thanks, I will." I've been wondering about the food situa-

146

tion. I had brought a big bag of peaches, but they had been consumed.

Lou comes down for the meal. It begins with Don's reading at length from a Bible and ends, rather late, with talk about the day's events. Then Don and Sandy go up to their loft, Lou leaves for his egg shed, and I spread my bag in one of the unfinished rooms so I can look up through the roof-beams at the huge redwoods and stars. I'd like to know more about Don and Sandy. They are more like fundamentalist Christians than hippies. But Don was uncommunicative about his background. He quotes from the Bible constantly and talks about the community as the coming Kingdom of God.

During the night, several people wake us up—first a kid who can't dislodge Don's big dog from his sleeping bag. Then one of the messengers returning from the Haight, together with a salesman from Chicago whom he met on the way. The salesman was intending to go to Las Vegas but ended up here. Don invites them up to the loft and talks with them for some time. Toward morning, another visitor—Nevada, a resident who has a day's job as construction worker today—comes to borrow Don's working gloves. I am angry each time at being awakened. Don and Sandy are calm and friendly each time.

The next morning, I go to look for the shower I heard was in the big house. But when I see the pile of dirty dishes in the sink and the dozen or so droopy people all over the floor and furniture, I decide I'd rather wash at the tap behind the vegetable garden.

Later, I find that the communal principle works pretty well as far as cigarettes go. Now I don't have any of my own, I feel free to bum from others. The only thing is—getting a cigarette becomes a rather large preoccupation, as it seems to be for most people here. It seems rather wasteful of one's attention.

The communal principle also works with food, it seems. I learn there is always one meal a day for everyone—cooked by whoever volunteers. The food is begged, bought or contributed. Some residents work occasionally and contribute their earnings. Others collect overripe or slightly spoiled fruit that stores cannot sell. Neighbors also contribute. Unidentified strangers bring food and leave it. But brotherhood is a bit flawed, even so: people on the hill complain that the parking-lot people always take the best for themselves.

The Love-in crowds from the city arrive at about midafternoon, with crates of vegetables, sacks of rice, and musical instruments. Maybe two hundred people show up, but the scene

147

never develops into much beyond staring and milling. So I start to talk with Jim (not his real name), the man who looked like a law student and gave up all his possessions last night. Not long ago, he was an elementary schoolteacher in New Orleans. If it weren't for a fluke, he says, he'd be an official with the Agency for International Development now. As it is, he's just being and grooving.

His tent is rectangular, with an open front, set on the forested hillside near the brook. We sit down near it and Jim tells me how he got here.

He grew up in Minnesota, he says, in an upper-middle-class suburban house, with a paper route and a puppy. Freshman year at the University of Wisconsin, he eloped during an Easter geology trip and pretty soon had a daughter. "The apartment and the child were beautiful," he says, "and everything was clean clean clean. I could be as big a slob as I wanted and things stayed clean."

The summer he finished college, he had a lifeguard's job on a lake. The rule was no talking, so he watched waves and sunsets. Then one day a girl sat down next to him and started to read poetry out loud to him. She came back the next day, at sunset, and the next. Pretty soon he was involved with her and confused about what to do. So he told his wife he had to get away for a while and, with $5 in his pocket, began hitching west. He never returned. "I was a compulsive worker, so I took all kinds of jobs—in a uranium mine, as a teacher. Sometimes I had two or three jobs at a time."

He met all the qualifications for the AID job, he said, but was turned down as a security risk. He figures it was because he once lived in an apartment where the previous resident had been the DuBois Club, a Marxist youth group. "So I thought of joining the Army, but then I read in *Time* magazine about Morningstar. I closed my bank account and came out here.

"At first I felt I should do something constructive daily. I worked on the shithouse. The guy who started building it was gone now and I feel like maybe the torch has been passed to me, but well, in that case I'll have to pass it on."

"You know they'll close this place if you don't build some toilets."

"Yes, I know it's important. But right now that isn't my scene."

"What do you do all day?"

"A lot of things. I'm making maps of this place." He pulls a sketchbook from under a sleeping bag and leafs through it. There are two or three sketches in it. "Well, I haven't done

148

much on this. I started a poem too, but this is as far as I got." He shows me two lines:

> Hills mosslike with redwood
> and scrubwood and deadwood.

"Things don't have to have permanence to be satisfying," he says. "Like tuning the brook. I tune it by arranging the rocks down there. Or drawing maps for tourists in the sand, that's tripped me more than once. Then there's the Easter Bunny Effect—like, I freed a kite from a tree and I didn't want to fly it, so I tied it to a lower branch and one of these days someone will come by and fly it. To be able to smile into the face of your executioner and dig him if that's where it's at, that's what I aspire to. I'm also learning about Robin Hood. Only I found out I was one of the rich."

"How's that?"

"One day I came back here, I was going to sharpen my knife, fix my guitar and get on with my music. But the whetstone wasn't here. Then the guitar disappeared, then my knife."

"You mean people steal from each other here?"

He shrugs. "Then somebody snapped a cable that it had taken me two days to fix so I could draw water from the brook. Then I had nothing left but this elaborate tea tin and all my possessiveness focused on that. When that went, I was free. So yesterday I gave up my claim to possessions."

"Yeah, but you can't play your music now either."

"To me, the scene now is getting in sync with the environment. There are a lot of things for me to do. Like watching the social structure, that's a trip. You know, people who live in different parts of the ranch are pretty different."

"I heard about the parking-lot people. What else?"

"Well, the people in the orchard tend to be long-time residents and quiet. They carry water all the way up from the creek but they like the quiet. Some of them have jobs outside. They eat alone a lot. Deputy Dog lives up there. He's called that because he raises chihuahuas and because he wanted to have a gun to keep out cars. He's a retired Army man. But we had a meeting and decided we'd rather have the cars and keep out the guns.

"Then there are the Redwood people, they're messy and tribal. They move into the redwoods to be with friends, not because they like the land. Down by the barn is sort of a family scene, couples and kids. They're a tribe and they have things going, like some of them are artists. The parking-lot people are a tight tribe too, like the barn people. They're united by the food. They get first crack at panhandling and contributions and a big breakfast is served every morning.

"The transients stay in the lower house and sometimes in the upper house. A couple of weeks ago the upper house was taken over by some drunks who made a lot of noise until the Gypsy Jokers came with their bikes and drove them out. I think someone must have called the Jokers for that."

"You could write a great sociological study."

"Well, that's not where it's at for me now."

It's rather far-out, but in essence, Jim is doing at Morningstar what others do at Esalen in different ways—learning to understand what Perls calls the now. If you thought of his previous double-job, double-clean life and this in terms of polarities, it made some sense. He is pursuing an education he somehow missed out on. I am sure he won't stay here after he learns what he came to learn.

That evening, I sit down outside the egg shed with Lou and he tells me how Morningstar came about. For years, he says, his life was pretty conventional. He was born in Los Angeles, the son of a Jewish physician and his Italian Catholic wife, got his B.A. from UCLA, married, had two children, served in the Army during World War Two, got a Ph.D. in musicology from the University of California at Berkeley in 1958. But then, instead of going into teaching or some other academic pursuit, he became an entertainer. First he did comedy acts, then headed a folk-singing group called the Gateway Singers, then became one of the Limeliters. The group had success during four years together, and hit big money when Coca-Cola bought a commercial from them and ran it for two years. In 1963, Lou took LSD, turned to yoga, and began to feel more and more unhappy about the direction of his life.

"In 1965 I got sick. I had drop foot—couldn't pick up my foot. I was so afraid of dying I went to every doctor I could find, the whole fucking panic. At the university hospital they tapped my spinal fluid and thought I had pernicious anemia. Oh man, I knew then that death had called. They shot my ass full of B-12. Death was knocking. I raced to a hematologist in Oakland. He had me swallow some tubes and he says—I stake my reputation on it, you don't have pernicious anemia. That's when I started questioning. When an illness is undiagnosable it's a thirst for the divine. If you're grooving with the environment, you don't need a doctor. And if you're not, you'll get more and more panicked and run from doctor to doctor where what you need is something else entirely. I

150

started reading Adele Davis, the nutritionist. She says there are forty-two nutrients a body can eat. I was trying to get a taste of each one, I collected a chest full of them. Man, that's when you're psycho."

Lou leans back in his chair. While we were talking, several people have gathered and sat down on the ground to listen. Lou is now no longer just talking to me but addressing an audience.

"Then I began to read Aldous Huxley's *The Perennial Philosophy,* and Gerald Heard. I began to meditate daily. Now I read any mystic who comes along."

"How did you start Morningstar?"

"It was a complete accident, *absolument,* my dear. In 1962, I was here and I saw an ad that there were thirty-one acres for sale here. I looked it over very carefully for about two minutes and started negotiating. The original plan was to cut it up into seven ranchitos, each with a swimming pool, and sell each for about $125,000 or so. It would have netted maybe $125 grand stonecold, as a hip community thing for climbing young executives of good family.

"The first of last year I was working as music reviewer for the *Chronicle*—that was my last job fling, it lasted three weeks—and I went out to cover the Trips Festival. Afterward, some people drove out here with me. The idea that access was not denied just sort of caught on. In mid-January I'm practicing the piano and a guy comes up and says, 'May I stay here?' Sure, why not? 'Here are these two people who brought me up.' Who were they? Don and Sandy."

The goat comes up to Lou, he rubs her behind the ears. "After that it started to grow. A month later one of the Diggers called, said he'd heard the place was open and was it Okay if he sent some people up. I said yes.

"In the beginning everybody stayed in what houses we had, nobody built anything. Then, when we started having trouble with building inspectors, I invited people from the University of California Architecture School to plan a design for us. My dream was that it would be interesting enough so that we could go to the building inspectors and get blanket approval as an experimental station. They came up with some nice buildings but, you know, I used to think there was a bridge but there isn't. Nothing the straight world has people here have any use for. If you want to build something here you just build it and see what it looks like. You don't make plans. It's really an alternate society."

"What happened to the real estate scheme?"

"It went with that fellow here," Lou says, pulling a New

York cabaret license out of his pocket. On it is a picture of a stern young man, clean-shaven, with short hair. It's Lou all right but at the same time it isn't. The face is obviously younger, but it looks older than the bearded fellow in front of me. We talk some more about Morningstar.

"The statement that you don't have to work is terrifying to a lot of people," he says. "Work defines so many people's relationship to reality. We must try not to scare anyone. Even bureaucrats must be dealt with in a way that won't scare them. Fear turns into hatred and hatred into violence.

"This sort of thing could be a beautiful alternative for people who are technologically unemployable and for other people it would be a retreat where they could come and re-create, I mean really re-*create* themselves. I can see ten Morningstars to every state, where people from straight society would come to live for a while in the 'alternate society,' a whole different culture based on noncompetition."

"What do you mean by 'technologically unemployable'?"

Lou gets up, goes into the egg shed and brings back a carbon of a letter he sent to a Sunday supplement publisher who asked for comment on an editorial about hippies.

"Technological unemployability is different from technological unemployment," I read. "The latter is an economic category, the former a psychological state. A person becomes technologically unemployable when he gets a job and, in the performance of his duties, it dawns on him that his job could be better done by a machine. That realization is a critical psychological transformation and prelude to 'dropping out.' Working for wages at a job that can be better done by a machine constitutes a massive, soul-withering affront to human dignity."

I thought Dick Werthimer's water robot probably caused some technological unemployability. But the theory did not fit some people here, like Jim, who clearly, from what he had told me this afternoon, had a good education and could choose his work. But the letter went on:

"The hippies are the first to confront a social problem of unprecedented historical importance, namely, the discovery and demonstration of a style of life appropriate for a future in which leisure will be compulsory and labor power—as we now use the phrase—superfluous. It is quite possible that the most valuable member of society in the future will be one . . . who can sit around . . . enjoying the bliss of being without doing anything."

Lou was a Communist from 1948 to 1954, but then decided that made no sense because the question of who owns the means of production is no longer relevant. The relevant question now, as he sees it, is the equitable distribution of the plenty that exists. And the answer, in Morningstar, is the Saint Francis story, he says, which "teaches that you beg for everything needed to erect the Kingdom of God."

"But what of the neighbor problem?" I ask.

"The man most set against us is a retired insurance executive. He understands about leisure, only he doesn't understand that everyone faced with it isn't a retired insurance man."

Later, thinking it over, I feel somewhat sympathetic with that retired insurance executive. But my view of the "alternate society" is blocked by those turds along the path. The Lady Macbeth complex—I still dig my utopia clean.

As I leave, a neighborly apple grower is helping Lou and some others collect the garbage. He gives me a ride toward the bus station, and tells me he feels well-disposed toward Morningstar since he gained a new perspective on life in an encounter group. But sometimes, he says, some kids do surprise him.

"I gave a ride to one fellow into town and also gave him a dollar," he says. "Then, as he was walking away, I noticed he was taking my sweater. I yelled at him and he brought it back, but he seemed resentful that I asked for it."

"He was acting on the Robin Hood principle," I explain. "He figured he needed it more than you did."

Morningstar continued to exasperate—and entertain—its neighbors. A few weeks later, the San Francisco *Chronicle* reports that Lou had, after all, been forced to arrest his friends for trespassing. Refusal to do so would have meant a $500 fine daily for violation of a court injunction against some forms of "being." However, some people returned and, months later, the battle still was raging and Lou was still quoting George Kateb. Meanwhile, I finally made my way to Tassajara.

Chapter NINE

Zen Mountain—Beyond Tripping

I WAKE to the sound of a bell's jangling and the heavy thuds of someone running outside. Opening my eyes, I see a window square of night sky. Surely it isn't time to get up. I pull my arms out from under the covers. It's cold. Quickly I draw them back under. But the runner with his handbell passes again. At the same time I hear the sound of the han—wooden hammer struck against a wooden board outside the zendo. It's 5 A.M. Twenty minutes from now we're to be sitting straight-backed and motionless in meditation.

This is the way each day begins here in the Zen Buddhist monastery at Tassajara Springs, deep in the wilderness of the Santa Lucia Mountains. Those who come to live here, under the guidance of the Zen master, are seeking much the same thing as some people at Esalen, Big Sur Hot Springs and Morningstar Ranch. But the way here is very different. Here there is no freaking, no tripping or emotional exploding. Zen students seek to find their true nature (or, in Esalen words, to expand consciousness and to develop their potential) through a strictly disciplined simple and quiet life of meditation, work and study.

The bell has stopped ringing and now I hear the second round of the han—toc silence, toc silence, toc toc toc. This means we're to be out of bed, washing and dressing. Already I hear people walking past my door. I fling back the covers, leap out—the floor is cold under my bare feet—light the kerosene lamp, wash and dress in one continuous motion. At the third round of the han I am outside, heading across the little bridge to the long low building at the end of which lamplight glows through a screen door. Toc silence, toc-toc-toctoc-toc, silence, toc.

The monastery is deep in a valley, miles from the nearest

neighbor, enclosed by steep mountains. The slopes are so steep all around that trees and bushes look like an avalanche suspended momentarily by an invisible force. We are only eight miles from the Pacific, but there are four mountain ranges in between. The telephone number is Tassajara Springs 1. There are no other numbers with that exchange. Some hardy people have hiked here from Big Sur. But I've heard stories of inexperienced hikers who tried to make it and didn't. The trail is faintly marked and there are precipices and ravines, snakes and mountain lions on the way. The setting here is perfect for its purpose, as Esalen's is. There, on the edge between mountains and sea, everything suggests explosion and out-reaching. Here nature calls for a turning within.

The narrow valley runs along the edge of Tassajara Creek. At the western end are hot mineral baths, at the eastern is a swimming pool. Rows of cabins, a guest dining room, the zendo and the kitchen house stretch between. Like the Big Sur Hot Springs, this was a resort until it was turned into an awareness center. There are seventeen hot mineral springs on the southern bank of the creek within two hundred yards. The water runs at a temperature of 140 to 150 degrees and contains sulphur, sodium, magnesia, iron and phosphates. Indians used to come here for healing long before it was a resort. In the 1890s, a road was cut through the mountains to allow horse-drawn stages. It took ten to twelve hours to travel the forty-five miles from Monterey or Salinas. In 1912, a better road allowed cars. Now the trip takes about two hours, because the last twenty miles, along a dirt road that winds along cliff edges, still requires careful driving. In the winter, it is sometimes impassable because of rain or snow. The San Francisco Zen Center bought the buildings and 160 acres in the valley in 1966 and turned the place into a monastery modeled after Japanese monasteries. Non-Zen guests are still accepted to help pay for the land and the cost of operations. But I'm here to sample life as a Zen student.

As I cross the little bridge on my way to the zendo now, it occurs to me that it must be pleasant to lie in bed, hear bells, hammerings and gongs, and not have to get up. But on the other hand, it's exhilarating to be up before the sun.

Dark shapes move toward the zendo. Outside its door, sandals and shoes are lined up in neat rows. People bow as they enter, facing the long room lit by kerosene lamps attached to the walls. At the zendo's other end is a platform on which stands an altar with an eight-inch golden Buddha statue set against a golden glowing circle on a background of a blue velvet cloth. To the right of the altar the priests and their assistants sit beside gongs, bells and drums used during the chanting of sutras.

A plywood partition, about four feet high, runs along the center of the room. Along either side of it, and along both walls, are low platforms covered with tatami mats. On these, at intervals of three feet, are round black pillows or zafus. I walk to one of these by the partition, bow to it with palms together in front of my chest, bow to the opposite wall, and settle, facing the partition, for forty minutes of zazen, or sitting meditation.

Most of the students are already sitting, still as statues, with eyes half-open and legs crossed. My legs won't go into half-lotus position. I can't even get my knees down to the floor as I cross my legs. With envy I glance at the straight-backed girl beside me who seems perfectly comfortable in a full lotus. But in Zen, I've been told, such things don't matter.

"Whatever you do is right. Nothing is wrong with what you do," Shunryu Suzuki, Roshi, said in one of the lectures I read. "But some improvement is necessary. . . . The point is not whether your posture is right or wrong. The point is constant effort or way-seeking mind."

When I asked a student how one meditates the Zen way, I was told to "just sit." The lotus position, in which the Buddha is usually pictured, is considered ideal. It is the posture in which the stomach area is least restricted, the vertebrae are atop one another, and one has a feeling of stability. But other postures are acceptable. I put my hands into a mūdra—palms up, the fingers of the left hand over the fingers of the right, thumbs touching and forming an oval. Looking slightly downward, I concentrate on my breathing.

The dawn bell rings—eighteen strokes during twenty minutes—outside the zendo. Then there is silence. About thirty people are in this room, yet the only sound is of the brook outside. A lantern behind me casts my shadow on the plywood before me. My body is stiff from sleep and resists the sudden rigidity. Within minutes both my feet are asleep from the ankles down. A pain begins in my groin, jumps to the back, slowly seeps into the thighs. In Zen meditation, I've been told, you allow your mind to go to the quiet alertness that precedes thought and knowledge. As you concentrate on breathing, thoughts gradually subside like ripples on a lake. When the lake is calm, you can see its bottom and observe your own image. That image, seen fully, is the face you had before you were born—the Buddha-nature which some call God immanent.

But my mind is jumpy with a vague anxiety of half-remembered dreams. My impulse is to move, to run, so that the mess in my head will fall into some kind of rhythm. It's hard to be still. After a while, the grain in the plywood before me blurs and its wavy lines begin to take on shapes. I see a face with open mouth and hands above the head, contorted bodies, bodies under torture, long flowing legs—shapes created from the pain of sitting. They mean nothing. Dick Baker told me, "You don't want to spend too much time at the movies." Zen is not meant to put anyone into a trance. It teaches perception.

Riding up here from San Francisco with Dick Baker, we talked about Dr. Joe Kamiya, who teaches people to control their brainwaves. "Wouldn't it be marvelous," I said, "if we could learn to control them so well that we could merge consciousness with one another?" He smiled. "Why? If you want that kind of special power, you first have to use fully what capacities you have now," he said.

But now there is only the pain of sitting. After an eternity has passed, I hear a rustling near the altar where the priests sit—Kobun Chino Sensei, Dick Baker and Phillip Wilson. Peter Schneider, an advanced student who might become a priest, is also up there. The Roshi is in San Francisco and expected back in a couple of days. Now Chino Sensei comes down the aisle between our ramrod backs—I see his shadow, with the staff raised before his eyes. He walks all the way around the room and then—whack, whack—there's the sound of the stick hitting shoulders. Whack, whack again. I look from the corner of my right eye, without turning my head. A girl bows, hands together, to indicate she wants a whack. It is administered. She bows again. Chino Sensei passes on. The woman next to me bows. Shall I ask? Do I need to be snapped into alertness from distraction or drowsiness? Yes. I bow. He pulls my hair to the left, whacks me on the right shoulder; pulls it to the right, whack. Not painful, invigorating. The blood courses faster, my back straightens, the mind grows calmer. But the pain in the legs gets worse. There is no time, I tell myself. I am not waiting for anything to end. This is it, this moment is my existence. But I cannot feel that. This is only my fourth time at zazen and all I have is what the Roshi calls "mechanical understanding."

At last I hear that someone is walking to the huge drum beside the zendo door. He begins to beat it, six times, slowly, and the deep vibrating sound goes right into my head and through my body. Then there's a bell and again the drums— three sequences. It is over. I can disentangle my limbs.

The next part is easy. We stand in the aisles to sing the Heart Sutra three times and make the perfect bow, with the forehead touching the floor, nine times. During the sutra, which is chanted in Japanese on one single note, Phillip Wilson, up front, beats a huge hollow wooden fish with a slit for its mouth with a padded mallet. Peter Schneider strikes a bell whenever a word of particular importance is chanted. "*Ma ka han nya ha ra mit ta shin gyo. . . .*"

This is the regular morning ritual at Zen Mountain Center and during the five days I am there it becomes as natural as brushing my teeth. But part of what helps me through is the thought of fifteen free minutes between morning zazen and breakfast, time enough for a quick hot springs bath. Looking forward to that is very un-Zen—it means I don't live fully in the moment—but if, as the Roshi says, "whatever you do is right," it is part of my perfect meditation. To me, these two statements are contradictory. But an enlightened Zen student would see both as true together, even while seeing the contradiction.

It is dawn when we emerge from the zendo. The mountains and trees hide much of the sky, but straight above some clouds are pink and, to the north, a couple of peaks are bright in sunlight. Over the swimming pool the pale old moon and a couple of stars are still out. I stop to look on my way to the baths, but only for a moment. In fifteen minutes, we're due back in the zendo for breakfast.

I run past guest quarters and the office, remove my sandals at a little bridge, and cross the creek to the baths. These baths are, in some ways, more luxurious than Esalen's, even though they don't have the ocean overlook. They include big steam rooms, showers, hot pools instead of tubs, and a creek to jump into when fully heated.

I slip off my clothes, sit on a step to the pool, and put my toes into the hot water. It's hotter here than at Big Sur and I spend quite awhile getting used to the temperature. Two girls are already bobbing in the water and talking softly.

"The thing I'm most afraid of is colds," says one.

"That and backaches," says the other.

"Colds give me a backache and zazen is murder then."

"I know a good yoga exercise to clear up congestion. I'll show you later."

A third girl appears (the baths are sexually segregated here) and I move over so she can sit down on the step next to me to dip her toes. But to my amazement, she dives right in.

"You'll get used to it," one of the other girls says to me. "It's like getting into cold water fast."

"I'm not that brave," I say, slowly lowering myself into the pool. There is just barely enough time to let the wonderful warmth seep in, then we all hurry out, dress and run back to the zendo. In the afternoon I can come back for the full pleasure of these baths. Now the breakfast bell is already ringing.

The schedule at Tassajara is rigidly structured and you move to the sound of the han, the drum and the bell automatically. "Our way of training," Dick Baker told me, "is to limit students in time and space so that their entire day is reduced to essentials. There is no opportunity for personal time. The student doesn't have to think about anything and we try to make it so that he can't. If he starts to think he can't keep up with the schedule. This forces the student to deal with himself and his relationships with other people. He is confronted with the immediacy of the situation and gets his identity from it. He ceases to be Chris or John and becomes a man getting up, a man getting a meal. Then he sees that all objects exist only in relationship."

"It's a kind of liberating totalitarianism," one student said. "You have to go inside to find freedom."

Every activity at Zen Mountain is held to be of equal importance. All is an aspect of the practice of Zen. There is no distinction between zazen and peeling onions. Nothing is preparation for anything else. Everything is what it is.

In cultivating this attitude, the student becomes aware that there is no distinction between the mundane and the spiritual, trivial and important, slight and profound. "It is within the domain of small things that you will find the Buddha-nature which you manifest," Suzuki Roshi said in a lecture.

The student also becomes aware how he and everything else is constantly changing and learns to go with the changes by accepting everything for what it is. Buddha taught that life is suffering caused by trying to hold on to what is transient —mainly one's self. The Zen student seeks "freedom from clinging" which will lead to realization of his Buddha-nature or, in Western existentialist terms, to self-actualization.

A lot of this becomes real to me in the ritual of the meal. We are now again in the zendo, this time facing the aisle, with our oryoki, the eating bowls, before us. They are wrapped in white napkins in the prescribed manner, together with eating utensils. After singing a series of gathas, or verses (". . . may we be relieved from self-clinging with all sentient beings") we untie the cloths and fold the ends under, forming a place-mat. We take the second napkin, which lay on top of the bowls, and spread it across our crossed knees. The rag, for wiping the bowls later, we lay beside the place-mat. The chopsticks and teaspoon go in front of the bowls, a little cloth-tipped stick, the setsu, to be used for washing the bowls, goes on the right. The three bowls are lined up, with the biggest on our left and the smallest on the right. Then we wait.

With a roll of the enormous drum, one of the cooks appears, holding high a symbolic food offering for the Buddha. He gives it to the priest, who puts it on the altar. The cook bows and goes out again. A few moments later, two kitchen helpers enter with huge pots. Starting with the priests, they dish out a gruel of barley rice and oatmeal. But they don't just go around slopping it into the bowls. They stop and bow, and we bow back, two at a time, with palms together before our chests. The bow is recognition of the Buddha-nature in each of us. Then they kneel, fill the bowls, stand up and again we bow to each other. The same happens with the second course, half a bowl of warm milk, and the last, half a banana.

The Chino Sensei begins another gatha, about rice coming from the efforts of all sentient beings, and we reply:

> First, seventy-two labors brought us this rice,
> we should know how it comes to us.
> Second, as we receive this offering, we should
> consider whether our virtue and practice deserve it.
> Third, as we desire the natural order of mind, to be free
> from clinging we must be free from greed.
> Fourth, to support our life, we take this food.
> Fifth, to attain our way we take this food.

At the last part, the spoon is placed in the bowl of gruel and it is lifted with both hands. Then we begin to eat.

Now I don't know what the seventy-two labors are, but as I taste the first spoonful I do feel at one with all that went to create this meal and, therefore, at one with the natural order. And, concentrating on the taste, I appreciate the subtlety of flavors in this simple food. Ground sesame seeds and sea salt are passed, again with bows, for sprinkling on the gruel. We eat in silence, without looking at each other, yet aware of the communion of the meal.

At the end of the meal, the servers bring kettles of hot water and pour some into the biggest bowls. We sing:

> The water with which I wash these bowls

tastes like ambrosia.
I offer it to the various spirits to satisfy them.
Om, Makulasai Svaha! (The last part is a
mantra, an untranslatable magic phrase.)

We wash the big bowl with the cloth-tipped stick, then pour the water into the second bowl and then into the smallest. The servers return with pails to collect the water. I don't learn until later that we are expected to pour only a little into that pail and to drink the rest as tea. When I do find out, I am shocked that we're to drink dishwater. But there I get another lesson in Zen and perspective: what to me is dishwater is also tea and an offering to the Buddha. The servers pour the collected water over a flower bed. And why, indeed, should it be dishwater?

With the bowls washed, dried and tied again, the priest chants one more gatha:

May we exist in muddy water with purity like a lotus.
Thus we bow to Buddha.

Nothing has been wasted or left behind. In the simple ceremony of the meal, we shared in the cycle of death and rebirth, and acted out freedom from karma, which means passage without traces. In Heinlein's Martian language, we have "grokked in fullness" what eating is. The Zen way is to grok in fullness every moment in the process of life.

This meal was exactly the opposite of the Tom Jones dinner at Esalen's Allowing seminar. No wonder Gia-Fu was so shocked. Also, almost everything here is in direct contrast with Morningstar. At the ranch, all is anarchy. Here, five hundred precepts govern every detail of life, from the way shoes are placed outside the zendo to the way a spoon is put into gruel. Yet from their opposite poles, Lou Gottlieb and the Zen master are both aiming at grokking in fullness. Zen Mountain, like Lou's commune, provides a way that may lead to discovery. Ultimately, the discovery comes from within. All those rules are only guidelines. Through the ages, Zen masters have repeated that there is no one way to enlightenment.

After the chaos of the last few weeks, I welcome the Zen way now. My first work assignment is as dishwasher and a more delightful site for the chore I have never seen. Adjoining the zendo, on a platform that is covered with a roof but open on the sides, a sink and some tables have been piled high with cooking pots and dishes used by guests. (The guests eat solid American fare and to the Zen students, the aroma from the kitchen is often tantalizing.) Beyond the platform's edge is the creek. On its other side the mountainside begins with its maples, oaks and sycamores. So, in washing dishes, you have the sound of the creek, of birds and wind in the trees and see sunlight on water and greenery.

A bearded fellow, John Steiner, is already elbow-deep in a caldron when I arrive. Barclay Daggett, a retired engineer, is sweeping the floor. Jim, a fellow who wandered in yesterday and doesn't quite seem to know what he's into yet, is wiping plates. Since they are all here for only a few days, their heads are not shaved as are those of most Tassajara students.

Barclay has toured the turn-on circuit. He has been to Esalen, to another center, called Bridge Mountain, to assorted gurus, and ashrams.

"I've had three ecstatic experiences in my life," he tells me. "One was a shot of morphine, in a hospital before major surgery. The second was in a womb tank, the third was a little satori on the seventh day of a seven-day sesshin in Honolulu." (A sesshin is a period of intensive Zen meditation. The word means mind-gathering.)

"A womb tank? What's that?"

"That was in the Sensory Limitation Research Laboratory of the Veterans Administration hospital at Oklahoma City," he says. "You float in body temperature water in a small tank. The room is dark, air-conditioned, and soundproofed. You have a face mask on and you float with a snorkel in fetal position. There's a mike in the snorkel and you're told, 'You're going on a trip. Please report all you encounter.' I was in it for eight hours and for five hours and fifty minutes I was completely quiet. Toward the end, my mind relaxed completely, but was still perfectly alert."

"How were your three ecstasies different?"

"They were all similar," he says. "They had in common that you don't care. You just don't care. Everything is perfect. There's nothing to want."

There's something faintly sad in the way that sounds to me. Barclay is a ruddy, healthy looking man in late middle-age. I wonder whether his search is building into anything. He says he plans to stay in Tassajara and be a monk.

A dark-haired girl named Patty joins us. She's a married woman, here for two weeks as a student, but she talks like a thirteen-year-old. "If only I could get Mortie to go on my Zen trip with me," she says. "I've been trying to get him to smoke pot. That might get him to see it a little. I feel it's my duty as his wife to smoke pot with him, even though I'm not supposed to. He just doesn't get it. You know what he says?

He says, 'This nonattachment sounds pretty selfish to me! Can you believe it? He's a physicist. When I give him a koan, like, 'Where does the sound go after it leaves the body?' he says, 'It gets converted into light and heat.' Do you think I can ever? Maybe if he smokes pot. Right now I wish the Roshi would come back."

"How come?" I ask.

"It's just different when he's here," she says.

"Yes it is," agrees John, who hasn't been talking much. He is washing the pots with meticulous attention, practicing Zen. I know he was here last summer, for two months of intense Zen training, and would like to talk with him, but now is not the right time.

"I'm going into tangaryo tomorrow," Patty says. "You'll have to do it too, Jim, if you're staying longer than today."

"What's tangaryo?" Jim asks.

"You don't know? Everyone has to go through it if they're here longer than overnight. You sit by yourself for a long time—at least half a day. If you're here for two weeks or more, you have to sit three days—from four in the morning until ten at night. I'm here for just two weeks so I don't know how long I'll have to do it," says Patty.

Dick Baker told me that the purpose of tangaryo is "to see if you can overcome mental and physical restlessness" and compared it to the practice, among Tibetan monks, of drawing a circle around oneself and sitting in it for a year. "It changes your concept of time and space," he said. Students who come to Tassajara just for a trip and are not serious about Zen generally are put off by tangaryo, so it's a way to weed out the dilettantes. In my case an exception will be made. Because I want to observe student life at Tassajara as thoroughly as possible in a short time, I will not sit in tangaryo.

When the last big spoon has been put away, the tables wiped and the floor mopped, it is almost time for lunch which consists of a barley broth with green squash, potato salad with peels and bread with jam. Afterward there are more dishes.

In midafternoon, John, Jim, Patty and I go down the creek for a swim in a natural pool that spring water has carved in the rock. John strips, dives in and swims around, just as the girl did this morning at the baths. But the water is ice-cold and again I hesitate. Afterward we stretch out in the sun and John tells me how he got into Zen.

He was a graduate student in city planning at Berkeley last spring, he says, when he became ill with mononucleosis and, confined to bed, too weak to read, was forced to reflect on his life. He found that it had been extraordinarily mental for most of his then twenty-three years. He had been active in a lot of social causes at Harvard and Berkeley, had spent a year in Guatemala on a Peace Corps-type project, but everything seemed to be in the same dimension as his studies. Now he craved something else, though he didn't know what. While recovering, he read Hesse's *Siddhartha* and the term "inner sanctuary" seemed to be it.

So he began to go to the Zen center in San Francisco, dropped out of graduate school—at least for a while—and, in the summer, came to Tassajara for two months. Originally, he thought that this time off would be valuable because it would make him a better city planner. But now it became important in its own right. He took an apartment across the street from the Zen Center, attended zazen daily and spent most of his weekends at Tassajara. He no longer knows exactly where he's going, but is certain that, for him, this is the right path.

John is intelligent and intellectual. In that sense, he is typical of the serious students I meet during my stay at Zen Mountain. Later in the afternoon, I get to talking with Taylor Binkley, a dropout from his last year at the Massachusetts Institute of Technology, whom I find watering the bamboo and the flowers beside the bathhouse.

Taylor, like a lot of people here, came to Zen by the psychedelic drug route. He attended the summer training session, when the schedule was much more vigorous than now, allowing only six hours of sleep and half an hour of personal time every day. At the end of a month, during zazen, he says, he experienced satori. "All the classic problems—greed, anger, pride—flew apart and I rose up into beautiful reds and oranges and came down green and blue." After that, at the baths, he felt his body turn into currents of color and saw ladybugs translucent in the sun against bamboo trees.

Then he left, he went to Berkeley and got into the drug scene again. "I had a marvelous month, one of the happiest in my life, but it wasn't enough. I had the satori but I didn't have the vessel to put in it. So now I'm back building the vessel."

Taylor now looks back on his psychedelic period as wasteful. "It's sort of nonsensical to throw your life away on something that doesn't understand that life is what's happening," he says. "A life should be carefully carved so that it lives up to its own inherent beauty."

His father, he tells me, is a biochemistry professor. "He

says you can't save the world by staring at your navel. You can't of course. That's not it. So I just wrote him—biochemistry is your quest. To me this has more meaning."

Like John, Taylor does not know precisely where he is going now, but has no doubts about being on the right course. "Most people here have no plans because they don't know where they'll be when they'll leave," another student tells me later. But most will not stay forever at the monastery. They will take their training back with them when they return to life on the other side of the mountains.

At zazen this same day—after a supper of rice, tomato and lettuce salad, burdock roots and carrots—my legs don't bother me as much. Now there is the sound of crickets together with the quiet rushing of the creek. I go to sleep, around ten o'clock, feeling that, somehow, things are right with the world.

But the following morning dream fragments again crash around in my head and the pain in my legs is so bad that I feel sick to my stomach. What use is this sort of torture, I wonder angrily. It deadens the faculties. Surely in Japan, where people sit cross-legged all the time, they don't go through this. How can I find unity with the universe if I can't get past what's happening to my legs?

When I meet Dick Baker later in the morning, I ask him about that. "I can't get beyond the pain," I tell him.

"Why go beyond it?" he replies. "The pain only exists as long as you compare yourself with someone who has no pain."

"But some people can sit cross-legged easily, others can't. I never could."

"It took me two years to get my knees to the ground," Dick says. "You discover you're much stronger than you realize, that you have physical and psychic second winds."

So now I feel challenged. I continue to sit cross-legged. That evening, beyond a certain point, the pain gets no worse and I can actually concentrate on my breathing. "When you are completely absorbed in your breathing, there is no self," the Roshi has said. The grain of the plywood before me begins to flow and, watching my breath and hearing the sound of the brook and the crickets, I become one with the flowing wood, the sounds, and the sap of the trees rising all around in the valley and the mountains. It is only a moment. The next morning, I wake with a sense of gladness just before the bell. But at zazen, the struggle begins all over again and my mind will not be still.

This is no easy road. But I sense that in this very simple

and very difficult life, there exists in distilled form all that is happening so chaotically at Esalen and on the acid scene. Here it lives in the single sunflower glowing in an earthenware pot outside the zendo, in the ritual of every meal, the attention that brings beauty and meaning to the smallest moment. "Actually," the Roshi said in one lecture, "Buddhism is nothing but living your own life, little by little."

One person who seems to know what that means is Phillip Wilson, who beats the big fish drum or rings a gong during the sutra singing after zazen. He is an advanced student and has spent about a year in Japanese monasteries. I've noticed that when he's talking with someone his face is somehow translucent and the expression is of a steady amusement and surprise. But it is a kind, not at all critical expression. One afternoon, I have a chance to talk with him.

Ten years ago, he tells me, he got a B.A. degree in medieval history from Stanford, and thought of teaching. "But I looked over the whole system, the way everything was being done, and I decided I couldn't do it that way. So I just cut myself loose and let myself wander until something happened to put me in the direction that was right. I went to graduate school for a while at Stanford and San Francisco State in anthropology and education, and then I went to Europe for a while and looked there, and then to the Art Institute and looked there. I had gardening jobs and teaching jobs. But it just wasn't right."

"What was missing?"

He laughs. "*Something* was missing. I had knocked out of existence, I had no respect at that time for what people were doing or for what I felt myself inclined to do. And I think that's a very bad condition for anyone to be in, a very sick one.

"Did you try psychedelic drugs?"

"Yeah, only again I didn't like the way people were doing it. I thought they weren't really going to the source, although I couldn't say what the source was. There's some kind of humanistic renaissance that's supposed to come about but there's no one with the strength. They get around people who have bad vibes or who aren't going their way and they get wiped out. You look at them on television and you love them. You see how beautiful and sensitive and *weak* they are. They can't make their garden anywhere, only on their own ground.

"So I asked myself, what would be the ideal condition? And it was to work with whatever you have wherever you are and to be at peace with whatever people you are with and still follow your own way. That's why I was happy when I

166

found Suzuki, because though he's a little guy and very weak-appearing, he's dynamite. He's like a thief and a mother. He's not held by superficial conditions of existence but he'll work with them and use them and transform them into a spiritual life. Now to do this without drugs and to do it with your everyday life to me is kind of a miracle."

About seven years ago, Phillip went to a lecture by Suzuki Roshi. "I had been looking at Russian ikons and I saw that he was a live one—in his stance, his movements. The look in his eyes was like out of eternity. He was very quiet and no one could understand his language, his images didn't follow a train of thought I was used to. At that time, I could tell how someone's mind was by the obvious—how they dressed, combed their hair, picked up an object and put it down, by a certain quality of feeling. But he had an unusual condition in his mind and when I tried to follow it, it would become invisible. So I said, all right, I accept the challenge.

"So I went to the Zen Center every day for a year, and I thought, how can he do it? I was going batty trying to get up at 5:45 every morning, while he was getting up at 5:45 and then working all day and doing meditation every evening and staying up till ten or eleven with conferences. After one year I got so I could do my morning zazen, a decent amount of work during the day and my evening zazen, and then I'd go out and have a beer or play around but he was still working and still more committed to life."

Phillip is a powerfully built man and, in the beginning, had trouble sitting cross-legged. "One day the sensei told me to put one leg over the other. I did that and after that when I did zazen I would sweat. My whole body would be a blanket of pain. But I kept it up and eventually my whole body became more limber."

"Is the pain important?"

"It's important to the student." He laughs. "If you look at the position you'll see it doesn't demand anything harsh from you. You're sitting, learning to be quiet, alert, keep your back straight, breathe from your stomach, hold your head high; and you're realizing that it takes courage just to sit, to eat, that it takes courage just to live and do the orginary thing. People have forgotten this and they need it.

"I was a very bad student," he continues. "Instead of being receptive, I was full of my own ideas. But to appreciate nature and things you have to become very quiet so that it can come into you. If you can be quiet and alert with some kind of helpfulness—the quieter you become, the more translucent you are. Things around you begin to do their natural pattern and accept you in that way. You become a kind of reflection of what they're doing, but at the same time you remain yourself."

"Now I listen to people differently. I see that they're expressing their nature or their confusion with it, or their understanding of it, or they're trying to complete themselves. I like people I used to avoid—like greedy, grasping businessmen or politicians, they show an unusual vitality. I see how they're struggling with their life. I don't feel separate now from anyone."

Zen Buddhism has no doctrine or creed. It is a mind-body discipline, a path toward the awakening to a truth that cannot be taught, explained or conceptualized. It is not accessible through the intellect, through obedience to rules or imitation of a master. The intellect, rules and master can steer a student in the right direction, but ultimately this truth must be experienced by everyone in his own way. It can best be spoken of in paradoxes and contradictions.

Zen stories tend to be illogical, irreverent and often seem non-sensical. Though they are not symbolic, they always point to something beyond themselves. They are always vivid, never abstract.

For example, some monks asked one of the ancient masters to speak to them about Buddhism. The master told them to first work in the fields. They did so and then gathered to hear him. He stood up before them and simply spread his arms.

Or, a monk asked his master, "What is the doctrine that goes beyond the Buddhas and Fathers?" The master held up his staff and answered, "I call this a staff. What would you call it?"

Zen teachers, in these stories, had no orthodox procedures. They were brusque and abrupt, replied to students' serious, thoughtful questions with laughter or slaps or by pulling their noses. The students, in turn, upon experiencing satori, proved they were enlightened by behavior that would be held irreverent in most religions. The masters were invariably pleased. As a result, Zen always remained in touch with simple, daily reality.

The history of Zen begins in 520 A.D. when Bodhi-Dharma came to China from India. At that time, Buddhist monks were busy meditating on the transiency of all things and seeking nirvana by transcendence of the world.

Zen brought the message that nirvana is to be found in daily life—that there is no difference between spiritual and physical, mundane and lofty. Seen through the third eye—the

168

eye of intuitive wisdom—daily life becomes a manifestation of the infinite.

Sometime after Bodhi-Dharma, the message of Zen was phrased as follows (in D. T. Suzuki's translation):

> Special transmission outside the Scriptures;
> No dependence on words and letters;
> Direct pointing at the soul of man;
> Seeing into one's nature and attainment of Buddhahood.

Scriptures, like all words, are a finger pointing to the moon, not to be mistaken for the moon. They carry the truth but do not open the third eye. The eye is opened in satori, which is always an abrupt, illogical experience. When the mind is ready, it can occur in the course of the most trivial incident. One ancient master experienced it when his master told him to wash his dishes, another when, sitting quietly in his office, he heard a clap of thunder. D. T. Suzuki, the scholar mainly responsible for bringing Zen to the West through his translations and writings, quotes a poem by the latter master:

> Devoid of thought, I sat quietly by the desk in my official room,
> With my fountain-mind undisturbed, as serene as water;
> A sudden clash of thunder, the mind-doors burst open,
> And lo, there sitteth the old man in all his homeliness.

If a man talks about his satori at all, he talks in such everyday terms. "When you have satori you are able to reveal a palatial mansion made of precious stones on a single blade of grass, but when you have no satori, a palatial mansion itself is concealed behind a simple blade of grass," said another Zen master quoted by D. T. Suzuki.

In the thirteenth century, Zen reached Japan and there was taken up by the warrior class. Fencing and Japanese sword fighting are influenced by it. In the 1950s, the Beats took up Zen in the United States and popularized it somewhat in their writings. Alan Watts popularized it still more. However, Dick Baker stresses that Zen cannot be understood through words.

The San Francisco Zen Center began in 1958 when the poet Gary Snyder's wife, and some other people began to come to the Japanese Zen Buddhist congregation at 1881 Bush Street to do zazen. Suzuki Roshi was, and still remained in 1968, the head of that congregation. He had come to the United States in 1958 and was one of about thirty Zen masters in the world.

He had his own temple in Japan and had been offered the

headship of a large monastery, but turned it down because he considered himself too young. He was then in his early fifties. Then he came to the States because the San Francisco congregation needed help. The visit was to be temporary, but the Caucasians who gathered around him so impressed him with their seriousness that he postponed his departure.

Among the early meditators was Richard Baker, a former Harvard student working on an M.A. in Oriental studies and Japanese history at the University of California, Berkeley.

"I read a lot of Zen," he told me, "but I never did anything with it until someone recommended I see the Zen master. I went to a lecture and couldn't disagree with anything he said. So I went back and saw that everything he did—the way he held his body, the way he moved his hands—was all of one piece. So I started sitting in 1961."

For the next two years, while working toward a doctorate and holding a full-time job, Dick Baker rose at 5 A.M. daily and went to the Zen Center. In 1967, he was ordained a Buddhist priest and three months later passed into the second stage of priesthood. If the Roshi finds that he has attained the third, he will receive a brown robe and be allowed to teach.

A priest becomes a roshi if a roshi acknowledges him as his successor.

Baker's talent in speaking of Zen in Western terms and his energy and ability in organizing and fund-raising led to the purchase of Tassajara Hot Springs for $300,000. It is the only Zen Buddhist monastery in this country. About four hundred students meditated there during the first year, April 1967–April 1968. Baker estimates that there are no more than a thousand consistently practicing Zen Buddhists in the country, though many more practice occasionally and perhaps millions have read books or heard lectures by Alan Watts.

"Zen has been in America for eighty years now and never had a real go," he said. "But some basic change in orientation is now going on. There is a readiness to study something like that and we have many more applicants than we can take."

LSD and the spread of the turned-on attitude have brought the sudden surge of interest. People who come to Zen from acid generally catch on faster, Baker said, but after a while they reach a plateau. Many of them expect their experience to be similar to the LSD trip and are disappointed. Expectation stands in the way of the Zen student as it does in the way of the students of Frederick Perls. Also, as in Perls' work, Zen students are at some point confronted by an impasse, Baker said. If they stay with what's happening, they reach what he calls "a more inclusive thereness." It is not dramatic but it is powerful: "You're not so distracted, you don't have moods or depressions. You're surprised when you find you don't have as many problems as other people—for you don't seem changed to yourself."

On my fourth evening at Zen Mountain, Suzuki Roshi returns from San Francisco. The first evening I watch him in the role of the diplomat. A couple of wealthy people, contributors to the Zen Center, are visiting. The Roshi, Dick Baker, and some students have dinner with them in the guest dining room.

"Was your monastery anywhere near Mount Fuji?" the woman asks.

"It is near Kyoto."

"We had such a marvelous time skiing in Japan."

The Roshi is a short, slight man in a black robe. He is polite, he laughs a lot and is gracious. But whenever a question becomes awkward, I notice, he suddenly fails to understand English. Nobody can get offended, the Roshi doesn't speak perfect English, it's well known.

The next day he works on his rock garden, carrying and placing huge stones with Phillip Wilson's help. I watch him from a distance. He works intently. In the evening he gives a lecture.

As he sits at the lectern, I can see what Phillip meant when he said the Roshi was a living ikon. His features are extremely well-defined and his expressions are never ambiguous. His face is mobile and has the kind of transparency ones sees in ikons. His gestures are never fuzzy. But he is not only spiritual, he also looks supremely practical, almost shrewd. I can see why Phillip said "he is like a thief and a mother."

He starts off by reminding the students that Zen is Buddhism, and talks about the history of Buddhism. That part sounds a bit routine to me. But when it is time for questions, he gives answers that leave a lot of people as baffled as the students in the classical stories.

A girl complains that she cannot concentrate during zazen because the weather has grown cold and she was chilled from inside her clothes.

"I understand how you feel," the Roshi says. "A cold or sickness won't kill you. No practice will kill you. So practice despite the cold. It is a good chance to practice. Take a negative attitude to your desires and you have a better chance of realizing your true nature. I do not mean annihilate your desire. So, if it is cold, you should not wear too much."

"Do you mean we should deny ourselves satisfaction when you say take a negative attitude to desires?" someone asks.

"Negative and positive are very important," says the Roshi. "You have to twist a rope from two strands. Positive is not always what it seems. Which is stronger, a man who beats or a man who is beaten? It is easy to beat but not so easy to be beaten."

"Is it ever all right to say yes to your desires?" a worried voice asks. "It seems to me that what's bad is to be attached. Isn't it all right to enjoy food as long as we can forget about it once it's gone?" It's Patty, the one who talked so much on my first day here. She's been quiet and reflective since she ended three days of tangaryo.

"Yes, that is so," says the Roshi. "There are no rules. There are rules but they are not always to be read the same way."

When the lecture is over, students cluster outside, trying to understand what the Roshi had meant they should do about their desires. They are uneasy. Zen is not supposed to be a rejection of the world. What did he mean? It is similar to the problem of the raspberry patch and the fig tree.

When the raspberries ripened, someone put up a sign by the patch: "To be free from clinging you must be free from greed." So nobody ate any berries, they fell to the ground and rotted. Now the figs are ripe and nobody knows how to reconcile freedom from clinging with the desire for figs and acceptance of their ripeness.

I do not stay long enough to learn the answer to the fig problem or get past the first glimpse of Zen. But when I leave, I understand a little better why one girl returned to Tassajara even though her father offered her a $4000 sports car and four years' tuition for art school if she didn't. I ride into Monterey with the monastery's laundry, with Taylor Binkley, Tim Buckley and a lovely longhaired girl who says her own father is embarrassed to tell the neighbors where she is. On the way, we stop once at an overlook to gaze at the vast wilderness. As far as we can see there are only valleys and peaks covered with forest. The silence is absolute.

Tim, who drives the panel truck down the cliff-side road, tells me how he came to move from New York to the Santa Lucia Mountains to further his spiritual discoveries. "I found I had a capacity for ecstatic experience and that's what I tried for with meditation," he says. "I figured that was where it was at. But I did not know what I was having or who it was that was having it. There are all kinds of subtle problems that develop when you try to hook that into your daily life without a teacher. And you can't keep up at that level alone.

One day I was driving along a back country road in Maine where there was a lot of pulpwood logging going on. Suddenly the forest and then the ground and then the car and I myself disappeared in something like bursts of white flame. Then I became aware of some danger. I blinked or shook or something and saw a logger leading a horse across the road about ten yards ahead of me. I swerved around them. In the rearview mirror I saw him yelling at me.

"When I started doing zazen I found out that many of the things I had thought were the basic core were not at all. There's a Zen poem: 'Getting wood, hauling water—how marvelous.' Now to me it's beautiful to be able to begin bringing it down to hot food and cold water and skin and bones."

On the bus from Monterey to San Francisco, I reflect that the one big question I still carry with me from the acid trip is —why do I hold on when it's time to let go? That's what Zen freedom from clinging is all about.

Back in the city there is the pleasure of a big meal eaten at a table with friends. But though I enjoy it, I miss the simple beauty of the Zen eating ritual. I also reflect on something Phillip Wilson said: "When you're nowhere, three steps in any direction are three steps from the center of the universe." Sometime, I might return for a longer stay at Zen Mountain.

Tassajara and Morningstar now appear as opposites, and also the same. Both force you to look at whatever is going on. Both are creating new attitudes. But so are a lot of people I'm meeting who live in no special community and follow no one leader or master. One of the most original among these independent pioneers is Joanie Summer, we'll call her, a friend of one of my new friends here. Her story highlights the changes that the institution of marriage is undergoing within the turned-on style of life.

Chapter TEN

Out-of-Sight Joanie and Sequential Monogamy

ON ONE of Joanie's occasional trips to New York, a friend bought her a purple feather boa because, that friend told me, Joanie is the only person in the world who can put on a purple boa and attract no more attention than she does walking down Fifth Avenue in her simple everyday clothes. It was the perfect thing for her to wear with the purple velvet cape, the Indian red blouse and the orange skirt. It also would have looked good with the black silk blouse and tiger-spotted silk harem pants Joanie is wearing right now as she dishes out spaghetti with grass-seasoned sauce in her tidy, warm San Francisco kitchen.

"I'm thinking of changing my name to Sequin Palladini," she says.

"Oh? Why?"

"Just because of the sound. I dig the sound. It suits me."

Over a mouthful of spaghetti—delicious spaghetti—I peer at Joanie with her newly red hair, the butterfly effect penciled out from the eyes, those pants, the gold chain dangling from hips to pelvis. Well, why not? Why should an intelligent, well-educated Jewish girl from New York not be Sequin Palladini if she so chooses?

Joanie is smiling, her eyes are laughing. Once again my astonishment turns into admiration. Two years ago Joanie was the proper-liberal dutiful wife of a social worker. Dinner was always on time, friends were employed and square, evenings were family scenes, weekends were busy. She was a wife-mother-career woman, one of those superfemales who seem to be always doing a dozen things at once, all efficiently. And all the while she was miserable.

Most of her friends were married and similarly miserable two years ago. They're still her friends now, but it's a new scene altogether. She sees them separately, them and the men and women they now live with. Sometimes they leave their children with her, to be picked up by the ex-spouse. With some of these old friends Joanie is closer now than ever, perhaps because, for the first time in years, she feels completely alive. A whole new world opened to her when, somewhat to her own surprise, she left Ed (also a fictitious name) after eleven years. Her old habits and hang-ups came off with her wedding ring. What remained was herself at last, going hip at thirty, Joanie only more so—Sequin Palladini.

Not that she flipped into an all-out hippie. She continued to work for a living, sent her two children to public school in neat clothes with homework done. She even enrolled her six-year-old daughter in dancing school, like a good suburban mother. But her entire outlook toward her work, her family, her friends and her possessions underwent a transformation. Now she is in the vanguard of a growing number of people who are spreading the turned-on life-style through middle-class society.

"Let's go into the living room, it's more comfortable," Joanie says, getting up and clearing the dishes. I follow her into the high-ceilinged salon filled with things draped and dripping and sparkling darkly in candlelight. Tinsel, cut-glass beads and long pieces of cloth droop from a mirror behind the couch; some handmade copper and silver pendants hang from nails on the wall behind the easy chair opposite, beside the fireplace. There's a batik print above the marble mantle, and below it, on the floor, a tangle of plants, straw flowers and reeds. The lower halves of the three tall windows that form a bay are covered with Persian print cloth, a cozy backdrop to the wooden window seat and its mirror-inlaid embroidered Indian pillows. A small light machine turns slowly, catching colors and flashes and letting them slip back into the shadow. The whole thing is more like some Persian courtesan's tent that the living room of a woman who grew up in New York's Westchester County.

Joanie lights a stick of incense, slips it into a ceramic candle holder on the mantel and then sinks into the rope hammock hung in the doorway between the dining room and the bedroom. In the dim light, her hair regains its natural darkness and her face becomes pale and soft.

"I was looking at that dresser the other day," she says, motioning with her left arm toward the recesses of the bedroom. "I painted the drawers different colors once when Ed was away for a month because of his job. I knew he wouldn't ap-

175

prove, so I did it when he was away. It was just one of the ways that the supercracks in our marriage began showing.

"We started off very tight and very close in values eleven years ago. Except that he came from this very liberal scene —his parents knew all these folk singers and stuff—while I came from a scene that wasn't really any one thing. We moved from the city to Westchester County before I went to high school, but though we had a big house there, only one room was really fixed up. My parents read the *Daily News* during the week and *The New York Times* all the way through on Sunday. That sort of typifies it. My parents were very uptight about money, they never to this day got over the Depression. My father has a degree in law and accounting but during the Depression he started putting together crystal radios and later he got a radio and TV store. My mother taught and did recreation work in camps. There were four kids and I was the oldest.

"I went to Bennington for three years and got married in my junior year. Ed worked with street gangs in New York at that time. Later we moved to San Francisco and he worked for the Oakland recreation department. I went to the California College of Arts and Crafts for a year and got my degree from Bennington *in absentia*.

"About a year after we married we got a job with the American Friends Service Committee to be leaders of a Peace Corps-type thing they had going in a Mexican village. The idea was to do what the village wanted with money the Mexican government offered. At first I was very unhappy there but then I really got to dig it. I ran some cooking and crafts classes and I dug that. Only I used to get, like, very restless with just beans and babies.

"So I started doing batiks, and I went into Mexico City a lot to spend weekends with a friend of mine who was a dancer. That was the preview of what was going to happen with Ed and me. In the kind of communal setup we had in the village you don't have enough privacy to run your own scenes down, there's always an audience around. And Ed has this thing of turning into an inscrutable Oriental.

"One thing I'm really into now—that I really got from a combination of therapy and acid and people—is leading as open a life as I can. Not having secrets. If I'm going with more than one guy, for instance, and one of them asked me about another I wouldn't hesitate to tell him. I don't see any sense in having those kinds of secrets between friends.

"With Ed it wasn't anything to do with other men at first. It was just that he would pretend that everything was fine when it wasn't, as if any problem would disappear if you just refrained from looking at it. So a whole lot of things became taboo and I got this censorship setup in my head. Before I said anything I'd run it through my brain like film and censor it. The habit started there in Mexico and got worse and worse until almost nothing was natural any more between us.

"We stayed with the Quakers for almost two years and came back to San Francisco right after our son was born. Right away I got pregnant again. But in spite of that, I decided to go to graduate school for a master's. You see, I was in a security bag and this whole 'feminine mystique' kick. I went to school with some talented and lively minds and then saw them fade into suburban obscurity. So I was determined that wasn't going to happen to me. The master's would help me to get a job teaching or something, and then I could always be economically independent if necessary. The fact that my pottery and my batiks were selling wasn't enough for me, in my super-feminist way of thinking.

"I decided to take decorative arts at the University of California at Berkeley. That was quite an experience after Bennington, which is a small place, very progressive, very personal and strong on the rights of the individual. Cal seemed just a big machine, big batches of IBM cards with teachers here and there in-between. A lot was going on there—the free speech movement and the start of the psychedelic music and the whole psychedelic culture, but I didn't have time to explore all that. I was on that whole American hardworking early Puritan kick, you know, extremely compulsive. When I think back on that now I get exhausted. What I was trying to do was be one of those amazing American women. I used to get up at six-thirty, change the diapers, feed the kids breakfast, feed Ed breakfast, see him off to work, deliver the babies to this girl's house who exchanged baby-sitting with me, park the car and be in class by nine o'clock. I'd take classes well into the afternoon and then come home and start with the babies and the food and the husband and then do the artwork.

"Socially we saw mostly people who did some kind of a social-worky thing. I could never get with that. I liked it as we lived it in Mexico and I liked it when Ed was working with street gangs. But now everything was all categorized and lifeless.

"It was somewhere in this period after our return from Mexico that it became apparent that Ed and I were moving apart. When we married we were mates. For a while we kept getting closer and swung together. But somewhere in those eleven years of our marriage the pendulum reversed in this superslow motion thing between us and we began to move in opposite directions. He started a reaction to his liberal childhood toward a middle-class secure thing while I started toward the place where his family was at when he was a child. It was like what happens in an eclipse—the sun's shadow moves toward the moon, covers it, and you see them for a moment together. Then they divide and you see opposites.

"All these signs began appearing. For example, I was halfway to a pilot's license and I never told Ed about it because I knew he'd freak. I had heard an ad on the radio for flying lessons and I started to think about the idea and thought I might just dig it. So one day after my classes at Cal I got into the car, went to the airport and somone took me up in a plane. I loved it. So I started to save money and whenever I had enough for another flying class I'd go to the airport in the afternoon and put in my hours and then go home and make supper and all that.

"We did a lot of interesting things together, Ed and I. But he is one of those people who can't stay home so we ran around every weekend. He seemed to mark time by moving himself around bodily—one weekend to Santa Cruz, another weekend to Mendecino, always going somewhere. He turned me onto that way of living but I really often preferred to stay home and make things. He kept saying I wasn't adventurous.

"So anyway, the supercracks became bigger. I flew a plane, I had an affair, one thing after another. We were building up a thing that was getting more and more secretive, as if in this way we could keep everything from crashing. We didn't talk about the big things but we argued about little ones. I'd want to put bead curtains in the doorways and he'd say that wasn't very practical, doors are to walk through. Or I'd come up with some lighting effect and he'd say that was very dramatic, but how can anyone read a book? He wanted to move out to Berkeley and get a house with a yard and a dog. I wanted to stay in the city.

"A couple of friends turned us on to grass but Ed wouldn't keep any in the house because he thought it was too dangerous. I thought he was being too uptight. I smoked more when he wasn't around and generally, I noticed, I was freer and more into what was going on around me when I wasn't with him. In every way, he was pulling in, I was moving out.

"We used to be involved in a lot of peace and civil rights demonstrations. But once a Quaker person came to the house and asked us not to pay taxes because so big a part went for defense. Ed thought that was a good idea in principle but he

178

didn't want to get involved with the authorities. I felt that we were being half-assed about our position and that we should either go far enough to risk arrest or not do it at all. The only place the authorities really can get you is in your mind.

"Now I've become almost apolitical, although I still vote in every election. But I can see where I might stop voting too. Like in this last election for the supervisors, one candidate was as much a turd as the next so it was really pointless to vote. But to me the answer isn't to run away with your children to the woods or to another country. The answer is to stay and fight, even if it's just by doing your thing. I feel with a lot of people that there's a giant battle for minds going on right now. Sometimes it's blatant and sometimes it's subtle. And I'm much more interested in where the minds of people now between ten and twenty are going to go than in the election this year or whatever. The crux of the matter is which way the next generation is going to believe. And I hope that —I certainly don't think that it can do it completely and I have no idea whether it can do it at all—but I hope that the spread of drugs and the things people will learn behind drugs will spread the number of people in the tribe, so that it has strength to protect itself. You have the tribe on the one side and on the other this scene where everything is becoming superclassified and divided. Like in social work—Ed is a group worker and so he's a vanishing phenomenon. Now all you have is caseworkers—unrelated individuals *treating* 'cases' individually, unrelatedly.

"Well, things got more fractured between Ed and me. I pleaded with him to go with me to group therapy but he wouldn't. So then I went alone to a shrink but not for long. He seemed so superficial. Meanwhile I finished graduate school and now had more of the economic security I had wanted. But that was of no help. I got more and more nervous until finally I was almost catatonic. I was scared. I knew I should split but I just couldn't do it. And then one day—I don't want to go into all the details—one day I just realized that I could. And none of the dire things I had imagined happened.

"Ed moved out. One of the first things I did was to rearrange the apartment. I moved the desk out and softened the lighting and hung a lot of things on the walls. Before, I had become compulsively neat. Now I began to like to have things I was working on lying around on the floor. Before, I even cleared the top of my dresser. As you see, this place isn't messy. But it would freak Ed.

"I went on seeing people and doing things as before because I never believed you need dates and escorts to go places. I felt that at age twenty-nine I was still young and there were many things and people still to try out.

"Before we split, Ed and I went to a few of the big psychedelic rock dances. They were the ones that followed Ken Kesey's acid tests—you know, where he gave out acid—the kind that later became popular at the Fillmore and Avalon ballrooms. When we went they were still being held at the Longshoremen's Hall. People came in beautiful costumes like they were straight out of the Middle Ages, and there were light shows and acid rock groups and the scene was very turned on. At first I saw only art student types there but gradually I became aware that these people and I had a kindered thing. So now when I was on my own I began to listen to rock and roll music and to look into the psychedelic-hip scene. When they had the first big music festival on Mount Tamalpais I did about eighty cloth banners for it. That got me pretty deeply into things that were happening and I began to move around with a lot of new people. And I began to see my whole life in a new light.

"I took my first acid trip soon after we split and saw myself on a dais that was revolving slowly in the middle of a round plane. All around me were all the important people in my life since I was an infant. I was spinning around and trying to talk to them—but at the same time I was throwing garbage at them. The words that were coming out of my mouth were 'garbage, garbage, garbage' and I was throwing garbage with both hands. And suddenly I realized that this is what I had been doing since I was little, dumping a lot of verbal shit on people. I had turned off people to protect myself and at the same time had turned myself off to a lot in life. I had done that with my mother and later with Ed. That's what the shrink had tried to tell me but I didn't see it until that first acid trip.

"Meanwhile, many of my old friends were going through parallel changes. All of us were reaching thirty and coming into our full selves and feeling that our marriage partners, in one way or another, were tying us down. Most of them also decided to get divorced. One friend, a painter who had been married to a sculptor, was now with a jazz musician. Through her, quite by accident, I met Trevor (a fictitious name), who's a very successful photographer and has been on the scene in New York for a long time. He was at Millbrook when Leary first started there and his head was much farther out than mine. He walked into my place and he dug it right away.

"Meeting Trevor was a real turning point for me because it meant I put my roots down in a new place. In some way or other I know that Trevor and I will be connected for the rest of our lives. We only see each other when he has an assignment on the West Coast, which is for about a week every few months or so. I know he has at least one other woman in New York and he knows I have other men, but when he's over here he sits at the head of the table. He has a special place and I make that clear to the kids too.

"I don't see the man-woman thing at all the same way as I used to. Like I don't see much point in marriage 'till death do us part.' Trevor and I are mates now the way Ed and I were mates when we married. Everybody is capable of finding several people in a lifetime whom he considers to be mates. A mate is just your true partner for any part of the life cycle, not necessarily for a whole lifetime or even the whole bringing up of a child. Most young people I know think the same way. There comes a point where you are ready for a new partner on a different level and then you move on. That requires a kind of inner freedom my 'feminine mystique' thinking hadn't opened up to me. If you get uptight and can't move on you begin to dry up and die.

"When I panicked at the idea of splitting with Ed it was mostly panic at losing my security, the kind of physical security I'd grown up to expect from marriage. There was a place that was my home, a man who said he'd stick with me 'for better or for worse,' a whole setup where I had very particular roles to play as the wife, the mother. I had always gone on the assumption that once I found my mate that would be it, from then on I would be able to stop worrying about a whole lot of things.

"Now I know I'll never have that kind of security because I don't believe in staying together with anyone 'for worse.' So I've got to find an inner security. I've got to replace the physical guarantee with a new state of mind. And I'm doing that through acid. I take it about every six months and each time I get a kind of reaffirmation. If I had taken acid before Ed and I split I don't think I'd have gotten into that panic.

"At first I wasn't sure how I was going to manage financially. I had my master's and could teach, but what I really wanted to do was work on my art. I spent a lot of my time hustling so that I always had a piece of work coming up and my income stayed as steady as possible. But now I'm dropping out of the security bag into this somehow-I'll-manage kind of scene. It's funny, just yesterday a friend reminded me how I used to say to him, 'You always talk about living on pennies. It's absurd.' Now I see the absurdity of thinking you need a whole lot of bread. When you don't have any, you start meeting other people to whom three dollars for the Fillmore is a lot. They're all from middle-class backgrounds and all of them find ways to live on less than they thought they could. It's an adventure, scrounging, if you never were forced to do it. And it's not really that different once you realize how many things you really don't need. There's a tremendous amount of affluence in the United States and a tremendous amount of duplication in ownership. Like, why should every family have a washer and dryer? If there were one in this building and the six families in this house and the two next door got along, they could do with just one among them. You can share a lot of things that way.

"I got into a semicommunal arrangement with this friend upstairs who had two children, the couple next door, and one or two others. We started to shop together and to eat at each other's houses, sharing the cooking. We shared a phone and a car and all the baby-sitting. The arrangement worked on the basis that nobody had much money but everyone had some at some point. We pooled our resources and found that we had more time that way to do whatever our thing was. It seemed so ridiculous, now that I looked back from a different perspective, the way Ed and I had lived, all that superficial socializing, the hiring of baby-sitters and running around.

"Later I moved to this apartment here and the communal thing ended. But I got into other similar arrangements. Like one day, when my car broke down, three guys heard me saying at the gas station that I had to get my daughter to dancing school. They gave me a lift out and back and we became friends. It turned out they live only about ten blocks from here. So now I go over there about once a week with the kids and they put at my disposal their washer and dryer, the refrigerator, their grass. We turn on and rap. Sometimes I go over there and cook supper while the kids watch the color TV. These guys are not hippies in any sense, they have regular jobs and they dress straight. They usually have a lot of things I wouldn't buy because of the price, like steak. But they can't cook well. So I cook a good dinner for everyone and it's an exchange.

"I shop carefully but I try to keep my kids from feeling uptight when money is scarce. I don't want them to feel deprived. They like yogurt and that's expensive but I'd give up all sorts of things before I'd tell them they can't have yogurt. On the other hand I won't get them certain toys because they're unnecessary and expensive and I don't think will

182

bring them the pleasure they want. For myself, I can't think of too much these days that I wish I had money for.

"Now during this last year and through all the changes, I found I developed a different attitude toward my art. I used to worry whether my family and all my duties and obligations would stop me from doing my thing, but now I just know that I'll do it because that's my life fiber—it's my river, my bag, to make things—tie dyes and batiks and pottery. That's my life trip.

"I used to worry about production but now I'm more focused on the process of making things than on having the tangible thing finished in front of me. And as a result I'm becoming a better craftsman. The urgency is gone. Right now I have to decide whether I want to take on a job or not. It's a choice. Last year I wouldn't have thought for even a minute, I would have accepted it automatically if I didn't have too many other jobs piled up. Now I have choices because I'm no longer worried about security and there are many alternative ways to spend my time.

"So I'm still myself only more so. Like, I always wore clothes that were a little off-beat but now I wear clothes that are outrageous, either because of the color or the design or because they're blatantly sexy. I do it on purpose. I'm convinced it's good for people if I go into the public library or the supermarket with my purple cape and, say, these pants. It cheers up their day and that's part of what dressing and jewelry and mojos are all about—to make life pretty or happy or lucky or more esthetically pleasing. A lot of people are misunderstood as exhibitionists when really they dress that way because it's fun and it's exciting, it makes you feel good like a sunny day. If the rest of the world finds it outrageous—so what? As long as they don't make a law against that too.

"You know, sometimes you find yourself getting into something more and more until you suddenly find you're really in it. One day a couple of months ago I decided I'd dress straight just to see what that felt like now. The first thing I discovered was that I owned almost nothing anymore that was straight-looking. And the second thing was that dressing straight was boring.

"My children dress the way they like. My daughter likes to dress very straight, in black leather mary jane shoes and tights and little dresses and pocketbooks. She's liked that sort of thing since she was two. My son, who's seven now, likes mirror vests and long hair and jewelry and the rest of the hippie man thing. He likes to parody it just as boys always parody men. They both have choices and they can see dif-

183

ferent styles of living because Ed takes them to his house and on his trips every other weekend. As far as I can see, they're comfortable in both places and that's because Ed and I still respect what we had together and don't run each other down in front of the kids or anywhere else. There's no need for that. We're just on different trips now."

Joanie drops her feet to the floor, gets out of the hammock and stretches. Then we go back into the kitchen and she puts on a pot of hot water for tea.

The children are with Ed tonight. I saw them all this afternoon. They're friendly children, alert and lively. For, though Joanie may look weird and have exotic adventures, she is a responsible mother. And despite the fact that other men stay in the house now from time to time, the children suffer from no confusion about who their father is. They seem to appreciate having two homes, both with a firmly anchored parent.

"I hear Ed is going to Synanon now," Joanie says as she reaches into the refrigerator for some cake.

"Yes. He's playing the Synanon games and he's very enthusiastic about them. Are you involved in Synanon too?"

"No, I don't join things. I like to find out about them and I know a lot of people who belong to all kinds of groups and movements, but that's not my bag. Though I would like to try living in a commune sometime. I've been to some but I haven't found one that's for me. I went up to Morningstar Ranch—you know, the place up near Sebastopol?—but I had a bad experience there. The Gypsy Jokers had come in on their bikes the day I arrived. I was walking past the house they had taken over and two of them came after me. They walked alongside and started bugging me. They didn't do anything, really, but just the way they looked I had this feeling that anything could happen and nobody would protect me. It was freaky. I felt I'd never been so close to being raped in my life.

"I've visited a couple of the Kerista groups too. The attitudes there are not exactly traditional. Like one night I was balling with this friend of mine in a room and a little girl walked in. For a moment I froze. I didn't know what to do. Then I thought that stopping would be worse than going on. So we continued and she sat down and waited and when we were through we rapped. She was perfectly at ease. Later I asked around and this was perfectly all right with everyone, her parents and everyone. Some of the Kerista communities have family groupings—this one did—others don't. I've looked around to other communities too but none of them is for me, and I'm not the type to start one. Well, maybe someday."

She sets out Darjeeling tea, cuts the cake and serves it. I listen to Joanie's report on the communal scene and wonder how Ed could possibly have thought her lacking in a sense of adventure. He must have seen only this comfortable human in the kitchen, the Joanie of the New York-Bennington accent, the P-TA meetings and the home-baked cake. Perhaps he was too frightened to make the acquaintance of Sequin Palladini. For now he has a house in Berkeley with a yard and is thinking of getting a dog.

Those who know her only slightly can dismiss Joanie, with her wild clothes and hip lingo, as a freaky parody of a hippie. To see the real Joanie is more threatening to a square. For in fact she is a revolutionary who says out loud and without hesitation something that most people already realize but hate to admit. It's perfectly clear by now that marriage is no longer the solid rock upon which men and women may build their lives. One out of every four marriages in the United States now ends in divorce. Yet most people still cling to the fantasy that nothing has changed. Most girls grow up believing that once they find a husband they can relax in wifely security. They divide their lives into two parts: the search for a man and life with the man. It's frightening to think that the home may at any time be abandoned by one of the partners if he feels the other is, as Joanie put it, tying him down.

And yet, though the traditional words are still spoken at weddings—"for better for worse . . . until death do us part" —what most people mean by them is not what their grandparents meant. They assume that the union will be "for better." If it proves to be "for worse," divorce is accepted as the healthy, positive answer.

There is no longer, for most people, any economic or social necessity to stay married no matter how miserable life becomes. Divorce has no stigma anymore. The ideal of personal growth implies that a relationship between a man and a woman should cease to exist if it goes dead.

Some young people, particularly hippies, have rejected legal marriage altogether and have replaced it with their own personal rituals. Others reject even personal ceremonies. A doctor's wife told me she had urged her son to "marry that girl before she gets away," and he had laughed at her.

"We're grooving together," he told her. "We like living together. What do we need marriage for? We don't need that kind of lock on each other. If one of us wanted to split, we'd stop grooving. So there would be no point in staying together."

Many non-hippies have similar views but marry when they want to have children, for the children's protection. But even with children, divorce is no longer looked upon as a disaster. "It all depends on how it is handled," said Dr. William C. Schutz, a psychologist on the Esalen staff who has been divorced twice and has three children, two by his first wife and one by his second. "Often the reason divorce is traumatic for children is that the children come to believe it's their fault. If you make sure they understand it isn't, they need not suffer any trauma." Schutz sees his children regularly or calls them regularly. He knows more about their thoughts and activities than many fathers who stumble in from work every night to perform fatherly duties automatically and without interest.

The high incidence of divorce has begun to create a new form of extended family, as in the case of Ed and Joanie and some of their friends. Children have two homes and, in their parents' new partners, a new set of relatives. If the adults manage to move from the first relationship to the second without bitterness, the children may well be better off this way than they would be with both parents in one home and unhappy.

The ex-mates, however, often part in bitterness and vent it on the children. Even when they make a deliberate effort to avoid it, they convey the idea that the other person was some kind of rotten bastard. Gerald Smith, divorced father of two children, does both marriage and divorce counseling in San Mateo County. Couples or entire families come to him to settle problems of breaking up and dividing property. The idea of saving the marriage is not even mentioned in these interviews. The aim is "to try to get through the divorce with as few mixed feelings as possible so that all that would be left would be the roles of mother and father. It's important to recognize that it is the relationship that gets sick, not one person or the other," he says. "The legal system does not recognize this fact. The adversary system, with two lawyers confronting each other in court battle, tends to set up vendettas. It would be much more helpful for them and their children if the divorcing man and woman were not pitted against each other legally as they are now."

Smith advocates that marriage be viewed as "an openended contract, a subjective commitment to the present not the outcome twenty years from now. For this it is important to keep an open door—the option of divorce. For you can't be close if you don't have room to be distant. You can't love freely if you feel trapped."

However, Smith believes that the marriage contract continues to remain important. "The symbol of commitment gives the marriage the resiliency needed to get through the pain in a relationship," he maintains. "Couples that don't symbolize the relationship have a brittle relationship. The tendency is to avoid pain and split over differences. But if worked out, the differences are the very thing that keeps a marriage together. They are the excitement in a marriage.

Margaret Mead has suggested that it might be useful to have two kinds of marriage contract. The first would allow a couple to live together but would not license them to have children. It would be easy to enter and easy to dissolve. The second would require some evidence that a couple is fit for parenthood. Everyone would go through the first relationship before—if at all—beginning the second.

The law usually lags behind social change, so it is unlikely that Margaret Mead's idea, or anything similar, would become the standard legal thing in the near future. Meanwhile, countless studies will continue to be published on why marriages fail, countless diagnoses and cures will be offered by popular magazines for the family's sickly condition and, quietly, daring souls like Joanie Summer will continue to experiment with entirely new approaches to the man-woman relationship.

To Joanie, LSD is a personal ritual to help her maintain the inner freedom—what Perls calls self-support, hippies call "centeredness" and what in Zen is known as freedom from clinging—she needs to live without relying on a permanent mate, a job or on other forms of external security.

For others who live in a style similar to Joanie, Esalen, Zen, and an assortment of sensory and mystical gurus provide the necessary reinforcement. During 1967 and early 1968, one guru who appealed to a wide variety of people and was much in tune with the entire new outlook was a tiny and clever Indian mystic, the Maharishi Mahesh Yogi. He rose to fame when the Beatles proclaimed him their guru and lost a lot of status when, nine months later, the lads announced they had made a mistake about him.

Chapter ELEVEN

The Practical Mystics

WHEN MAHARISHI Mahesh Yogi spoke at the Berkeley Community Theater September 25, 1967, the price of admission was fifty cents for any seat in the house. Four months later, when he appeared at the new Madison Square Garden's Felt Forum, tickets sold out at three to ten dollars.

It seemed obvious to a lot of people that His Holiness was a con man out to make a fortune: he was asking a week's salary for instruction in his meditation technique; he was courting publicity, going after the rich and famous, building luxurious ashrams, staying at the Plaza Hotel, hiring public relations men. What kind of holy man could he be? Why didn't he preach for free out in Central Park instead of selling his message at outrageous prices?

It was irregular, highly irregular. But what his detractors failed to appreciate was that Maharishi was a practical man. He was out to turn the West on to transcendental meditation and was using the most effective techniques—Western techniques—to get his message heard. Had he spoken in Central Park, who would have come on a cold winter day? A lot of hippies who were already meditating, a few curious people, some reporters who would have called the scene a freeze-in or something. If meditation was to become a daily ritual in the West, a different approach was needed. So Maharishi tuned into the popular success machinery and became the yogi who makes it like a movie star, using glamour power and the mass media with a smoothness any promoter would admire.

He was not selling anything new. "I am only summarizing the already tried experiments in different parts of the world," he himself said. But to many Westerners, meditation was utterly irrelevant—they thought of it as self-indulgent navel-gazing—until Maharishi got them to consider it as a practical necessity in their busy lives.

LSD had paved the way. A lot of people were turned on to mysticism and were looking for something that would help them find their way without drugs to the realms psychedelics had shown them. They wanted a technique rather than a faith or creed. Most of them were unwilling to spend much time on the quest. Tuned more to the idea of flash than of satori, they wanted something that worked fast—a quickie shortcut to mystical reality. And that's exactly what His practical Holiness came to offer.

The acid-sparked way of thinking had affected the attitudes of non-heads too. Four months ago, in Berkeley, Maharishi's audience had been almost entirely students and hippies. Now, at the Garden, it was diverse. Young East Side elegance—stylish tinted glasses, wigs, Dr. Zhivago midi-coats—prevailed over Lower East Side hobbit-garb. But there were also quite a few straight, square people in dark suits, coats and ties, come to hear the man *The New York Times* had labeled "Chief Guru of the West."

Between the Berkeley and the New York appearances, Maharishi's beaming countenance had appeared on the covers of the *Times* Sunday magazine and of *Look,* on the *Johnny Carson Show* and the *Gary Stevens Show.* He beamed also from the jackets of two record albums that were prominently displayed in many stores. One was a collection of his lectures, the other a recording of jazz flutist Paul Horn with musicians he had met at the Maharishi's Academy of Meditation in Kashmir. Horn dedicated the album to His Holiness and put in a plug for his meditation method inside the jacket.

The yogi's success, which had begun when the Beatles announced, in early September 1967 that they were giving up drugs to become his followers, was at a new high on the day of the Garden event. (Nine months later, they were to announce they made a mistake about the man, though not about meditation.) The 3,600-seat hall was full despite the high admission prices. A pack of newspaper and TV reporters and cameramen waited by the stage on which a three-sectioned white couch and a low table had been placed in front of a microphone, against a background of five bouquets of yellow and brown chrysanthmums.

The apperance had been scheduled for 3 P.M., but at 3:15, aides said Maharishi was still in his dressing room, meditating. Only at 3:35 did he appear in the rear of the hall, a tiny man with curly shoulder-length black hair and a white beard. He was, as usual, dressed in a flowing white dhoti and held a bouquet of seven yellow tea roses. Briskly, he made his way toward the stage, surrounded by dark-suited assistants.

One of the aides stepped behind the couch and spread a deerskin. Maharishi sat down on it, placed the roses on the little table, drew up his legs into lotus, folded his hands, closed his eyes, and became perfectly still. Photographers began to run around, dragging their equipment, flashing lights. Maharishi sat unmoving and there was no sense of unease in the scene, no sense of offending a holy man with the crass paraphernalia of publicity. This yogi cheerfully welcomed the scrambling press: this was the way ideas were spread in the West.

I had heard the Maharishi in Berkeley for fifty cents and was looking at him now from the five-dollar seat in the center of the mezzanine. As I looked, I sensed a smile spreading through me. Others in my row also looked suddenly pleased. Something was unmistakably radiating from the tiny guru far below. When the photographers dispersed at the command of one of the yogi's PR men, a pile of flowers, mostly yellow ones, became visible at his feet, put there by admirers. He picked up a hyacinth and began to speak:

"If I were to tell you the condition of my heart, it is bouncing with bliss, with great happiness," he said, his high voice bouncing over syllables as Indian voices do. The cause of his joy, he said, was the "simple technique" that he was about to present and which could "create a natural situation of lasting peace in this generation."

He made it all sound incredibly simple: approaching the problem in its immensity is not efficient, since peace keeps escaping us. So, why not reduce the big problem to its particles? "If each individual takes care of his own peace, the world will be in peace." For personal peace, we must be free from tension and suffering. These come from desires for more—more power, more happiness, more possessions.

On this, many mystics would agree. The traditional answer is renunciation of desires and concentration on the spirit. But Maharishi was saying you don't need to give up a thing. All you need to do is to tune in through transcendental meditation. This will free you from tension, enable you to use your abilities fully, bring your desires into harmony with nature and lead to their fulfillment. Tension is contagious and leads to competition and conflict. But if you meditate, you will radiate bliss consciousness, peace and joy, and spread that all around. If only one percent of the world's population would meditate for half an hour every morning and evening, a lasting peace would result.

Never mind the defense establishment, the racial riots and the Bomb. Those are merely symptoms of tension. They will resolve in due course under the rays of expanding bliss consciousness.

The yogi disagreed with the traditionalists who say it takes years to get into meditation and question whether the Western mind is suited to the adoption of Eastern techniques. His technique, he said, is so simple that anyone can learn it within fifteen minutes from a trained teacher. It is a matter of finding the right mantra (he uses sound syllables, such as "ram"), learning to sit quietly, in any comfortable position, and letting thoughts range freely through the mind. With the help of the mantra, the mind will naturally go to the source of thought, energy and joy. This source is being or pure consciousness. Western man has lost contact with being and, thereby, with his inner nature and his relationship to the world. Transcendental meditation frees his mind to rediscover being.

Maharishi sat on the couch, toying with a flower and selling meditation in a voice that occasionally rose in a birdlike inflection or burst into a giggle. "The thing is there," he said, "The moment we start using it, we begin to get benefits from it." He sounded, at times, as if he was advertising vitamins. Only he was coming on casual, without high pressure. A man who doesn't find time to meditate is like a man who has no time to pull back a bow and throws the arrow instead of shooting it because his enemy is approaching too fast, he said.

Some people walked out before Maharishi had finished speaking and later called him a phony and a simpleton. But a lot of others dug the 105-minute address. For what the yogi said was, in essence, what all the turn-on gurus say in their particular ways: to grow we need to return periodically to our roots for new energy and we must go with the changes. It was what Frederick Perls said, what acid makes people realize, what Zen is all about: what is is. All is now, all is one, all is change and flow. We are God. Tune in and dig. That message still held later, even after some of the yogi's most glamourous followers became disenchanted with the enthusiastic way their guru seized on Western promotion gimmickry and marketing methods to get it across to the populace.

Maharishi drew supporters from all factions of the turn-on circuit—businessmen, artists, hip gypsies follow him—partly

191

because he had a talent for using the right words in the right context. In Madison Square Garden he stressed freedom from tension and peace. A leaflet distributed at the doors referred to transcendental meditation as "depth therapy." In Berkeley he talked more of the fulfillment of desires, and said, "A few days with a trained teacher and one gets into the groove of diving within."

There was time for questions at Berkeley and he fielded them with grace and humor. "If two men desire a promotion and there's only one spot and both meditate transcendentally, what happens?" someone asked. The yogi answered promptly, "The corporation will expand and meet the needs of both."

Asked about LSD, he said, "It is unrealistic, very unrealistic, and moody. And then it is injurious to health and to the nervous system. That is why," he said with a smile, "medical system does not recommend these drugs."

Both in New York and in Berkeley, Maharishi talked about development of one's potential, using the familiar phrase of the Human Potentialities people. He also said repeatedly that evolution proceeds through freedom and change and that control is damaging to life. He spoke casually and without urgency, like a teacher laying out the elementals of physics. This generation has a chance to end suffering and to create peace with hardly any effort at all. It would be a shame to pass by the opportunity. But there will be other generations. The message was too obvious to be ignored forever.

The Maharishi did not willingly discuss his personal life, but a few facts are known about him. He was born the son of a government revenue official, graduated from Allahabad University with a degree in physics, worked for a while in a factory, then went to the Himalayan Mountains to become a holy man. He studied there with Guru Dev, who taught him transcendental meditation and said it should be passed on not only to monks but also to people of the world. He had been spreading that message since 1952.

In 1958, he decided to try turning on one percent of the world's population. To do that personally would take two hundred years, he figured. He was then in his mid-forties and didn't think he had that much time. So, to speed up the process, he founded the Spiritual Regeneration Movement and began to train instructors in the method. He came to the United States because he thought people in this country would be more receptive to a new idea than people in more tradition-bound cultures, he explained. And he was not disappointed. By early 1968, more than twenty-five thousand

Americans had taken instruction in transcendental meditation and instruction centers had been set up in twenty-five cities. Germany, however, turned out to be even more receptive. Two hundred centers sprang up in that practical country, he said, "because Germans went around whispering, 'Production increases.'"

Many people I met were ready to praise the practical value of such meditation. My friend Bob Sherman, an artist from Pine Bluff, Arkansas, now living in San Francisco, was one. He had become interested in meditation when he read Hermann Hesse's *Magister Ludi* and was looking for a suitable method when the Maharishi came to town. Before that, he had attended some meetings of the Krishna Consciousness Society but found that was not for him. The swami there, he said, had talked about giving up material things and turning to an ascetic religious life. Bob was not interested in that. So, when he heard the Maharishi talk about enriching the life one had rather than abandoning it, he thought this guru was worth a try.

He signed up after the Berkeley lecture, and soon got a postcard inviting him to another lecture by one of the yogi's instructors. He went and, a day later, returned for his initiation. For this he had been asked to bring flowers, fruit, some article of clothing and either a week's salary or $35. The money angle bothered him, it seemed inappropriate, but he accepted the explanation that it was an offering and part of the ceremony.

At the initiation, he filled out a questionnaire stating his name, age, occupation, marital status and similar data. Then he went into a room with the initiator, was given his mantra, and taught how to use it. That process took about ten minutes.

The initiator left the room while Bob practiced meditating for the next ten minutes. Then he returned and asked Bob to describe his experience. It had been quite extraordinary for a beginner, Bob was told.

"I could feel myself physically sinking," he later recalled. "I felt waves. As each wave came over something different would happen. There was a point that was highly visual. I saw an eye that was bright purple and bright green. Beautiful. This happens to me almost every time now. Sometimes it will change scale and have little flamelike things around it. Then sometimes after that I will have very brief visual scenes —very brief, like one frame of a movie, but clear. I don't try to hold onto them so I don't even know what they are. After that it's pretty hard to describe, there's nothing that con-

193

sciously happens. But when I come out of it I feel very clear-headed, very refreshed. Occasionally I can't get into it, I don't even get to the purple and green eye, and then I don't get much from it.

"The most interesting thing about it to me was the change that I noticed right away. After the first day my head was completely clear. When I talked to someone I was completely 100 percent there with nothing going on in my own head. Then, when I needed my mind for something, I could bring my whole mental force to it."

After the initiation, Bob attended the six lectures that completed his instruction. There he learned that his progress had been unusually fast and that the burning tingling he sometimes felt in his head as he meditated meant that he was reactivating unused nerve centers.

The total-presence effect he experienced in his first days of meditation did not stay. But after a while it began to return. Three months after beginning to meditate, he said, "I still have times when I'm like I always was, when there are a thousand thoughts shooting through my head. But these periods of being 100 percent in the here and now seem to be getting more frequent. Generally, I'm much more tranquil, less easily frustrated, less tense in my relations with people. Which doesn't mean that every problem is solved, but there is an improvement.

"Also, I don't know whether it's a coincidence or a result of it, but my work has never gone so well. There don't seem to be any more periods when I'm unable to work. I can work all the time, and really well. I don't know whether that's because of the meditation."

Bob, like other Maharishi followers, is expected to keep his mantra a secret. He does, though he thinks that may be a bit of unnecessary hocus-pocus. "It doesn't matter though," he says, "because the method as a tool works and that's all I care about."

Similar views are voiced by others. A well-known psychiatrist in the human potentialities movement, told me after using the method for three months that he was "absolutely sold" on meditation. Sometimes he meditates while traveling. "On the way to the airport on the bus, for example, I'll turn on and come out with renewed vigor. It has changed my metabolism, given me much more energy and a positive outlook."

Another San Franciscan, who has been in the insurance business for ten years, found that, after a month with the method, "You can't lose your temper. It's very hard even to raise your voice because it jars. Prior to this I used to be rather high-strung and I could never keep up with my thoughts. Now they come one at a time and they're stronger."

When the Maharishi launched his worldwide campaign in 1958, he intended it as a ten-year program. In the tenth of those years, though his followers still did not number one percent of the world's population, transcendental meditation had gained a firm footing in the West. When at a press conference in early 1968 someone saw fit to mention that Jesus didn't use public relations men, the tiny yogi could smile as he answered, "That is why he took so many hundreds of years to be known." A couple of months later, however, it was the turn of reporters and editors to smile and laugh. Abandoned by Beatles and Beatle-lovers, Maharishi had become a target of ridicule. His reign as chief practical mystic in the West was over.

Though he had the widest appeal for a while, the Maharishi Mahesh Yogi was not the only Eastern mystic to emerge in the West in the wake of the LSD phenomenon. Quite a few others also picked up a following. Among hip young people, another popular guru was Meher Baba, whose name translates as Father of Compassion and who is believed by his followers—who call themselves Baba lovers—to be the Avatar, a reincarnation of Rama, Krishna, Buddha, Jesus and Mohammed.

Vedantists believe that the Brahman—pure consciousness, reality beyond appearances, the Godhead—sometimes becomes incarnate in the Avatar. He takes multiple forms and always, in different ways, brings the same message. However, the status of Meher Baba as the new Avatar is by no means universally acknowledged. His rather far-out appeal is to people who seek a master rather than a technique.

Baba lovers say that Meher Baba has not uttered a word since July 10, 1925. He has layed it all out in previous incarnations, they explain, and this time wants to be heard through his silence. Before he dies he will speak, and then the world will know his love. Meanwhile, however, in his seclusion in India, he seems to talk a great deal through gestures which his disciples translate into words and sometimes even publish under his name.

Sufism Reoriented, Inc., with headquarters in San Francisco, follows Meher Baba. It is headed by Murshida (teacher) Ivy Oneida Duce, the widow of an oil company executive who was an Episcopalian and a Red Cross volunteer before she became a Sufi. She still sounds and looks like a motherly church matron. Many of her students are young people who used to take acid but came to heed Baba's dictum that drugs are physically, mentally and spiritually harmful.

A pamphlet, "God in a Pill?" issued by Sufism Reoriented, states, "LSD apparently stimulates certain centers of the brain which are usually activated only as a by-product of the development of the spiritual seeker. In such a case activation is a normal process, and the seeker has then developed the capability to exercise safeguards. If these centers are artificially stimulated, the result is something like the forcing of a locked door. Then one is not certain that the door can be properly closed again."

Instead of LSD, Mrs. Duce says she offers "Meher Baba and a purpose in life. I show them why they're here and what they should do when they're here." Her students are expected to follow the master's teachings and learn to tanscend their selves so that they cease to compete and engage in conflicts and learn to live in cooperation and love with others. All rivalries and competitions, according to Meher Baba, are the result of an incomplete understanding of the unity of all life.

One young man, a graduate student who was raised as a Morman, found many lost comforts when, after LSD and wandering through various cults, he found Murshida Duce and Meher Baba. He was relieved when the Murshida told him to go back to school. Here was someone to tell him what was right once again. Here was a new Jesus to follow and obey. The one of his childhood lived so long ago that his teachings were easily misinterpreted, he figured. The new one, Meher Baba, spoke in modern idiom. This student began to spend half an hour every evening in repeating Meher Baba's name, just as, years ago, he had prayed.

Obviously there are many differences between Maharishi Mahesh Yogi, Meher Baba, and the other swamis and yogis now active on the turned-on scene. But all those who have recently come into prominence share the same basic outlook. In their various styles and metaphors, they all talk about flowing with life, of God immanent in man, of freedom from clinging to forms, structures, rituals. And they all offer some technique for self-renewal that can help to sustain the turned-on attitude. Some people will always go farther—into monasteries and more demanding disciplines. But for the many Americans who are not ready to go that deep but suffer a spiritual hunger because the mystical factor is totally missing from their lives, the practical mystics are valuable. For them, even brief daily meditation sometimes means important changes—decreased tension, expanded ability to listen, a new awareness of previously unrecognized ways of seeing. Likewise, for people who flashed to cosmic consciousness on acid but then were left floundering, gurus like the Maharishi and Murshida Duce may provide a badly needed framework for living. Just how badly that is needed was apparent one Sunday when I walked through the Haight-Ashbury and Golden Gate Park.

I intended to go to Sunday morning zazen but only made it to the Zen Center in time for the lecture that followed. Afterward, when I was putting on my shoes again outside the zendo, someone called my name. I looked up to see Chris, the Harvard graduate I met at Esalen just after his month at Tassajara.

"Chris! What happened to you? You vanished."

"Yes, the deal of working for Fritz didn't work out. So I went to Mexico for a while. Now I'll be starting at State pretty soon."

I remember he was going to the San Francisco State College graduate program in creative writing. He looks healthy and tan now. The gaunt pallor he had acquired during that month in the Zen Mountain Center is gone. But his head is still close-cropped and he still wears the same black sweater and yellow beads. We go out for a cup of coffee.

Chris is exploring the mystic scene. He not only practices zazen but also belongs to Subud, a group that meets evenings for self-realization and mystical unity and that allows no visitors and requires all prospective members to sit outside the door for a couple of months before being admitted. Next week he has an appointment with a Chinese yogi. Last week he was at the Krishna Consciousness Society.

"I'm going over there again today," he says. They have a feast very Sunday at noon. It's a real feast—all kinds of sweets and spices I'd never tasted before. After the brown rice at Tassajara it was like food for the gods. You want to come along?"

"Yes, why not? Krishna Consciousness—are they the ones who chant Hare Krishna all the time?"

"Right. That's their way of getting to pure consciousness."

We take a bus to the edge of Golden Gate Park and walk to the little storefront that is the Krishna Consciousness temple. But it's locked. A notice on the door says the feast is at four o'clock. So we decide to walk around for a while.

On Haight Street kids are flaked out on the sidewalks, bums from suburbs and colleges lying along the walls with their heads on blanket-rolls and satchels, trying to peddle grass and hash or pan-handling from the tourists. A lot of them look stoned and sickly. After Big Sur, this scene is depressing. When we wander into the park, we find a freak-out festival.

At the bottom of a hill just inside the entrance off Haight Street, a red-faced, bulbous-nosed man in a cheap suit stands waving a Bible and shouting up the hillside where hippies sprawl in the sun, nuzzling each other, sleeping, listening.

"Turn back to God! Get some purpose into your life! Jesus will save you but you have to give up these ways, you have to lead a life with a purpose."

Someone blows a horn so that it sounds like a Bronx cheer, just once. The others just let the man rave on.

We go on, through a little tunnel and onto another meadow. Here we hear chanting, drums and a drone and walk to the place it's all coming from. A crowd of maybe a hundred people is sitting and lying on the grass. In the middle of it four flags wave—Star of David, a cross, a moon and star and a yellow flag with writing I can't discipher. As we approach the sound becomes clear: "Hare Krishna, Hare Krishna, Krishna Krishna, Hare Hare, Hare Rama, Hare Rama, Rama Rama, Hare Hare." Over and over.

Just behind the flags, a young kid with an enormous brown bead necklace and an intense expression on his face is chanting into a mike. Beside him, a stoned-looking girl in a sari beats finger cymbals. Another kid is handling the drone with one hand, holding another mike with the other. This is really the same scene as the hip gypsy lawn at the Hot Springs, except that here there are more people and more instruments. "Hare Hare. . . ." The chant goes into your head for a while. It makes muscles relax until the sound begins to pour in directly, as if some screen had been knocked out inside you. I can see why that girl looks stoned. "Hare Krishna, Hare Krishna. . . ."

"Do you think it ever occurs to that guy over there, that Bible pounder, that this is religion?" Chris wonders. "He's shouting for it but here they're doing it."

"I doubt he thinks about it. This would be devilishly pagan and dissolute for him. Want to go ask him?"

But at that moment a blast of sound hits us from the back. We turn and see a jazz band, and walk over to listen. It's a small group but has a good sound, somewhere between jazz and rock and roll. Just as they start to swing, though, an elderly man with a trim gray beard and a faded blue beret takes the mike and they stop. They were playing to collect a crowd. Is this another evangelist?

The guy starts talking. "Those ionized clouds forming over there—that's from the flying saucers. You know the earthquake last week, that came from the imbalance of forces causing the earth to rock and roll. The saucers have been neutralizing the imbalance but they won't do it anymore."

His name is Allen Noonan and, it seems, he has intimate contact with the saucer people who are superior beings controlling the world. Those who are turned on can feel their vibrations, he says. He talks a mish-mosh with echoes of militant pacifism, civil rights, all kinds of liberalism interwoven somehow into the thing now going on, the hip acid thing.

"We're coming into a world where we hold all things in common. We're gonna rise up against fear and overcome it because there is no enemy. The enemy is in ourselves. We're gonna get the police on our side—of course there are no sides ['a problem, that,' says Chris. 'Funny how that does become a hangup.'] but we will get them to support us.

"Next door is another organization." Noonan nods toward the Hare Krishna group. "They've been sitting there all day long but they haven't directed their energies. . . . The Messiah is already turned on . . . Steve, you want to say something?"

At this point the French horn player takes the mike. He's a good-looking fellow, in his late twenties perhaps, dressed in light brown corduroy trousers, cotton-velvet shirt of the same color, with an amber chain around his neck. Black shiny hair falls over his forehead over shining brown eyes. He tucks his horn under his right arm and takes the mike in his left. But —can I be seeing right?—in that same hand, together with the mike, he is holding an unlit joint. He stands there with the eyes of the crowd on him, in the middle of the park, with a joint in his hand, oblivious, apparently, of the fact that people *do* get arrested for possession of grass.

But when he starts to talk it all fits together—this guy is under the Messiah's protection. For the Messiah Allen Noonan just referred to is Allen Noonan.

"Three months ago I was standing on the street wondering where my next joint was coming from and I didn't know the Messiah," Steve says. "Then I started to work for him and for weeks I still didn't know. Since then I've been aboard a spacecraft. . . ."

The guy seems to believe what he's saying. "LSD was given by the highest spiritual forces to release all that energy. The truth about acid is that it's a tool for unleashing energy." And he goes on about the spacecraft, and about how the space command took him out of his body and showed him telepathy. "The twelfth dimension is being beamed in by the spacecraft . . . those who are turned on can hear. See those clouds over there? They're formed because of the ionization of the atmosphere at the passage of the spacecraft."

Chris turns to look. Then he says, "Let's go." As we walk off Steve is talking about the Messiah's plan, which seems to be to turn everyone on to acid, and invites everyone to come to the Here and Now macrobiotic restaurant, which is just down the street from the I and Thou coffee shop. The whole scene strikes me as a distorted reflection of Fritz Perls and my acid trip.

"You know," says Chris as we walk toward a nearby group to listen to Afro-Cuban drums, "I could almost see those spacecraft. That guy makes me want to subscribe to *Scientific American*. I'd like to have those experiences—it would be groovy to go aboard a spacecraft—but I'm afraid if I let it happen I'd believe it. The world has been like this for centuries. Are we going back to that, do you think, or are we going on?"

"Both ways, from what I see. I've met a lot of people who have gone from acid to superstition and a lot of others who've really learned with it. Perlsian polarities again."

"Yeah. Master Suzuki says you can't get illumination through the intellect but it's better to have a good intellect than none. I guess what you do with the experience depends on what you bring to it."

We wander back through the tunnel to where the fire and brimstone Bible man was. Now he'd been replaced by another speaker, a bushy-headed, wild-bearded fellow dressed in gray bermudas, gray and white-checked short-sleeved sport shirt, gray sneakers, gray socks—a square's clothes. But a godseye dangles from his top buttonhole and yellow beads are around the neck. He's standing on a metal milk-bottle rack and holding a mike. Beside him stands a shopping cart with a loudspeaker from the mike inside and a neatly lettered small poster: "Ashleigh Brilliant, P.O. Box 1485, Personal Platform for responsible freedom of speech and pursuit of happiness." We stop to listen to him.

He's talking about a girl named Barbara, who, it seems, refuses to see him. "I wish you would go and explain to her," he says. "I understand that we've both changed but I still care for her. If she would only send some small sign that she also cares for me—that's all I ask. I want us to be friends. I don't want to break up her marriage. If necessary I'll be friends with her husband too."

Incredible. This fellow is acting out the fantasy of every

200

rejected lover. He's actually standing there pleading his case with the world. He's down there addressing The People sprawled on the grass.

"I know that trip," Chris says.

"Anyone have any questions?" Lover asks, smiling up the hill. Chris raises his right hand and is recognized.

"Why don't you give up?" he asks.

"I have given up," says Lover. "I haven't seen this girl for five years."

"But why don't you let go and go on?"

"You mean forget about her? Not think about her? I can't do that, that's impossible!"

He pulls a sheet of paper from his pocket and reads off the girl's name and address. "The song 'The Girl I Left in Berkeley,' in my song book is dedicated to her. I don't even know if she's happy. If, say, twenty-five of you would contact her this afternoon, that would be fine, that might help."

Lover is an effective speaker. I can see him chairing a meeting of some organization. He's completely clear in his madness. People ask questions, he answers. It's the ultimate in hip openness and group therapy I'm witnessing—a surreal scene.

From somewhere on the right, three boys in blue jeans and white shirts approach Lover. They are holding a sheet of white cloth on which is stamped three times in black "Vote For Me." Silently they approach and stand to Lover's right, looking at him. He doesn't see them, absorbed in pleading his case. They step behind him and squat, holding the sign like a backdrop to his milkrack platform. They don't speak and don't smile. After a while they walk away toward the tunnel. The sign would go as well behind the acid Messiah and the Bible yeller as behind this fellow. Vote for me. Golden Gate Park is the living theater of the surreal.

It's nearly four o'clock by now and we head toward the Krishna Consciousness place for the feast. Inside the little blue and white storefront we find a crowd of people sitting on a faded Oriental rug. A transparent plastic runner has been laid lengthwise in the middle of the room. On it stand bottles and jugs filled with asters. People are sitting cross-legged facing the runner, some on pillows, others on the rug.

Against the back wall a blue curtain has been hung. Through an opening in it I see some painted Indian statues. In front of it stand huge bowls of crumpets, rice, bananas and other food. Women in saris are ladling out the food into paper plates and sending the plates down the runner where people place them edge to edge. "Hare Krishna. . . ." More people come in, filling the place wall-to-wall. When the entire runner is covered with plates of food, the chanting stops. Someone speaks a few words about the temptations of the tongue and of rich food. But this food is good, he says, because it's a Krishna feast.

It is, indeed, very good. On each plate there's rice, watermelon, a few grapes, a few pieces of banana, a round biscuit with curry inside, a few round sugary balls, a banana and nut cookie. At the end of the meal, a jar is passed around and some people drop a little change into it. But there is no pressure and the jar doesn't even make it halfway around the room. The free feasts are part of the religious practice of the sari-clad chanters.

This is only one of several places where free food is to be had in the Haight. The Diggers serve a daily meal in the park and distribute food contributed by merchants and individuals to communes and groups. More food is offered than the Diggers can manage to pick up and give away. This is a fat land.

And yet, in this fat land, there is the craving for something indefinably mssing. Chris, and I, and a lot of the people at Tassajara, and Esalen and Morningstar have been traveling around in search of that elusive absent something. A lot of the people we've seen today, who seem mad or far-out, must be driven by the same hunger.

We stop at the I and Thou coffee shop and there I meet someone who is just about to embark, perhaps, on a similar quest. At first, when she comes up to the table where we're sitting, I can't remember her name. She's a college classmate I haven't seen for twelve years. But I do remember her smile —she was always smiling in this same fixed way.

"Molly?"

"Right."

She introduces her companion and they sit down with us.

"I've been wandering around. My friend wanted to see the Haight-Ashbury. Actually, I haven't been here myself for many months and I'm shocked—it's so dirty. All that dog shit on the sidewalks. It's really awful."

Molly has been teaching at Berkeley for the past several years. But right now, it develops, she's between things. Last spring she got a job offer from a Midwestern University, which meant financial and professional advancement. She didn't want to go to the Midwest and was luke-warm about teaching, but she accepted because she saw no good reason not to.

Then Molly took a summer vacation in Canada and had such a good time there that, she says, she did a foolish thing on impulse. She wrote a letter to the Midwestern university saying she would not come after all. It was an act committed in a moment of abandon. She was having such a good time up in Canada that she lost her perspective. But now, when it was too late to change her mind, she was panicked. Just the thought of waking up in the morning and not knowing what she was going to do during the day scared her.

"Do you like teaching?" I ask.

"I left Berkeley because I was doing a bad job. The students kept saying I was teaching as if I didn't know *why* what I was teaching should be taught," she says, smiling. "They were right."

"What would you like to do instead?"

"I don't know. Maybe I'll write some articles for the journal. The credits would look good on my resume."

"You prefer to write?"

"Not really. But it would be useful professionally." She is still smiling.

"What for, if you don't like teaching?" I ask. "Sounds to me like that was sanity, not madness, what you did in Canada. Why don't you try something new, find out what you want?"

She shrugs.

"But Molly, you're only thirty-two and you're single. Why should you do something you're bored with? Weren't you Phi Beta? You can do a million things!"

I try to tell her about Esalen. But I see it sounds mushy-headed to her. She considers herself a capable person, an intellectual who can use her head to figure out her life. I understand her reaction, it would have been my own a few months ago. Yet Molly is ready to be turned on. She is ready to take the first step. The chaos on Haight Street and in the Park put her off. The Maharishi Mahesh Yogi would put her off. She'd certainly never go to Morningstar and probably not to Tassajara. But an encounter group—maybe. I start to tell her about Bill Schutz's truth lab, to which I was sent on a magazine assignment, went with a negative attitude, and which turned out to be my first step toward this whole trip.

Chapter TWELVE

More Joy

THE LITTLE I had been told in advance put me off at the same time as it intrigued me. I was to go to a house in the country, meet thirteen strangers, and spend two days with them trying to be completely open and honest about everything that happened between us. We were to talk, move, touch each other and through all that somehow become free in mind, body and spirit and capable of more joy.

Before taking this trip I went to see Dr. William C. Schutz, the leader, in the West Side Manhattan apartment where he was staying at the time. He looked like some yogis I'd seen in photographs—bald, the remaining hair shaven, relaxed and distant. He sat back in a deep leather chair with a glass of orange juice in his hand, fixed me with his pale green eyes and explained the theory behind these weekends he calls "More Joy Workshops."

"Joy is the feeling you get when you realize your potential," he said. "It comes natural to infants but later, under the stresses of life, we lose much of it." The weekend was to be a combination of therapy and education to liberate perception and emotion and expand the capacity for experience and, therefore, for joy.

All that sounded to me like a lot of psychological wishful thinking, particularly since Schutz himself did not strike me as a joyful person. His eyes seemed cold. The way he held his head suggested severity. To be sure, his credentials were good. At age forty-one he was a psychologist who taught at the Albert Einstein College of Medicine, at Harvard, the University of Chicago and the University of California. He had run workshops in New York, Bethel, Maine, on Big Sur, in Boston, and even in Nigeria. He had a book coming out called *Joy*. His techniques, he said, came from the creative arts, particularly dance and drama, from psychotherapy and group dynamics, and from Eastern religions, especially Zen. He said he used nonverbal methods a lot because most people are skilled in using words to hide experience from themselves and others.

The following Saturday, a windy spring morning, I made my way to a rambling white Victorian house on a hill overlooking the Hudson River, where I found the other participants already assembled.

We were seven men and seven women, ranging in age between the mid-twenties and the mid-fifties. Several people knew each other from other workshops or as colleagues—fully half the group consisted of psychologists and human relations experts here to learn from Schutz. The rest were in business, teaching or other professions. Only three of us had never been to a truth lab before.

We settled in a circle on couches and chairs in the high-ceilinged living room and Schutz began:

"Why don't we start by giving our first impressions of each other."

Nobody moved for a couple of minutes. Then a pudgy fellow of about thirty-five leaped up and positioned himself in front of the window like a prisoner before a thirteen-judge court. We saw him in silhouette for a moment, then someone drew the drapes and the face became clearer. His wide lips were fixed in an uncertain quarter smile, his head was bent forward like a victim's, his feet were planted firmly but the arms dangled helplessly at his sides.

"He's much better than last time. He looks happier," someone said.

"He's scared and worried about himself," I said and immediately regretted having said it. "As who isn't?" I added. A burst of laughter broke the tension in the room. Well, I thought, this could be fun. Charades.

As they stepped up one after another to be examined and judged, I began to understand what Schutz meant when he told me, "Sometimes these groups turn on too, without drugs." I seemed to see each person better than the last. Never before had I seen strangers so clearly.

Phil, tall and skinny, in his mid-fifties, looked like a slap-on-the-back type with that saggy reddish face and hearty manner. But there was something else too. Effeminacy? No, something blurred but attractive. It made me reserve judgment. Others, who knew him from a previous weekend, said he had changed a lot but that some of his obnoxious manner still hung on.

Bob was soft lumpishness, vagueness, an innocuous bumbler

who saved himself by laughter. Chuck—alert, boyish, wiry and tense. Irma, plump and motherly, would be so solicitous you'd gasp for air. Karen was timid and sleepily pretty; she drooped as she stood like a broken-stemmed flower. Mary's delicate face was taut, her mouth smiled with a learned sweetness, her eyes had cried a lot, probably in secret.

By the time half the group had been up, my concentration began waning. If I didn't get up now, I thought, they might be too tired to be attentive. So I rose, hoping that my mouth wouldn't start to twitch as I faced them.

Thirteen pairs of eyes pinned me. I had a terrific urge to say something funny to distract them but realized that would be a copout. Nothing twitched. But could they see through me, I wondered. Could they tell I was a phony?

"Her body is sexy but I don't know about her face. It seems separate," some man said.

"She says something and then flicks it off, puts a phrase to it and is on to something else." Ugh—yeah—a dilettante.

"She's so attractive and yet no one comes up and hugs her. She keeps us off somehow."

A man came up and embraced me. It was awkward and my spine was frozen, so I responded only halfway. More comments were made. At last I sat down. The confrontation had melted the stiffness between us and now I could watch more at ease. I felt I had gotten away with something, though with what I didn't know. Mike, David, Sara; Jill, then Mona, a thirtyish teacher who spoke with great control as if she were holding back some very violent emotion. She had come up several times to melt petitely into various men's arms, always the same way, like a puppet. It was now, when Mona was up, that the action got rolling.

From the back of the room a cold voice spoke. "She's a bitch." I turned to look at Jill, a pixyish young woman whom I had liked right away. She had a good laugh, she was bright, perceptive and enthusiastic. But now I saw only fury in her clear brown eyes. Mona stared at her, then lost her cool. "That's all right," she said slowly, " 'cause I think you're a bitch too." Then she sat down.

Schutz stood up last. I had been wary of him before, but now, suddenly, I disliked him intensely. People were saying he was sympathetic, understanding, kind.

"A little boy."

"Someone you can trust."

It made me angry to hear them say such things. The cold bastard. "Not at all, I wouldn't trust him one bit," I found myself saying. "Why does he have his head shaved? Trying to look like some guru! It's phony. What's he doing to people? He sits there so detached, and gets a kick out of this show he'll make us put on." My virulence surprised me, so that I didn't even hear what was said next. Some man went up to Schutz to comfort him with an embrace.

By the time we had all been presented we were loosened and ready to move to the joy music. But it was still unclear just how far we could go with this openness. Schutz took care of that question by asking Jill and Mona to walk toward each other from opposite ends of the room and do what they felt like doing when they were face to face.

They started walking. High Noon for more joy! What would they do? Shake hands? They no doubt felt ashamed by now about that "bitch" episode. After all, they had just met.

They stopped maybe four feet apart. Jill reached out, yanked on Mona's sweater and simultaneously kicked her in the pants with her left knee. Mona pushed her off, then stuck out her right hand. Jill stepped back and began to scream:

"Nah! I won't shake hands with you, you bitch, you don't know what you do to people, always manipulating, twisting them around, playing your little games. I know your kind, you . . . !"

She wasn't screaming at Mona, it was someone else she saw there. Her mother. The girl seemed half mad.

"You boy," Mona replied evenly, with contempt. "You're not a girl, you're a boy."

Suddenly they were down, rolling on the floor. Jill had Mona around the middle with her legs, she had Mona's head down on the floor. My God, what was this? Schutz and some others were hovering over them, others had moved out of the way. Nobody stopped them. But then Mona went limp. Of course, why should she fight? I liked her. No, not anymore. Ten minutes ago I liked her but now her face was distorted and ugly. But it wasn't her fault! Still, my heart went out to Jill.

By the time they got up—Jill's hand-knit blue sweater was ripped—and we went to lunch, the tone had been set for the rest of the weekend. I was thinking that I'd certainly have a good story to write, but I was also shaken and a little frightened.

During lunch we chatted. It was as if by going from living to dining room we had crossed the border from some strange country whose strange customs we were just learning, back into the world we knew. We sat stiffly at the long table, with oil portraits of someone's stern ancestors staring down at us.

After lunch we returned to the living room. The drapes had been pulled back and sunlight streamed through the windows.

"I have no more suggestions," Schutz said. "It's up to you now."

For what seemed like ten minutes there was silence. Irma got up to get cigarettes from a nearby table. Bob took off his shoes. Chuck, the tense boyish one, moved from chair to floor. We were all tense and curious. Then Jill jumped up, bolted across the room and installed herself in Chuck's lap. She began to whisper in his ear.

We were relieved that someone was at last doing something, but she made us uncomfortable, behaving that way. Mike said, "Jill, what are you doing?"

"I'm trying to get close to him," she said, little-girl-cute, "only I'm scared he'll get mad." She tossed her head toward Schutz. Then she began clowning, like a spoiled child provoking her father. For a while we laughed but then the comedy began to turn grotesque and we became distressed at the desperate way she was playing the fool. People started telling her to stop. But she kept on, as if waiting for someone to stop her or punch her. Finally Schutz said, "Jill, I think you should leave the room for ten minutes." She went immediately.

We turned to Dave, a pale, tired-looking man whose gentleness struck me as deadness. He was gentle, I thought, and worked hard to be kind because he was so weary he could no longer give or take anything more. His smile was sad and seemed to appear through an upward tug of strings attached to the corners of the mouth.

Dave wanted to talk about something but didn't dare, or couldn't. Schutz suggested that "breaking out" might help. Six men linked arms surrounding Dave in a human-walled cell. We women moved out of the way. Dave pushed and pulled; the twelve-legged prison swayed about within the circle of couches and chairs. The furniture. That lamp! A floor lamp crashed and broke under the human mass.

In surges the battle went on until Dave was puffing and panting. He stopped, sat down between all those legs and smiled—a real, stringless smile. Then he got up and began to fight in a new way, punching and kicking with no more regard to where the blows fell. And he was out.

Flushed and exhilarated, he sank into a couch and began to talk. The technique had worked. By breaking out, he had overcome not only a physical obstacle but also, somehow, the emotional one that held him back from speaking as he wished.

I was seeing all this as if I were high. Afterward, at home, it would probably all seem absurd, but this was the way the world was now. Strange things were happening in this room and in my head and they all seemed perfectly natural. But the night's big drama was yet to come.

After dinner there was first a little talk that didn't go anywhere. I told Phil I couldn't fit that good-Joe Kiwanis part with the rest of him. He had been emerging as a thoughtful, perceptive person throughout the day.

"Well, I'm trying to change," he said. "This is all very new to me. A few months ago I didn't know anything about this sort of thing. It was 'How are you?' and 'That's great.' There weren't any problems because there wasn't *anything*. Then I realized that I'd been living a fraud. I'm trying to change now. It's late at my age, but I'm changing. This is my second time here and I don't think I want to say much more just now. I took up a lot of the group's time last session."

Then it began. We all probably knew dimly that Jill was building up to something. That fight with Mona, that little-girl business after lunch, was clearly only a beginning and an explosion was inevitable. But if anyone had told me that Phil was the one who would force her to explode I would not have believed it.

Now Jill was chiding Irma for her motherliness. "You're always going around taking care of people. What's the matter with you? Aren't *you* worth taking care of?" What she was saying made sense but she was very wrought up. Phil kept saying, "Sit down, Jill," but she ignored him. Finally Phil's tone changed from tolerant-gentle to firm. "Jill, let's wrestle," he said. "I've known I'd have to wrestle you since you came in that door this morning."

Jill stopped short. "You didn't. How'd you know that?"

Phil rose, they faced each other and began to shadowbox. Then Jill slapped Phil and he grabbed her. He got her down on the floor. She was fighting like a wild animal. "You queen!" she screamed. "You goddamn queen! I've had enough of you queens. Get away from me!"

But Phil was coming on like a man. He got her legs down and pinned her. She kept screaming but he was talking to her: "Help me, Jill. I want to help you." And over and over like an incantation: "You can help me and I can help you."

"I don't want to help you, you fucking queen," she screeched, tossing her head from side to side. "Get away, I'm tired of helping everybody!"

Finally she stopped struggling. Phil let her go and returned to his chair. She stayed on her back in the middle of the room, weeping. Schutz came up to her, held her ankles a moment, then brought her some wine. She sat up, buried her head in her arms and began to sob. Schutz got on his knees in front of her, bent over her, put his head against hers. When she looked up her face was puffy. She was a woman in her thirties now, nothing of the coy little girl was left. Directly in front of her she saw Mona, her enemy.

"What do you know," Jill said. "The first thing I see is the bitch."

At this Mona started crying, Karen started crying, Mary started crying. I looked around and for a moment I felt like laughing—but only for a moment—for here was Jill going through all this for some desperate reason. I wanted to help her but was a bit scared she'd push me away. I got up from my chair, came up to her and sat there a moment. Now I was in the middle, with Jill. Everyone else was at a distance, sitting in a circle and looking. Only Schutz, Jill and I were out here. I put my arm around her shoulders.

"I want to be your friend, Jill," I said. The words, once out, embarrassed and scared me. They were a commitment.

"Why? What do you want from me? Do you want sex or what?"

Good God, what had I gotten myself into? But I couldn't pull back now.

"No, I don't want sex with you," I said, keeping my arm around her shoulder. "I just figured you might need a friend." Then I got up and brought her some more wine. She wiped her nose with the back of her hand and started to talk about men and how they only wanted sex from her for one night, and how everyone was always playing games, and how, since men wanted nothing but sex, she'd had sex with girls who wanted affection too. But she'd rather have a man and get married. Her mother, "the bitch, wouldn't give the old man nothing," she said, so he wanted it from her instead. Now Mona was just like her mother and Schutz just like her father who didn't want her to be with boys other than him.

Phil couldn't bear it. He got up, staggered toward the door, hid his face against the wall. His shoulders trembled. Mary went over to him. Meanwhile, Schutz took the role Jill wanted him to play, as he had done in the morning when he sent her out of the room. He held her hands and told her, "I want you to like the other boys. I want you to go to them now." He motioned to the men to approach. All did except Phil, who sensed she wouldn't want him near her now.

Jill made Schutz repeat what he had said, then let the men take turns holding her. She became the clown again. After asking Dave to unbutton his shirt she said, "Hey, that's nice. That's the greatest stomach I've ever seen. Pretty different on top."

We all laughed with her. But this was too classic. This girl had to be sick. What was she doing at a weekend that was supposed to be for normal people—or normal neurotics—anyway?

"What's going to happen to Jill when she goes home?" I asked Schutz as we broke up at one in the morning.

"She'll be all right, don't worry," he said.

Jill was in the same room with me. She fell asleep like a baby with her arms above her head the moment she hit her bed. The next morning I was amazed. She was calm and relaxed and even teased Phil about his "pretty pink shirt"—Phil was proud and delighted—and took part in things without asking to be the star of the show. Now she didn't seem any sicker than anyone else I knew. Perhaps last night was what she needed. Perhaps we all carried some sort of hell inside us that would look as sick as hers if it were uncovered.

The second day turned out to be athletic. Two of the men wrestled Bill (to test their masculinity, it seemed) and lost. One of the women attacked another and, in the fight, broke two toes. It began to get monotonous and, I thought, rather inane. I kept thinking that until, in the midst of something I was saying, Jill came across the room, grabbed my ankles and wiped up the floor with me. I had never fought a girl in my life. She locked her arms around my belly. I tried to get out, couldn't do it, gave up.

"All right, Jill, let go. I don't want to fight you."

"Does it hurt?" She tightened her leg lock.

"Let go!" I couldn't breathe. It hurt all right. I began to feel nauseous.

"It hurts, ah? It hurts?"

"Let go, Jill." Was this some Lesbian kick for her? I refused to have any part of it. "Let go!" I was trying to sound firm and cool but it came out like a scream. She let go.

When I sat up I realized first that Jill and I were now friends. Whatever I had been saying before wasn't making sense to her and, by attacking me, she was trying to shake me out of the senselessness. A little later I realized that I took the easy way out by not fighting back, just the way Mona had when she stopped fighting yesterday. Still later I reflected on how much self-pity there is in taking the easy way out.

It was six o'clock now; the end was in sight. Everyone except Phil had had the group's attention for a longish interval during the twenty-five waking hours we had spent together. Now Phil spoke up with an urgent plea.

"I want to ask the group to help me. I have a very difficult situation I'll be going to and I want to take the group with me. Would you mind rolling me around a bit?" Rolling him around?

"First, before we do that, let's talk a bit," Schutz said. (Later, he explained to me that the rolling and rocking technique helps to bolster people who feel deprived of affection. But, like the other techniques he uses, it only works if used at the right moment. He wanted to build a better connection between Phil and the group.)

So now this tall, middle-aged man, a successful and prosperous businessman, who was so wise and kind with Jill last night, walked to the center of the room. There, to my astonished dismay, he fell on his knees and elbows, buried his head and began to cry. People moved in around him and stroked him. Jill stared, scared.

"I'll tell you, it's Jill," he said. "It's not that she called me a queen, I know I'm not, but it's that today she ignored me and after what happened last night I was hurt. I wanted to help her last night and now that she's changed she won't have anything to do with me."

Jill was silent.

"Jill, would you be willing to go up to Phil and do what you feel like doing?" Schutz asked.

She looked thoughtful a moment, then an impish look came over her. "All right, let's go," she said. She put her arms out and grinned. "Let's dance."

What a conclusion! They waltzed around the room, smiling at each other. However, this scene wasn't following theatrical principles. Phil needed something more. He stopped dancing, closed his eyes, crossed his arms on his chest, hunched his shoulders and once more began to cry. Again people surrounded him, patting and stroking. I came up too, for during the past two days I had come to like him a lot—that jolly-good-fellow aspect of him seemed to have vanished entirely —and I admired him for the struggle he was making. I put my arms around him and pressed my cheek to his chest.

After a while the group formed a circle and passed Phil, who went limp, from hand to hand, round and round. Then many hands lifted him in horizontal position and rocked him gently, very gently, and lowered him to the floor. When he rose and said thank you, I was sure he would be all right. I was also sure that nobody in his office on Wall Street would

212

ever believe he had ever done what he did this weekend. It was now six o'clock.

What had happened? In that short time we had become intimates. I now had real affection for some people here; others I disliked, still others I did not know any better than before. For Schutz I had developed trust and respect. He was an able practitioner for he had made things happen and had kept them from blowing us to pieces. All of us, together, were now a community suspended in space and time. I did not want to leave these people who only yesterday were total strangers.

We said good-bye with embraces. I rode into the city with Phil and a couple of others. We met their wives and had dinner together, gradually returning to our accustomed lives. But when I finally got home late that evening and closed my door behind me, I was seized with uncontrollable shaking. My teeth chattered, my knees knocked together. I was exhausted and the creeping horrors were closing in. Was this more joy? Where had I been? Had I really taken part in all that?

That weekend was my first step on the trip that led me to Esalen, on the LSD trip, to Morningstar, Tassajara and unexplored regions within myself. After I got a good night's sleep I experienced that sense of heightened perception and diffuse inner freedom that was so strong some months later, after the LSD trip. But I also had misgivings, at first, about the weekend. "Isn't it dangerous to go this deep on a one-shot weekend?" I asked Schutz.

"If someone knows how to run the workshop, the deeper you go the safer it is," he replied. "If you go deep the group gets close. People begin caring for each other and supporting each other. The leader has many assistants then. Generally I see one or two in each group afterward, individually. I'm available but I'm not used much. If they seem to need something more I usually direct them to another workshop." It was important to remember, he said, that the weekends were not intended as therapy but as occasions for normal people to increase their emotional and intellectual understanding.

"With all that violence and anguish—normal?"

"If you get anyone to this deep a level you'll get at least this much," he said.

I spoke afterward with several of the people who took part in that weekend and all of them told me they were glad they had gone. Chuck soon thereafter decided to leave a frustrating job and do something he liked better. Jill noticed many changes in herself and said others had noticed them too.

Dave felt the experience had improved his work because he was now more aware of his inner state. I myself could not pinpoint the weekend's effects, because so many new experiences followed soon after. However, I found myself recommending Schutz's workshops to all kinds of friends and acquaintances.

When I went to another truth lab just after I got to Esalen, it proved a disappointment; partly because I was not in the mood for it then, partly because the group failed to come anywhere near the dynamic intensity of that first one with Schutz.

"At the end of these labs I often have mixed feelings," Schutz told me. "There's exhilaration and warmth, for this is what human relations could be like. And then I have a feeling—how pathetic that we need workshops like this. What happens in them should be a way of life."

Chapter THIRTEEN

Love Labs and Hate Labs

ON THE West Coast, truth labs are so widespread they have become a social institution. Many people live more or less nomadically—all over urban America and especially in California—and their neighbors, friends and even marriage partners keep changing. They have no stable community to rely on. So the truth labs, offering instant intimacy and instant belonging, become a substitute. In times of transition, as just before or after divorce, they provide emotional support and a chance to make new acquaintances. Attended regularly, they can be emotional gyms for reinforcing and practicing turned-on attitudes. Many people use them in the same way that Joanie Summer uses her LSD trips.

Like all turn-on games, the truth labs aim at developing self-style and expanding awareness. The basic idea is that a group of people gathered for a weekend, a week, or a regular session, shall respond to each other with complete candor in the context of the here and now. This process creates a mirror game. Reflection and reality comingle in multiple images showing oneself and others in new perspectives. One becomes aware of the flow of change and realizes that what one is changes from moment to moment, with the changing context. The illusion that anyone or anything is ever separate disappears.

These groups come in different formats and with different names. Dr. Carl Rogers, a key figure in the Human Potentialities movement, calls them basic encounter groups or intensive group experiences. They are also known as personal growth groups or workshops. One variety, offered by the Synanon Foundation, is the Synanon game. Another, developed by Drs. George R. Bach and Frederick Stoller in Los Angeles, is the marathon, which usually meets nonstop for twenty-four hours or more. I call all of these groups truth labs because they are all concerned with the search for authenticity and meaning.

Truth labs grew out of group therapy and the T-groups or sensitivity training groups that were first conducted in 1947 at the National Training Laboratories of the National Education Association in Bethel, Maine. In the T-groups, which are now widespread through business and industry, the focus is on individuals as they relate to others in some organization. In group therapy, the focus is generally on overcoming emotional problems and neuroses. In the truth labs, the focus is on expansion and personal growth. However, the dividing lines are sometimes blurred, for the T-groups become truth labs if they go deep enough; therapy, if successful, also leads to expanded awareness and personal growth, and truth labs often must deal with emotional problems before they get to further possibilities.

Little research has been done on the groups' effects and they are controversial. Carl Rogers has found that they lead people toward becoming "more spontaneous, flexible, closely related to their feelings, open to their experience, and closer and more expressively intimate in their interpersonal relationships." In a paper, "The Process of the Basic Encounter Group," prepared at the Western Behavioral Sciences Institute, he wrote, "If we value this type of behavior, then clearly the group process is a valuable process. If, on the other hand, we place a value on the individual who is effective in suppressing his feelings, who operates from a firm set of principles, who does not trust his own reactions and experience but relies on authority, who remains aloof in his interpersonal relationships, then we would regard the group process . . . as a dangerous force. Clearly there is room for a difference of opinion on this value question and not everyone in our culture would give the same answer."

In following up with questionnaires 425 people who were in his groups during one year, Dr. Rogers found that, two to twelve months later, 65 percent felt the experience "had made a continuing positive difference in their behavior." There had been changes, but only temporarily, in 16 percent; 15 percent saw no change, and two people did not like the changes they observed in themselves.

Lack of statistically documented evidence of the labs' usefulness, however, did not prevent their widening popularity. By 1968, they were running in universities, churches, special centers, therapists' offices, homes. In most of them, people sat in circles and talked. In some, they also used sensory awareness, movement, music, clay and paints, psychodrama, and other nonverbal self-games. Some of the labs were gentle and might be called love labs, others—especially Synanon's—worked more like sledgehammers and could qualify as hate labs. But whatever the form or technique, they all led toward attitudes associated with the turned-on style of life, at least toward the yin-yang principle and paired opposites.

With the yin-yang principle, one becomes aware of a movement in nature like the swing of a pendulum. But as awareness continues to widen, the pendulum flips over and the movement is that of a wheel on which all points are equal, there is no beginning or end, and opposites cease to exist (as in a mandala). At this point the self and the universe are one, the interdependency of all existences ceased to be an abstract concept and becomes an experiential reality. The statement "Thou are God" becomes relevant.

Most truth labs are not powerful enough set-breakers to get the pendulum movement to flip. But they lead toward that point. Many people who begin with a truth lab later move toward meditation or mystical groups. Ministers and priests have begun to organize them in churches.

A unique expression of the link between truth labs and religion is San Francisco Venture, a loosely knit community in the form of a network of ongoing encounter groups. It is a religious community because its leaders keep in mind that I-Thou meetings lead to questions that are usually called spiritual. Aside from that, religion is not much talked about and theological words are avoided.

Venture is quartered in a slightly shabby Victorian house on the fringe of the Fillmore ghetto. About 150 people come there once or twice a week for potluck supper and truth labs. They also listen to music, paint, do sensory awareness and meditate together, and spend occasional weekends encountering in a country retreat.

Venture members tend to be, like most people along the turn-on curcuit, middle-class. For most of them, earning a living is no problem. They gather to find out what else there is to life. Many are attracted and titillated by hippies but find them too far-out. Even if they wanted to become hip, they would not know how to go about it. So Venture becomes a small, safe step in that general direction.

I visit Venture on the first meeting of the fall year and join a group called "To Choose Life," led by John Levy and Jane Rhyne and composed of a dozen people who will spend the next eighteen weeks examining values, decisions and choices. Levy begins by asking whoever wants to do so to say something about some crucial choice in his life.

"I just follow the same old routine," says a proper-looking old lady with bluish white hair and a dark, tailored suit. "Too many things involve my four children, my dog, my job. I should be correcting papers tonight but I thought I'd try something different."

"I just follow the same lack of routine," says a younger woman with hair pulled back in a bun and wearing a folksy skirt and blouse. "Just like I've always done, I fly around looking for the next mess to get into. I need someone to talk things over with. I don't have children, like you."

"Oh, they're all gone, the children, and the dog is in the car," replies the old lady. "I have no one to talk things over with."

"That's one of the terrors of our society," says someone.

"Nothing but loneliness," says the old lady.

A slump-shouldered middle-aged man speaks up. "I work in an office, a large office. Do I want to do this for the rest of my life? No. But I don't do anything about it. The secondary benefits are good. I'm pretty close to some people but. . . ." His voice fades.

"Do you expect to be in the same company a year from now?" a woman asks.

"Yes," he says, apologetic, uneasy.

"It sounds just luke-warm, just a job," a man says.

"Not bad, just second-best," adds a woman.

During the next eighteen weeks, this man will be made to examine his attitude and either look for another job or seek creative satisfaction with it somehow. In the process, he might lose his lethargy and open up to new experience. As if to encourage him now, a teacher says:

"I was bored stiff with an education course I was taking at State. And I thought I should do something about it. The first thing that occurred to me was that if we sat in a circle instead of in rows with our backs to each other, something might happen. But every time I decided to suggest that, my hands would start shaking, my heart would beat very fast. But I had picked up some things at Venture and I was determined to use them. So finally I did it, and it changed the whole group. Other people started coming up with suggestions, we turned it into a course with a lot of discussion, and I enjoyed it and learned a great deal those six weeks."

John Levy, a rather formal, dry man who is one of the founders of Venture, offers his crucial choice:

"Ten years ago I decided to get out of the construction business and do this kind of work. I'd been following the American dream pretty much down the line. I was going to be president of this company and for that I was putting a lot of things aside. It got to where it looked like I was making it. I was very excited and caught up in what I was doing. I love competition. I knew it was a game, but it was a good game.

"But I had a lot of anxiety. I thought I should do something more worthwhile. So finally I left the company, feeling noble and covering that up with a lot of humility. I was noble and dutiful and dishonest. Because after I made that decision to leave it dawned on me that I was doing exactly what I wanted to do. I had played this game out. I had lived up to my father's dream and there was no place to go from there, it was a dead end. If someone had thrown that at me then I would have said they didn't know what they were talking about. So now I'm very interested in being more aware of what I'm doing and less dishonest."

This is the first meeting, so people are mostly polite to each other, feeling out the situation. But confrontations begin, even so.

The lonely old lady speaks again. "My life was worthwhile. I had a husband and three children and I divorced him, I married again and had another child and left him. But we were so busy, I and my children, I was alive. Now they're gone and I'm not living anymore."

A fat man in his thirties turns to the old lady. "You talk about your life being great before, where actually it was pretty shitty. All you lived for were your children and there's more to life than that. You were gutless."

A woman turns to him and attacks the fat man for speak-

218

ing that way to the old lady, but another man jumps to his defense, for he senses the old lady was not being honest with herself or the group. She sits, straight and nonchalant, smoking a cigarette.

"It doesn't hurt me," she says.

"He made a pretty telling comment on your life," another woman says.

"It only hurts if you listen," the fat man says, bitterly. "If someone other than a fat slob had said that she would have listened."

"You called yourself a slob—why?"

Now the focus is on the fat man. The group has passed the preliminaries and moved into the here and now of a basic encounter. Before the meeting ends, Jane turns to the old lady. "I throw you a challenge," she says. "If you were alive with your children and aren't now, was Frank right? Did you live only through them?"

It is gently asked, and next week or the week after, it might be asked another way. Compared to a lot of other groups, Venture is mild—deceptively mild, according to Mike Murphy, Esalen's president. For a lot happens in these meetings after potluck. Many, like the old lady, come out of boredom and loneliness. But the groups will not simply pat and soothe them. Levy told me that after they become acquainted there is a tendency to stop at acceptance and closeness. But the leaders try to coax them further, so that nobody leaves the eighteen-week sessions without having taken some step forward. That might mean any number of things. For the teacher, it meant speaking up with a suggestion to transform a boring course. For the old lady, it might be the end of self-pity and the start of a life that will give her more than the memories of her children and the affection of her dog.

Venture began in 1963, when Levy and six others—including a minister, a lawyer and another businessman—broke away from Sequoia Seminar, a Stanford-based movement that has been described as an effort to give Jesus one last chance. The seven had been taking LSD together for spiritual reasons. They found they were more interested than the Sequoia group "in helping people find their own way and recognizing that the ways may be different," Levy said. They bought the house on Page Street and opened it as a kind of noncredal church where people might, as their statement of purpose declared, "move toward greater creativity, authenticity and involvement in living . . . exult in the joy of being alive and . . . face squarely the burdens, the responsibilities, the suffering that are also ours."

People who seek out Venture, Levy said, "are pretty much committed to finding their own way and willing to go through some discomfort in the process, not people who want someone to tell them." Some began to turn on at Esalen but, having neither the time nor the money to go there often, came to continue their discoveries on Page Street.

"It's a place where you can find something and move on," said Louis Sloss, another of the founders. Most people do not stay beyond a few months. "That's good," he said, "we don't want it to become too ingrown."

Many of the Venture people (it is not a membership organization, you pay your fee and bring something to potluck, that's all) are professionals or businessmen, but they tend to be dropouts from the status race. "If you're interested in success, this tends to mean you get involved in the company's values," Levy told me. "So I think there's a tendency to either stay identified with the business community and not ask too many questions, or drop out, or to compromise—continue to earn your living but without taking it too seriously."

"Many people here are in the process of withdrawing from that world and opening up others," Sloss said. A missile expert, who recently began coming to Venture labs is, for example, beginning to think of his work as meaningless. Sloss, who runs a property-management business, spends less time on that than he used to. He meditates for half an hour daily, reads more, attends labs. As a result, he says, his life has become richer and has gained "a sense of wholeness, connectedness—the religious element."

Levy, who is a Quaker and active in the American Friends Service Committee, originally wanted Venture to take part in social action but found the groups were not interested. "They come because they need something," he said. "We used to batter away at them about getting involved. We don't anymore." Another disappointment, he said, was lack of interest in Venture among neighborhood residents. "It should have been obvious why," he said. "People operating at a survival level don't ask the kinds of questions middle-class people ask." Venture does cooperate with AFSC work in the neighborhood, which is about 80 percent Negro, and makes its facilities available to community action projects, such as tutoring.

Group leaders at Venture are carefully chosen from among participants and come from different backgrounds. "We've often found that psychologists are the worst," said Levy, who is also president of the Humanistic Psychology Association.

One group leader is Alby Doan, a petite, well-groomed

middle-aged woman who until recently was married to an executive in a large industrial firm and lived in one of San Francisco's wealthiest suburbs. She used to spend her time at the country club, the bridge club, in golf and volunteer work. Now she frequents Esalen, Jungian seminars, assorted truth labs, sensory awareness sessions and considers Venture her community. Some of her new attitudes might shock her former bridge partners—her lack of interest in another marriage, the tolerance of a young daughter's hip way of life, her gladness that her son, who had enlisted in the Army, later applied for conscientious objector status. "My children, young people generally, they're so alive," she told me. Venture has become a stepping stone for her into that kind of aliveness.

Somewhat similar to Mrs. Doan's is the background of Jane Rhyne, an elegant and intelligent woman who at age fifty-four looked no more than forty. When I met her, she struck me as a sequel to Joanie Summer–Sequin Palladini. Like Joanie, she had swung from a super-middle-class life into a bohemian one. But later, as a member of Venture, she had found a self-style between the two extremes.

Jane Rhyne grew up in Marianna, Florida, married her brother's best friend right after college and for the next seventeen years lived comfortably, as the wife of an oil company executive and mother of two children in a suburban community in Pennsylvania. "I gardened and sewed and cooked and had a Girl Scout troup and was a Cub Scout mother and belonged to committees of the P-TA," she told me. "Outwardly I was a mature, well-adjusted person. But I was dead."

After struggling to overcome what she thought had to be a neurotic sense of dissatisfaction, she left her husband, taking her children with her, went back to Florida State University for a masters in art and anthropology and married a painter. "The next ten years were mad and adventuresome, absolutely the opposite of everything I had known thus far, for my second husband was exactly opposite my first," she told me. "He was erratic, creative, marvelous and terrible all at once. Sometimes our life was hard, at other times ecstatic."

They lived in Mexico, Spain, and a community in the Canadian wilderness. Jane Rhyne became an accomplished painter. Then, when she was almost fifty, the marriage broke up.

After a year of confusion and unhappiness she came to San Francisco with one suitcase and the determination to make a new life for herself. Almost by accident, she found Venture and became deeply involved in its activities. She now lives in a rambling old Victorian house in the Haight-Ash-

221

bury, and is again active in her community—the hip, turned-on community this time. She is a group leader at Venture and, with the San Francisco Gestalt Therapy Institute, offers "gestalt art experiences" where people play self-games with clay, paint and paper. Among those who come to take part are psychotherapists, social workers, nurses and others who welcome the chance to express themselves freely after work that requires supreme self-restraint. For Jane Rhyne, as for many others at Venture, the truth labs remain a reinforcement for an expanded and exploratory attitude toward life.

Another community built around truth labs is the Synanon Foundation, which started in 1958 as a self-rehabilitation program for drug addicts. Ten years later, it was calling itself a social movement that incidentally stopped junkies from shooting dope. Nonaddict members (squares, in Synanon lingo) outnumbered resident addicts by more than two to one and the foundation had prospered—it controlled an estimated five million dollars worth of real estate in Santa Monica alone and operated also in San Francisco, Marin County, New York and Detroit.

Squares came to Synanon mostly for a chance to play the Synanon game. By early 1968, more than 2,500 people were gathering at the various Synanon houses at least once a week. Some came two, three, even four times a week. For the game was as absorbing and amusing as a choice gossip session. The chance to become verbally intimate with ex-junkies also had a certain glamour to many safe-living squares.

Synanon's brand of truth lab has been called "a verbal street fight," "attack therapy," and, by an advocate, "the human sport." Like all truth labs, it can be gentle and sympathetic. But what distinguishes it from all other varieties is its verbal violence. It might be called a hate lab, while love lab would be more accurate for groups at Venture. Both, in their way, aim to strip away masks and defenses and free people to become authentic and strong. But while the Venture people use some delicacy in that operation, Synanon game players tend to rip and tear.

The game, together with Synanon, began with Chuck Dederich, who in 1958 was living on a $33-a-week unemployment check on Santa Monica's beaches, trying to stay away from liquor. A member of Alcoholics Anonymous, he followed A.A. tradition by gathering a discussion group around him. Junkies soon outnumbered alcoholics at the meetings and Synanon was underway. Dederich was an inventive natural leader. He found that if addicts hammered at each other's illusions and "dumped their emotional garbage" (again

Synanon words) they began to grow up and become responsible. He refined the group discussion into a game and built around it a program that has gained national fame. Ten years later, Synanon had admitted some 2,300 addicts and people with "character disorders." About half left before they were judged ready, and may or may not have gone back to drugs. Some 380 were graduated. Nearly half the graduates remained to work in Synanon.

But if the game was therapy for addicts, to the squares it was offered as entertainment. It was to be played for fun, like golf or tennis.

I attended nine Synanon games, in New York or San Francisco, and my most vivid recollection later was a roomful of people, their faces distorted, screaming abuse at me. It was —well—a growth experience that taught me something about standing up under group pressure. I wondered if some people don't collapse under it but Synanon leaders insist that, since it's all for fun, nobody can get hurt. That seems to mean that bruises will heal if you keep coming back and understand what the game is all about.

The only rule in the game is—no physical violence. But there are many techniques and plays. It begins with groups of ten to fifteen people sitting in a circle and looking at each other. Someone will levy "an indictment," such as "Marcia, you sure look like an old maid, what's your story?" With that, the game is on Marcia, who will defend herself as best she can. If she gets uptight and says, "What do you mean?" or something, the group will know they got her in a weak spot and will pounce upon her, trying to get her to reveal something that bothers her. If the attack does not bother her, they'll try to find another opening. Marcia will either break down, or she'll want to talk about her appearance, or she'll manage to swing the game to someone else. She may say to her attacker, "Oh yeah? You're not married, are you? You like to play with boys?" The homosexuality attack seldom fails to get an inexperienced game player.

It's the greatest sport ever, afficionados insist. Dan Garrett, director of the San Francisco Synanon House in 1967, compares it to the Olympics. Men used to run for their lives, he says, but now they do it "as an end in itself. There are side effects, of course—your legs get stronger, you eat and sleep better." Others compare it to tennis or a boxing match. You fight with all you've got, they say, and after it's over you all go off together for coffee. It reminds me more of a game called "The Law" described by Roger Vailland in his novel of that name as common in Sicily. One man becomes law giver in this game and another the scapegoat. Led by the law giver, all players try to make the scapegoat lose his cool.

It's 7:30 on a weeknight in San Francisco's Synanon House. The big main room, where most of the socializing is done, is crowded with maybe two hundred people. You can't tell the residents from the squares, except that the residents tend to look squarer than squares, and neater. A jazz combo is playing—Synanon has many supporters who give of their talent, and also has musicians in the house. People sip coffee from paper cups and chat at the many formica-topped tables.

At 8 P.M., the night's game players divide into game groups and scatter into the many gamerooms in the building. I am assigned to a small office where I find an empty folding chair in the circle and settle with ashtray and coffee. There's a bit of desultory chatter, then it begins.

"How come you're such a lousy game-player, Charlie?" (names of game players are fictitious) someone says and all eyes turn to Charlie. He is thirty-seven but looks fifty. His hair is graying, his body is slumped and spreading, his face is droopy, particularly around the eyes. Now he puts on a nonchalant mien.

"You're a sack of potatoes," says a woman with long, polished nails. "You think you're a role model or something?"

Charlie shrugs. "I don't know, maybe I am." People try to be role models in Synanon, like super-model Chuck Dederich, whose short, brush haircut, and tough-cool manner are mimed by many in the organization.

"Ha!" says a nervous young fellow. "And what makes you think you can be anyone's role model? You've been playing games for years, you're a lousy player, what else are you?"

"He's gutless," says the woman with the nails.

"He'll never do anything for anyone," a man adds.

"Well, there are some pretty stupid people around here," says Charlie. "They might see me as a role model. How can I tell?"

"Oh yeah? You think people around here are more stupid than you? What makes you think that?"

Pretty soon Charlie is against the wall, squirming.

"Just what do you do?"

"I'm an accountant."

"Are you good at it?"

"No."

"Why don't you get better?"

Charlie looks worried. "It's boring. I don't like the work."

"Why don't you do something else?"

"Well, I've been thinking of law school but I have these debts. I owe more than three grand in gambling debts and that comes first. If I can survive a year and a half and pay them off, then maybe I can do something."

Tomorrow maybe. The dream is comfortably out of reach, there are so many obstacles between now and the dream that all Charlie does is stay miserably bored. In a year, maybe he'll have more debts. And so it will go, on and on. A lot of Synanon game players seem to be characters out of *The Iceman Cometh*. There's Richard, a husky heavy drinker who lives with Jane. For them it's a settlement with Jane's former husband that keeps the dream away. As soon as that's done, Richard says, he will put his foot down, he'll tell Jane she has to quit talking with that ex-husband of hers every night and they'll marry. It's sort of understood.

"Have you asked her to marry you, Richard?"

"Of course I have," he says, with the belligerency of the weak.

"Did she say yes?"

"It's understood."

"Did she say yes?" yells Charlie, getting his licks in now.

"Yes, she said yes . . . conditional on my stopping drinking." Charlie smiles.

So, as for Charlie, in moments of despair, there is gambling, for Richard there is drinking; and the gambling and the drinking comfortably, miserably, keep away the dream.

"Why don't you fuck it, fuck that settlement, Richard?"

He shrugs, he squirms. If he keeps returning, the pressure will get heavier. Maybe he will be forced into taking a step out of the vicious wheel. Maybe the result will be similar to what might happen at Venture to a person who favors a gentler style.

The games last for about two and a half hours and seldom focus on any one person for longer than fifteen minutes. Many innings certainly do turn out to be more entertaining than most TV serials.

"This is very hard for me," says Bitsy, a pretty young social worker, when her turn comes. She says it with eagerness and enthusiasm. "It's hard to talk about but things are just terrible. I'm sleeping with two guys and I don't like either one of them but I do want a meaningful relationship and . . ."

"Wait a minute, stop that bullshit right there," another girl yells. "You're making no sense."

Bitsy, it seems, was seeing a black psychiatrist and fell into a state. "He told me how sex should be an animal sort of thing and he got me all excited just talking about it. Only I couldn't sleep with him—even if he had offered—because that would knock the image. But I met a Negro man where I work. I didn't know him very well, we just had lunch, but I thought maybe it . . ."

"You needn't go on. Do you think you're unique?" says Pat, the girl who earlier stopped her. "You're a neurotic Jewish girl who has this thing about black men."

"I know," says Bitsy, "it's terrible."

"You enjoy it," says Pat.

"No I don't. I *don't!*"

"If you didn't you wouldn't fuck them."

"Bet you have one orgasm after another," says Richard.

"Nah, she doesn't have any," says Pat. "She's looking for a black shrink to give her one. You're not unusual at all," she says to Bitsy. "I did the exact same thing, maybe not that extreme. It happens to the best of us."

Bitsy says she's been seeing a psychiatrist for six years and she knows she doesn't want to do what she's doing, but then again maybe she does because . . .

"Listen, you gotta start with the basics," says a Synanon resident. "You're confused and you're stupid." Bitsy nods. "I went to a psych for years and I could play you the same record—I want but then again I must not want. You gotta stop doing that. Stop sleeping with those guys."

"Will you do it?" asks Pat.

Bitsy nods. A black resident has been listening. "How come you're silent?" the other resident asks. "They were talking about you, you're the only black man in the room. You must have some wild reaction. Here she's talking about you all having big dicks."

"I should be mad?" says the black resident. "I'm proud of being black."

"Yeah, I'm proud of being Jewish," says the first resident, who had been in Synanon longer. "As long as there's a goy around I'm proud. Up at Santa Monica they once got all us Jews into one room and after a while it turned out different."

"I'm proud," the black man insists.

"Forget it then," says the other one, angry. "I don't even want to talk with you."

Whenever the interchanges are between Synanon residents, it seems, the game turns into something deeper and there is a lot of concern, affection and understanding beneath the jabs and barbs. But with many of the squares, it struck me as mostly a chance to vent a little venom, something like the Joe Pyne Show. Some married couples seemed to save up their quarrels and then get the satisfaction of a super-scene by bringing them out in a game.

Donna and her husband, Lester, come two or three times a week and almost always have something to offer. Usually it's Donna who brings out the moment's grudge. One evening someone starts off by saying to her:

"You two, you came in like you'd just had a fight. What's the story?"

"No, we didn't," says Donna, pulling down the miniskirt a little toward her fishnet-covered knees. "But it's true, we have had a bad week." She looks across the circle at her husband who, as usual, is dressed in a cheap bright shirt that fails at being hip-chic. "Lester, you just don't give yourself to the family," she says, whiny. "Like last Tuesday, you were over at Jimson's when I was all ready to go to the beach. I got everything ready and then I had to go over and *call* you."

Lester sits impassive, as if tuning her out.

"It just bugs me," Donna says. "You could have helped me but you just . . ."

The rest of the group backs up Donna like a lot of housewives from behind a fence:

"It's something you should know, Lester."

"Your responsibility."

"How selfish can you get?"

"And another thing," says Donna. "You put me down. Like last Wednesday, when those friends of yours were over. You don't respect my intelligence, Lester, you still don't. Sometimes I feel you just don't care."

He sits with head to one side, sullen. Pretty soon Donna is in a rage. "You asshole!" she screams. "You're nothing but a fucking asshole!"

Watching them, I think that surely their marriage is done for. But Lester gets his licks in too, later, with community backing, and they leave with their arms around each other.

Synanon leaders freely admit that the game can be addictive. But they're proud of it for they believe that if people "dump their garbage" they eventually get through hate and hostility and emerge honest, strong, self-reliant and accepting of others. I never got that far. In several games I was attacked for nonparticipation. In the last one, the group turned on me for daring to write about Synanon after what they all considered too short a time. The scene turned into a roomful of bursting eyeballs. Someone yelled, "You're a prostitute—you're doing this for money." "She's been leeching off us," someone else shouted. A lot of what was said I never heard, for I blanked under the verbal barrage. However, I was glad that, before coming that evening, I had decided it should be my last. When the game began, I felt no hostility toward any of the people in the room—at least any I was aware of. When it ended, I had plenty. I knew that if I came to another game, I would have plenty of garbage to dump. One leader in the Human Potentialities movement, who had explored the Synanon scene, told me, "I used to go home after those games and cower in bed—literally. Then I found myself thinking about how I could get back at those people. That's when I quit."

Whatever reservations one has about the game, Synanon is a dynamic organization. Part of its strength come from the solidarity of its members, who find a community in it. Part is achieved, it seems to me, through group pressure. "What have you done for Synanon?" is a standard question in games. A person who has not contributed much beyond cookies and a few dollars will be reminded that Synanon has a waiting list of people eager to play the game. I saw a middle-aged sociologist start out saying she did not feel obliged to contribute more than her monthly dues (these were later reduced from $10 in San Francisco and $15 in New York to a penny a month) and end up promising to buy gas at a Texaco station run by Synanon, even though it was considerably out of her way. In another game, a legal secretary was violently attacked for refusing to take Synanon's side in a hassle with Santa Monica neighbors before she knew the neighbors' side. A game player who belonged to left-wing groups in his youth told me he saw the dynamic of Synanon as similar to that in a Communist Party cell.

Dan Garrett insists that no label fits Synanon because it is constantly changing. Synanon is a way of life, he says, that teaches self-reliance and decent citizenship. "This is a true Socratic socity," he told me. "Socrates said the unexamined life is not worth living and we have means of examining everything we do in common and everything we say in common intensively." People in Synanon have as much say in the community's affairs, he said, as they can make heard, for anyone is free to criticize anyone and anything in a game.

Leaders in Synanon foresee a time when every major city will have a Synanon house where any member can find instant intimacy. If that happens, Synanon will be the first group to set up a national network of truth labs.

A Far Eastern scholar I talked with suggested that the Synanon game and other truth labs may be a Western way—parallel to meditation in the East—of getting past the verbal and into a deeper reality. We are so hung up on words, he said, that perhaps we need to talk until we become sick of verbiage and burst through into something real.

With their verbal and emotional gymnastics, the truth labs are often a first step in the break-up of mind-sets. They tend to lead to an awareness of ways in which we are self-prisoners in mind and body and to a further search for inner liberation and harmony. Some people continue this search with mystical groups or gurus who work with the senses.

Chapter FOURTEEN

Charlotte Selver — Sensory Awareness

"So WHAT do you do in these classes?" a friend asks. I'm hard put to explain. "We stand, we sit, we lie down, we breathe, we play with little red balls. I know it sounds inane. We don't do any exercises and we usually don't move around much. You see, it turns out we're all clutched inside, we're masses of tight knots and snarls, strangling and squeezing ourselves. We're self-prisoners. The idea is to let go and find a natural balance and freedom. To learn to go with it, whatever *it* is."

"A kind of relaxation technique?"

"No. You can call it a turn-on or awareness expansion. Someone at the San Francisco Zen Center called it 'a kind of formless Zen.' I've only been to a few of her classes. I can tell you what happened, but it's not describable. Like Zen, it's something you have to experience."

The self-imprisonment begins in early childhood, according to Charlotte Selver (and to her teachers, Elsa Gindler and Heinrich Jacoby). For in Western society, "the parent invades every aspect of the child's development," and so prevents him from growing naturally. It's a four-way invasion, she explains in an article, written with her husband, Charles V. W. Brooks, in *Explorations in Human Potentialities,* edited by Herbert A. Otto: First, the child is taught to place a value on all he experiences. He is taught "when and how much it is *good* for him to eat, when and how long he *ought* to sleep, what parts of him are *bad* or *dirty*. . . . When he falls and cries he is taught not to allow the pain and shock to go their way but to seek instant distraction from them and to expect fuss and anxiety from the parent rather than quiet sympathy: 'you *good* boy, that *bad* banana peel!' A little later he will be taught that exposure to cold or getting wet in the rain is *unpleasant* and *dangerous,* as it will actually become after the lesson has been thoroughly learned." The child grows up unable to experience without judging.

Second, parents convey the notion that exaggeration is needed for everything. They sniff fiercely at flowers when they want the child to appreciate the fragrance, they smack their lips over food when they want him to eat, they talk in caricature of baby talk. The child gets the idea that the natural way of doing things is somehow insufficient.

Third, many parents tend to coax children constantly toward some effort, even when none is needed—toward seeing, listening, speaking, walking, learning. The child learns that effort is needed for everything and grows up believing that nothing happens without "trying" or even "trying hard."

Fourth, parents tend to interrupt children at what they are engaged in, stressing that a *good* child comes when called, no matter what. This confuses a child's innate sense of rhythm.

And so, through this parental invasion, the child is boxed into the social mold and the social norm and into himself. Instead of perceiving and discovering the world and himself in it, he comes to be ruled by ideas and images. He does not know how to allow himself to see, hear and feel without interfering with his perceptions.

"In our work in sensory awareness," Miss Selver and Mr. Brooks explain, "we gradually and patiently sort out what is perception and what is image. We build upon sensations, particularly the proprioceptive sensations, the cultivation of which has been neglected in our education so that they no longer come easily."

Miss Selver—like Frederick Perls, yogis and Zen students—has discovered that if you stay with what is happening within yourself, distortions dissolve and natural rhythms return. She therefore seeks to cultivate an attitude of open attentiveness: a kind of concentration that allows things to happen; a listening, watching and following. Usually, when we are engaged in what we call concentration, we do just the opposite. We glue our energies to an objective and seek to effect changes by force of will.

It's a drizzly morning when I set out for Miss Selver's studio on West Seventy-third Street in Manhattan. I'm late, the bus is slow and crowded, and by the time I reach Seventy-second Street I'm in a foul temper. The address is an old brick building in the heart of junkie land. Almost running, I fling open the door to the lobby—and flinch. A tall black man in trenchcoat and shades stands just inside the door. New York paranoia! Immediately I'm ashamed. Did he see my nervous twitch? He looks at me with a sardonic smile. Yes, of course. What a place for sensory awakening! Yes, here, not idyllic Big Sur, is the place to test its worth.

I hurry up the stairs to the second floor and enter a narrow little hall, part of which is cut off by a cotton curtain and serves as a dressing room. I hang my coat in the elbow-cramping compartment, take off my shoes and walk into the studio. It's like walking out the door of a subway train into a garden.

Japanese rice paper covers panes in the large window to the south and the two smaller ones to the west, filtering and softening the light that falls on plants, flowers and twelve people in leotards and sports clothes who sit cross-legged in a semicircle on brightly patterned tatami mats, facing Charlotte Selver. They are men and women of assorted ages in the tenth week of their twelve-week sensory awareness course. For me, it's the first of six classes.

Miss Selver, in a long beige gown made of drapery material, is also sitting on the floor. She is a woman in her sixties with something of the old-fashioned demure German schoolgirl about her. Her dark hair, slightly graying, is cut straight and hangs to just below her ears, framing a mobile face with gentle, live brown eyes. A set of stereophonic earphones lies beside her, attached to a microphone that stands in the center of the room. She is nearly deaf and must use this elaborate equipment when conversing with a group. Now she speaks in a slow, calm, German-accented voice:

"I do not believe there is any limit to waking up," she says, "for instance for the weather. Today it is raining. This is usually not accepted. When we see rain we classify it as bad and then shut ourselves off from it instead of experiencing it. We judge and try to control everything. We even control our breathing, as if the breath would stop if we did not pull and push it. The breath is something we don't possess. It comes and goes, a natural power. We let something old out of ourselves and something new into ourselves. If our whole being is ready to receive it and dismiss it as it comes and goes, then our breathing flows naturally.

231

"Would you lie down now and quietly follow your breathing." We stretch out on the mats and close our eyes. My tight nerves begin to relax. "Let it happen without supervising it or changing it—without trying to breathe 'right.' When something which was not conscious comes to consciousness, we must be careful that we do not immediately try to manipulate it." I focus my attention on my breathing. Soon the crowded bus, the street and the man in the lobby cease to exist for me.

"Could you become so peaceful and permissive that you let your exhalation satisfy itself completely?" asks Miss Selver. There is a long pause. "Could you gradually allow your head to become more a part of you, not something special or separated?" Another pause. "Could you give up watching?" During the pauses I find that some of Miss Selver's questions translate themselves into changes inside me. "Could you experience without immediately labeling the experience . . . Is it possible to get rid of 'the little man in the head' [the phrase is Wittgenstein's] who is watching? When you are all awake you don't need to have someone in the head watching. Gradually allow the changes needed until you feel—I am a clear passage."

I know what she means about becoming a clear passage, but I don't understand how it is possible to be aware without mentally watching. When she directs our attention to the feet, for example, I see my feet in my mind. Should I stop seeing them? Would that make me more aware?

"Thank you," says Miss Selver and we open our eyes. "What did you experience?" At that, I realize what she means about that "little man in the head." I was so busy arguing with myself I had not sensed my feet at all.

"The constant effort to perceive kills much of perception," says Miss Selver. "The more peaceful we are in our heads, the more possibilities of perception are available to us."

Yes, she is right, I say in my head. But during the next few minutes it becomes clear that here, as in Zen, verbal answers and mental agreements lead only to rephrasings of the same questions. The true answers have to come from each person's experience.

Miss Selver picks up a satchel that stood beside the low couch behind her, opens it and asks us each to take a small red ball out of it. We are to roll the ball on the floor and discover what happens just before it stops. I watch. It rocks and balances. She next asks us to put the ball in front of us and to stand so as to see it. Then, without ceasing to see the ball, she asks us to notice what else we see.

I have been looking only at the ball. Now I unglue my

eyes from it and broaden my focus to take in its surroundings. I look at it now the way a driver looks at a red light while also seeing the road, other cars and the scenery. The change is amazing: the space in my view expands until I see almost the whole room, a kaleidoscope of red balls, legs and bright tatami mats in filtered light. The legs sway and rock gently like reeds in the breeze, like the red balls before stopping. Everything is alive, even the still objects are moving in stillness. It is beautiful. Stillness and motion are one. My vision has expanded just as it did the first time I tried marijuana. At that time I noticed that I could see almost 180 degrees around me and that there was life in objects. But here it is again, without the help of grass. All I had to do was to stop attacking that ball with my eyes.

"It's amusing, isn't it?" says Miss Selver.

"Now would you let the ball roll again and move with it, coming to standing when it comes to rest." We begin to move around the room. "Could your breathing be interested in the ball? Are you moving with the ball? Is your saliva flowing with the ball?"

These are Zen words. But is it possible? A perception, an awareness, exists when a connection runs from wherever in my body I sense it to my mind and is there recorded. Doesn't it? It is recorded as a sound, a feeling, a picture, a set of words. Is it possible to be aware of this little red ball with my breathing, without making that translation? Could I sense it so clearly that my breathing would respond to this object?

"Don't try to see," says Miss Selver. "Let your eyes be a threshold through which what you see passes and let it be received by your whole organism."

I let my eyes go out of focus and take in shadows and shapes, colors and movement as though through a screen. "Let your eyes and your ears and your nose be thresholds." No, but that's impossible.

When we sit down I say, "I don't understand how awareness with all senses simultaneously can be possible. I shift my attention from one to another, that's all. All I can do is vary the speed at which I shift it."

"*You* do not shift it, *it shifts*," she replies. "It happens, that's the way we function if we only allow it. This notion of having to *produce* everything! If you had seen the group just now you would have noticed that some people were awake for what they were doing and others were not."

If you had seen—but of course, she is right. When she asked us to let the eyes be a threshold I deliberately set my vision out of focus. I made an effort to look instead of simply

233

allowing myself to see. This realization, like a flash, illuminates vast new ranges of possible awareness. But how stupid of me to have doubted when I had already been to the place Miss Selver was talking about. In my encounter with the doctor during the LSD trip, sensation and movement and music and vision were one. Even he and I and all in the room were one, everything existed as part of one immense flowing pattern and yet nothing lost its identity.

As if guessing my thoughts, Miss Selver now says, "The moment your breathing becomes free. all kinds of things are possible. Drugs just make the mind quiet so that you experience everything more fully. If you let the world come in through the threshold of your senses, then everything—the colors. the movements, all that is happening—every moment becomes new." She turns to the middle-aged woman beside her. "How would you like that. Martha?"

"It would be beautiful," Martha says with nostalgia.

"It is yours." Miss Selver's voice is now rich and full of promise. "You have it. You need only to use it."

As I leave the studio. Miss Selver's words mingle with those of my LSD guru. "It only opens the door," he had said. "It's all in you, it only opens the door." Zen had shown me another door. And here, a woman from an entirely different tradition knew of still another. All three led to the same spaces.

The originator of sensory awareness work, Elsa Gindler, knew nothing of Zen; nor did Miss Selver until 1957, at which time she had already been conducting her classes for more than twenty years.

"The first time one of my students said, 'Charlotte, you are teaching Zen.' I said, 'What is Zen?' " she recalled during an interview. "Then one of my students went to California and wrote me that she had met a man who spoke of what I did. She sent me Alan Watts' book *The Spirit of Zen*. I recognized the kinship immediately and visited him on my next trip out west."

"We had an immediate feeling of connection. In Alan Watts' office, behind the desk where he sat, he had a big scroll. On it something was written in beautiful Chinese characters. I asked what it meant. He said, "Mountains are mountains.' 'What do you mean? Of course mountains are mountains,' I said. He told me an ancient Chinese proverb: Before I studied Buddhism, I thought mountains were mountains and waters were waters. After I studied awhile, mountains were no longer mountains and waters were no longer waters. Now mountains are again mountains and waters again waters.

"This is what happens in sensory awareness work too. People come to it with concepts that separate them from experience. Gradually, they go from the word to the experience. The process is the same as in Zen in that it happens through practice. You have seen Mrs. S. in class, the older lady with dyed hair? She is delighted by everything but only as an interesting idea. She is not yet conscious that she isn't responding. I was the same when I first began to study with Elsa Gindler. I thought she spoke from the depths of my heart and was overwhelmed by what she said. Only I didn't really understand. A year and a half after I first began to study with her she at last came and put her hand on my shoulder and said: 'The first movement.' I was flabbergasted. And then I began to feel that ever so often I made empty gestures. I did not really experience what I did, what I said, or what happened. That was the beginning of going deeper."

However, Miss Selver said, the similarities between her work and Zen must not be overstressed. Zen grows out of thousands of years of philosophy and the entire Eastern way of life, while sensory awareness work began when Elsa Gindler, a Berlin factory worker's daughter, decided she did not want to die of tuberculosis at the age of twenty-one.

The way Miss Selver tells it, this now legendary woman decided, when she was so ill she had been given up by the doctors, that there had to be a way she could let parts of her lungs rest while others breathed so that through rest she would heal. She began to experiment and, in the process, discovered a lot about the self-directive and self-healing capacities of the organism. Following them, she recovered and soon began to gather students with whom she continued her explorations. Eventually it became apparent to her that the whole question of creativity—and of all healthy functioning—was involved in these organismic capacities. Musicians, teachers, dancers and other artists came to seek her out and she moved beyond therapeutic work. She never published anything about what she did, believing it could not be passed on with words. Whatever notes she had taken were destroyed in an air-raid fire in her Berlin studio, together with seven people she was hiding from the Nazis. She died in 1961, without giving a name to her work. It was Miss Selver who called it sensory awareness.

Miss Selver studied with Elsa Gindler about eleven years. The manner in which she came to her teacher is reminiscent of stories told about Zen students and masters. She was teaching rhythms in Munich when someone mentioned that there was an amazing woman doing related work in Berlin. During a visit to that city some time later, she went to the Gindler studio.

"Elsa Gindler was working with her class with her back to the door and she didn't see me," Miss Selver recalled. "I sat and watched and suddenly realized that all I was teaching and learning was wrong. I felt I had to start all over again. So I went up to her after class and asked if I could study with her. She asked what I was doing and I said I was a teacher of rhythms. She asked, 'Are you successful?' and I said yes. 'Continue what you are doing,' she said. I protested but she cut me off. 'I'm sorry but I can't accept you.'

"Six months later I came back. She asked, 'Are you still doing what you were doing?' I said yes. 'Continue.' 'But why?' I asked. 'Why don't you take me?' She said it was too much of a responsibility, I would have to unlearn all I learned. So I went away a second time but again returned after a few months. This time she said, 'I can predict it will be very hard for you, but if you really insist, come.'"

Miss Selver continued to teach rhythms according to techniques she had learned from Dr. Rudolf Bode, a former student of Jacques Dalcroze and the originator of the Ausdrucks-Gymnastik still popular in Germany. But at the same time she began to study in the Gindler school.

"I was born in 1907 in Duisburg-Ruhrort am Rhein, in the Ruhr, where we had nothing but smoke in our lungs and every meadow was gray," she recalled. "I had never been young. Now working with Gindler as an adult, I became a child. The simplest things became enormous new experiences. Once, I remember, she asked us to climb up on a fence. It was quite high, in a meadow, and I was terrified. I clung to it trembling. She asked quietly, 'Do you feel what is under you?' I had only seen the empty air. Now I began to feel there was something solid under me. By and by my legs and feet began to give to the roundness of the tree trunk that served as a rail. I gradually came up to standing. I stood freely on the fence. It was a wonderful feeling."

She began to adapt her own work in rhythms to what she learned from Elsa Gindler. Eventually, she ceased to work with music and concentrated on sensory awareness.

She married, divorced and came to the United States at the end of 1938. At first she made her living as companion and nurse to a wealthy old lady. After a while, she met people from the Alanson White Institute of Psychiatry and most of its leading members became her students. Erich Fromm, the existential analyst, studied with her for years and sent analysts training with him to her. They, in turn, sent patients. It was Erich Fromm who interested Frederick Perls in Miss Selver's work. Perls studied with her also and incorporated sensory awareness into his Gestalt therapy.

Another student was Charles Brooks, the son of writer-critic Van Wyck Brooks. He had planned to become a writer and had gone to France for that purpose but found that all he did there was fix up his house. So he returned, became a carpenter and then a cabinet-maker. In Miss Selver's classes, he found he could reconcile the many conflicting intellectual, social and emotional tendencies in his life. In Miss Selver, he found a wife. Now he shares in teaching the classes.

About 1950, Miss Selver joined the faculty of the New School for Social Research in New York. Mr. Brooks followed in 1964.

"Would you now come to standing," Miss Selver says to the group on the tatami mats. "Could you feel yourself standing in the space around you? Are your fingertips awake to your standing?" Each question is followed by a long pause. "Does your neck allow standing? Your shoulders? Your groins? Your head? Your breathing?"

The questions light on different parts of me, bringing more and more of my body into my awareness. "How much space is there between your shoulders and the floor? What of you is between your shoulders and your feet? How much space is between your feet and the top of your head?"

I sense the space around me, feel the air touch my skin. My feet are solid on the rug, which gives to my weight. Above my feet I am somehow out of line, weaving to maintain balance. My head is vulnerable so far out in space.

"That was beautiful," a woman who used to be a ballet dancer says. "Before this I always had a problem of standing. I felt that my pelvis stuck out and didn't support me. This time for the first time I found out what standing is. I didn't want to give it up because I was afraid I wouldn't find it again."

"Forget it," says Miss Selver. "When you want to make a note of it and produce it again you are in the devil's kitchen. This moment will never be again. You cannot reproduce it. You can only be awake to the moment and respond."

A pretty blond woman, who looks like a Westchester matron still remembering herself as senior prom queen in high school, had trouble finding her balance.

"I have a feeling you have a mental image of yourself standing," Miss Selver tells her. "Rather than allowing the simple act of standing, you watch the image of a film star or

237

someone with an especially long neck. You follow the mental picture rather than what wants to happen. You have to get away from a performance of standing and come to natural standing."

Sometimes a class can be disturbing, for the simple activities, when fully attended to, arouse long-buried feelings. This morning Charles Brooks leads the session. There has been some talk last time about the center of balance. Brooks asks us to stand and touch with both hands what we feel is our center. I place my right hand on my waist in front, my left slightly lower on my back. It feels right. Others find somewhat different positions. Then some of us stand still, with eyes closed, while others put their hands on what they think is our balance center.

I marvel at the difference in people I can sense through the touch of their hands. One is afraid, tense, and touches lightly. Another presses heavily, as if he were trying to show he wasn't afraid. In their own way, both are holding back. The third has strong and gentle hands. But I feel too vulnerable under this touch. I want to pull away, to shout—let me go! It's as hard to be still and keep breathing as it was, months ago, to meet Gia-Fu's direct gaze without speaking or moving.

When it's my turn to do the touching the experience is equally intense. One woman expands and contracts freely and I sense she must trust me and herself to do so. Another sways, jerks, agitated. A man moves only in front. I feel no breathing in his back.

When we sit down I am flushed and tired. Then two people say they were disconcerted by someone who held them unevenly. "Yes," says the young girl, the one I thought I sensed trust with, "it was strange." She makes a grimace of disgust.

That's me they're talking about! Suddenly a feeling comes from way back in my past, from a time when I was particularly awkward and miserable. Together with that I realize I held them unevenly through some familiar perversity: I knew better where the middle was and would show them. But no —wasn't I gentle, respectful? Which was it? It spins me into a tight ball. I pull up my knees, put my chin on them and wrap my arms around my legs.

We go on with other activity but I am preoccupied with what just happened. We are now doing with knees what we just did with "centers." We cup the hands around another's knee and hold it awhile. I can do the holding, but as soon as someone gets a hold of me I tense and begin to tremble. Yes, it is easier to touch than be touched, easier to give than to

238

take, to put on a good show than let down your guard. But this is ridiculous. I decide to speak about it.

"I find it very hard to let someone hold me like that," I say at the next opportunity. "And I wonder, does anyone else?" There is silence, then one woman says hesitantly that she finds it difficult. I look across the room at a man whose knee I had held. He had been extremely tense but had made a desperate effort to seem relaxed. Now he looks away from me and says nothing. I realize that it was so hard for him that he can't even tell me he understands what I'm taking about. His face is blank. I suddenly feel sympathy for him and forget my distress.

One morning I wake distracted, with a tightness in muscles and head. Something is out of focus. I really look forward to the class.

The big white studio with its sunburst of mats is serene and still. People lie and sit in a circle. Miss Selver's inexpensive tan gown looks rich and golden in the morning light. A vase of many-colored flowers stands beside her. On her other side lies the set of earphones from the hearing aid. Today is the last session of the twelve-week Friday morning class. There is a guest, a priest from the New York Zen Center. Most people at the Zen Center, he says, have taken classes with Miss Selver.

"There is a possibility of going toward things clear-minded, without distinguishing into pleasant and unpleasant," she says. "Let it speak—feel it out without diminishing it by categorizing. One of my teachers, Henrich Jacoby, used to say that people are like those huge chests with hundreds of little drawers that homeopathic doctors use—every time they come across an experience they classify it. Ah, number 371, they say and put it into the drawer with that number. Yet how much significance everything could have—even the most common thing—if we really took it in. It can speak to us or we can pass it by, it's up to us. We can stand in the middle of an event, with a wider focus, so that we do not cut it off from its past and its future. And to this, breathing can help us. I found that I learned an enormous amount of patience and deeper experience by following my breathing. Have you noticed that the moment you feel warmer toward a person you can feel that in your breathing? You can feel you are afraid before you know you are by your breathing. Find it out for yourself."

We stand, close our eyes, and sense ourselves standing in space breathing. "Bring your hands to your neck on both sides and feel if the muscles are elastic or rigid." Rigid. "Do you feel a need for changes in your neck, in your head, to allow your breathing?" Something is clamped tight inside my forehead. "Is it possible to allow the tightness to dissolve?" No. My head is held tightly in place by muscles that stretch rigidly from skull to shoulders. "Would you touch your head just below your left ear. What do you feel?" Nothing special.

"Would you tap with your fingers all around the ear. Then tap out in all directions from the ear, starting with strong tapping by the ear, letting it become lighter as you go away from it." We do so. When I stop I feel, standing there with my eyes closed, that the ear has expanded and is now open and huge. Life radiates from it. The right ear seems shriveled by comparison. Now the right ear. Waves of life go out from each ear. "Each tap is an event that arouses a process," says Miss Selver. I open my eyes. The head sits easily atop the neck now, nothing is rigid anymore, the breath flows easily.

She takes a brass gong and strikes it once with a mallet. The vibrations go on and on, changing, fading, going into me through my wide-open ears and through my whole body. Again she strikes it. This time it is different but equally beautiful.

"This is only metal," she says. "But we have all those nerves and cells. When you tapped around your ears you began a process that may still be going on unless you cut it off. Most of the time we don't allow a process to come to its end. We live like this." She strikes the gong, which she is holding on a string, and immediately cuts off the sound with her hand. The effect is jarring.

Then she takes a silver Mexican candlestick from the windowsill, puts it on the floor in the center of the room and lights the red candle in it. "This is the beginning of a process," she says. She sways a little before it and the flame follows her. "This is like your breathing." Then she bends and blows out the candle. A wisp of smoke rises upward. "You see, nothing ends suddenly. This is a phenomenon of nature. Don't make a philosophy out of it, it is simply a natural phenomenon. After I finish speaking, you still hear my words. Yet we seldom allow this process to take its course. We do things abruptly. That's why we read so many books—as soon as we have read the words, they cease to exist for us and we immediately start something new. But the natural way is—it is not exactly a waiting, it is this." She bows slowly from her waist. "I give you the right to your own suchness," she says, quoting D. T. Suzuki. Again she hits the gong. "This will never happen again and it only sounds this way because I happen to hit it this way." She gives the gong to the person nearest to her who hits it and passes it on. Each person's sound is different. "If you try to remember how something is done and try to repeat it, if you rely on some formulation instead of your own experience, you will never go very deep, you will work second hand," she says. "Let us again come to standing. Allow your eyelids to close." We stand still. I feel happy and peaceful. "Let your eyes open." We do. "Goodbye."

The old lady with orange-dyed hair goes out with me. "I'm going to take Charlotte's course in Mexico over Christmas," she says. "I still haven't told my family, they wouldn't understand. They still think I'm taking my same old courses at the New School. But I knew there must be a better way to live. I was getting by all right, of course, I got as far as being a grandmother and the children turned out fine. But when I saw this course in the catalog it intrigued me and I went right into it like a fish into water. Well, good-bye."

She hurries toward Broadway, I go in the opposite direction. As I walk toward the bus stop, feeling the cold wind against my face, it occurs to me that there is too much clutter in my apartment and I want to hurry home to throw out most of the furniture, the paintings and books, and leave only a few lovely things in a large open space. Like Zen, Charlotte Selver's sensory awakening leads to the taste for a single flower rather than the elaborate bouquet.

Through the bus window I watch other buses glide past each other like fish in an aquarium. My eyes are a threshold through which they pass. Normally I would be thinking ahead and planning my day during this trip. But now I am "all there for the experience," as Miss Selver would put it, and see only the street scene outside and the bus scene around me. If I were fully awake, I might also be able to do my day's planning at the same time, but these six classes have given me only a taste of what that's all about. Around me I see weary New York faces, worn and pulled out of shape by the constant shoving, shouting and grabbing that is so much a part of this city's way of life. A fully awake person, Miss Selver says, would stay free even in this environment.

Charlotte Selver's work is in the field Michael Murphy, quoting Aldous Huxley, calles the nonverbal humanities. She has influenced many on the turned-on scene, including Richard Baker, president of the San Francisco Zen Center, who studied with her and remains an admirer. In the spring of 1967 and 1968, she joined with Shunryu Suzuki Roshi in leading a seminar for the benefit of the Zen Center, so bringing even closer together the Eastern and Western paths toward expanded awareness.

Another lady who works to free bodily processes, though in an entirely different way, is Ida Rolf. I've been told that her technique of structural integration is as rough as Charlotte Selver's sensory awakening is gentle. I met Dr. Rolf at Esalen, but did not get a chance to find out much about her until I returned to New York. Her office is only a few blocks away from Miss Selver's.

Chapter FIFTEEN

Rolfing

EVERYWHERE she looks, Dr. Ida P. Rolf sees out-of-shape, twisted, warped bodies locked in battle with gravity. She finds it pitiful—all that energy wasted on fighting the pull of the earth.

"These are average people I'm talking about," she told me. "I'm referring to random bodies, people who think of themselves as normal and whom their friends see as normal. It's rare to find a person with structural integrity, a body stacked properly with respect to gravity, free to move. Most people never *were* integrated, either. That's myth. Children are born with imbalances and dislocations and have to go through life with them because in spite of all we know about body chemistry, we know very little about body mechanics.

"Mind, I'm not talking about posture, I'm talking about structure. Posture is holding your structure as well as you can. When the structure is properly balanced, good posture is natural. A man slouches not because he has a bad habit but because his structure doesn't make it easy for him not to slouch. Structure implies the relationship of parts and it implies gravity. In school they never make you feel you are living in a gravitational field. We know about gravity in architecture. We know that buildings show strain to the degree that they deviate from an optimal relation to gravitational pulls. In buildings we recognize the origins of these strains but in bodies we don't. So we talk about back trouble, indigestion, a bad heart, bursitis, when what we are really talking about is a maladjustment to gravity. People spend an enormous amount of energy fighting their bodies because we ignore gravity. So that's our work. We align bodies with respect to gravity."

We sat in Ida Rolf's Esalen workroom down at the baths, next to the massage room. I had heard many stories about her treatments, which she called structural integration and postural release and her clients called rolfings. The stories had to do with cures for backaches, headaches, even alleviation of a serious heart ailment; with straightenings of slumped, pot-bellied frames, sudden gains in vitality, and with pain. Rolfing hurt, people told me—but if you really wanted to get down to basic potentialities, it was worth it. Rolfing hurt, others added—and you feel so good afterward only because the pain is over.

With such stories I had conjured up the image of some witch. But this gruff-friendly old lady was more like an Amazonian grandmother. I knew she was more than seventy years old. Her hair was completely white, her face was lined with fine wrinkles. She was of sturdy girth but no taller than five feet five inches. Yet she looked strong enough to knock over any youth. As she spoke she was dead serious. But there was a sparkle in her light-blue eyes that revealed kindness and humor.

"How do we become so misshapen?" I asked her.

"Through accidents, mostly. A child falls out of a tree, then off a bicycle, then out of a car. These things take their toll, even without apparent injuries. A bone may be slightly displaced and when the swelling goes away, this bone and the muscle structure around it are left in a different position— just slightly different. But now there is a new balance. Other parts begin to compensate. The way the body is stacked shifts. Some muscles shorten and thicken, others become rigid. Fascial sheaths lose their ability to slide over each other. Eventually the body loses its freedom of movement and develops all kinds of stresses and strains.

"The trouble can also start with an emotional problem. A person who is afraid or sad or angry dramatizes this state in a body attitude. If the feeling becomes habitual, the muscular arrangement becomes set. The emotional and physical attitudes then reinforce each other and the man is restricted in many ways. If the balance is dislocated badly enough, the

243

supply of blood and oxygen to various parts of the body is cut off and you get a loss of energy with or without all kinds of ailments."

"So you cure ailments by rearranging the body structure?"

"We don't stress illness," she said. "People come with 'belly-aches,' bad shoulders, bursitis, heart conditions. Those are reasons why they are willing to part with money to come to us. But we're interested in making better people. We don't compete with medics. Our eyes are turned on well-being where theirs are on what's wrong. What's wrong often disappears spontaneously in the process of righting the structure. And personality changes occur at the same time. The psychological barriers break down along with the breaking of the physical barriers to movement."

"Sounds like what osteopaths and chiropractors do."

"No. They see the body as an aggregate of segments and work mainly with the relation of structures to adjoining structures. We see the man as an aggregation of blocks—head, thorax, pelvis and legs. These blocks must be in balance if the smaller units are to work well together. So in our work we align the blocks. The smaller units then can fall into place spontaneously. A back pain often occurs at the extreme point of misalignment of blocks.

"But let's talk some more in New York, since we're both headed there," she said. "I work there with my son. If you like, you can come to a demonstration and then experience what I'm talking about by taking a processing yourself. You're not as bad as some," she said with a smile as I got up to leave. "But there's hardly anyone who can't profit from it."

Apparently Dick Price, Esalen's vice-president, agreed. For though he looked beautifully aligned to me, he was waiting outside the door for a rolfing.

Most of the Esalen gurus have undergone rolfings. Perls, who came from Los Angeles with a heart ailment, credited Ida Rolf and the Big Sur air with saving his life. Ed Maupin, Bill Schutz, Price, and Bernard Gunther, all of whom seemed in excellent shape, found the treatments beneficial in smaller but still significant ways. Among other Rolf clients are skeptics and devoted Rolfites. The Rolfites say the treatments are a liberation and a blessing. The skeptics call some of Ida Rolf's procedures hocus-pocus. "She talks such a good game you don't know what to believe," said one man who had returned for numerous treatments. But I also met people who came with no special mind-set and went away singing her praises.

244

Perhaps the most dramatic case is that of a thirty-five year-old woman, who lived with her husband, a poet, in a tiny cabin on Partington Ridge, a few miles from the Big Sur Hot Springs. She worked part-time in Esalen's kitchen. At age three she had suffered polio, which had left her with her left leg three-fourths of an inch shorter than her right. This caused her to limp and suffer back pain.

"My parents spent thousands of dollars on physical therapy and the hip got straightened to where the leg was just a quarter-inch shorter," she told me. "But I'd often snap it out of place and then it got stiff and hurt horribly. That happened last year while I was down here. Someone said, 'Go see Ida Rolf.' I didn't know anything about her then but I went down to look for her down at the baths. She said she was too busy. But then she looked at me standing there in obvious pain and told me to come in. I lay down on my back and she lifted me several times in the middle. The pain didn't stop completely, but it wasn't nearly as bad. The next day she called me. She said, 'I couldn't sleep last night because I said no to you. Come on over today.' She gave me seven treatments in all. On the fifth, I think it was, I was lying down and she was working on my ankle when suddenly my whole back felt like it cracked. It was excruciating and I couldn't help it, I kicked her in the head. She just said, 'I can honestly tell you I never cracked a back in my life.' After the seventh treatment I felt fine and I was straight. She told me as she left for New York that if I ever snapped my back again she would pay her own way to come back and fix it. But I haven't had any more trouble."

Outside the self-realization circuit, Ida Rolf is little-known except among osteopaths and chiropractors, even though she travels extensively in the United States, England and elsewhere. This is so partly because people tend to be wary of physical manipulations that don't have the stamp of approval from physicians, partly because she has trained only a handful of disciples, partly because she is impatient with demands for documented proof of the effectiveness of her work. She has stated in articles, that laboratory tests had shown that "an immediate and lasting shift in the homeostatic equilibrium" accompanies the body's realignment; and reported that changes had been observed by taking urine tests, blood counts, stool cultures, and measures of blood cholesterol, blood enzymes, redox potential, protein-bound iodine and various proteins. Measures by the Cameron Heartometer had also shown changes in the pulse rate, peripheral circulation, heart and body rhythms, she has written. But the results have not been compiled, nor have any outsiders scrutinized her treatments with scientific measuring tools.

In Dr. Rolf's apartment on Riverside Drive, I looked at albums of Polaroid snapshots of bodies before and after treatments. Dramatic changes seem to have occurred on nearly all of them. Paunches are gone, legs and necks stand vertically instead of slanting, backsides look smaller. People look younger and thinner although no dieting accompanies the treatments and Dr. Rolf says no weight changes are involved. "A paunch usually means that the lumbar spine is displaced, tilting the pelvic basin which then can't hold the viscera and they sag out," she explained.

Most of the photos show bodies before the start of treatments and after the ten sessions she considers the minimal unit. But there are also some taken before and after one treatment and a few taken a year after a ten-session rolfing. These don't look quite as good, but not nearly as bad as the initial picture.

"Look at this child," she said, pointing at a series of pictures. "He's brain-injured and ten years old. He just sat in a rocking chair by the window. He didn't even go to the bathroom. He was doing first-grade work with a special teacher." The photo showed a little boy standing limply, with his arms dangling at his sides, in an attitude of someone treading on uncertain ground. In the photo after ten sessions he stood firmly, alert and self-confident. At the end of the sessions with her son, Dr. Rolf said, the child was promoted from first grade to fifth.

A bulletin of the Foundation for Brain-Injured Children, headed by the child's mother, reported that after the treatments the boy was no longer afraid of falling or of noises. "The protruding teeth assumed a more normal attitude and the voice quality changed from animal-like sounds to the normal voice range of sounds. The desire to talk was facilitated and although speech had not emerged his total involvement and understanding of language is evident," the bulletin reported.

"All this with just your treatments?" I asked. "How did it happen?"

"How? God knows how. We know very little about how things happen in this or in medicine. It happened and let's be grateful it did, that's all."

Coming from a tent preacher, such words would sound naïve. But Dr. Rolf is a graduate of Barnard College, has a Ph.D. in biochemistry from Columbia University (1920) and spent fifteen years in chemical research at the Rockefeller Institute for Medical Research. A personal problem in her family led her into her later work and into becoming one of a growing number of people who believe that Western medicine has lost sight of the whole man in its great thrust toward specialization.

"The data available through modern research methods to anyone capable of interpreting them is beyond the wildest dreams of the medical scientists of even fifty years ago," she wrote in the June 1963 issue of the British journal *Systematics*. "But this information has been derived from, and applied to, isolated bits of human tissue. . . . Where is the Man?"

The evening Dr. Rolf gives a demonstration, about twenty people are present, mostly as my guests. They include a couple of dancers, a physician and his wife, two lawyers, a reporter interested in medicine, and my friend Mel, who is to be the demonstration subject. She talks a bit, shows slides of the pictures I saw in her album, then calls for Mel, who stands before us all in his worn underpants. At this point, Dr. Rolf turns on something that is known as "the bedside manner" when practiced by physicians but referred to as "the pitch" when used by other healers. She looks at Mel with amazement and pity.

"What do you do for a living?" she asks.

"I'm a sculptor."

She drops her arms and steps back. "Man, you really believe in working for a living with a body like that. Look at him," she says, turning to the audience. "You see how his feet are?" They are turned out. "If these were wheels, would anyone ride in a car with wheels like that?" With feet turned out, ankles cannot function properly, she says. Neither ankles nor knees can act as true hinges. "You can see how much energy this poor guy loses in the course of a day."

Mel's left shoulder is considerably higher than his right. His ribs sag. His back curves in a severe scoliosis. His neck is thrust forward so that he has to hold his head rather than just balancing it. By the time she has pointed out all these deficiencies, it seems that any improvement would be a godsend. She spreads a sheet on the rug and asks him to lie on it on his back.

"Take a deep breath," she tells him. His chest rises and falls. "Well, at least your breathing is all right," she says. Then her son, Dr. Richard Demmerle (licensed as chiropractor) kneels beside him, picks up his right wrist, raises the arm and drops it above the head. He does the same with the other arm. The elbows seem to get stuck in the air above Mel's head.

Now Dr. Demmerle begins to press, push, dig his fingers in between muscles, slide the heel of his hand along the demonstratee's body. Mel grins in pain. "It's not possible to make changes without pain," says Dr. Rolf. "But as soon as the pressure is off, the pain is gone."

Dr. Demmerle eventually sits up, picks up Mel's left arm and drops it over his head again. This time it flaps out farther, showing more balance in the shoulder muscles. He continues to dig, prod and slide about while Dr. Rolf provides a commentary:

"You see this man with his curved back, his left shoulder higher than the right. Doing sculpture aggravates the condition because it strengthens the strong parts of him and increases the imbalance. It's the same with exercise. Exercise is fine if your body is properly aligned. If it is not, it aggravates the misalignment. The difference between what you see here and exercise is the difference between training and education. In training you install a pattern which is not natural through repetition. Education comes from the roots *e ducere*—to lead out. It does not require repetitious training but an organization of your assets. Once led out, you operate in the new way because it is a joy to do so and much easier." Similar words were said by John Dewey about F. M. Alexander, who developed a method of "creative conscious control" to improve posture and make possible what he called "the proper use of self." Dewey favored inclusion of some such system in education. Dr. Rolf studied a version of Alexander's technique.

Dr. Demmerle drops Mel's left arm above his head once again. This time it continues moving outward in a semicircle until it lies horizontal to his shoulder.

After an hour of what looked to one man in the audience as slow-motion karate, Mel is asked to breathe deeply again. His rib cage has expanded, the ribs are more independently visible. When he stands up, his feet are more parallel. There is no visible change in the shoulder levels or the scoliosis. The neck is much more vertical.

"He will not keep all of this, but he'll keep about seventy-five percent," Dr. Rolf says. The demonstration is over. As Mel goes off to get dressed and be photographed, the physician, a young and humorless internist, gets into a hassle with Ida Rolf. He wants to know how she measured that 75 percent.

"It cannot be measured with a ruler. This is a process, an experience," she says hotly.

"You said 75 percent."

"Figures, statistics! You can't put this in figures."

"You said . . ."

"Analyzing! Didn't you see the changes? How would you measure what you saw? How would you measure what that man feels now?"

"But this has been the cry of religion through the ages," complains the exasperated young man. "Don't question."

"No. Don't *measure*," Ida Rolf says, turning away. The physician addresses those around him:

"There is no evidence. She did not show us what she was going to do before it was done. She showed his front and his back before starting but did not say what changes might be expected. At the end she did not show the back where the scoliosis was as visible as before. The pictures were taken from the side, but she did not show his side. There is no evidence. You have to have controls. You have to check how much is explained simply by the power of suggestion. You have to compare this with other methods."

"What other methods are there?" I ask. He doesn't know. Orthopedics had not come up with much recently, he says. He is here, as a matter of fact, because his wife, who had a whiplash injury, had found Ida Rolf helpful after medicine had failed to alleviate her pain.

But what about that 75 percent? I ask Ida Rolf as we leave. "I meant the bulk, of course," she says, "what does it matter, exacty—60 percent, 80 per cent, 75. Who knows? He'll keep most of it." And there it is—the basic difference between the scientist and the intuitive healer, or perhaps rather—the specialist and the holist.

To my surprise, Mel signed up for another treatment, and then another. He did not know what percentage of what he kept, but he found that his back pain lessened and a leg pain disappeared. I had a rolfing, found it painful but not unbearable and afterward felt I had a balance that had eluded me as well as more flexibility in the rib cage. It did not seem to matter whether manipulation or suggestion brought the change, for it was beneficial, and it remained for at least three months. Unfortunately, because of the scarcity of Rolf disciples, rolfings are available only to a few in the vast multitude of random, warped bodies.

Chapter SIXTEEN

Self-style into Art as Life-process

ONE NIGHT during the 1967–68 season at the San Francisco Dancers Workshop, audience and dancers together took part in an event called "Atonement" that required them to stay totally still for one hour while a drum played very loud. It marked another step by Ann Halprin, the Workshop's director and founder, in breaking boundaries between theater and life.

Before entering the large loft where the event was to be held, the audience met in a studio next door and was told that what was about to happen would be an ordeal, not something pleasant. They were to choose a position—standing, kneeling or whatever—and remain that way for one hour while the snare drum played without stopping. Nobody opted out of the experience, and only one of about fifty people left before it ended.

When the sound went off they remained completely still, absorbed in what had happened. Then, returning to the other studio, they were asked to divide into small groups, choose two words that came closest to describing their experience, and tell them to others.

"We found people had paradoxical experiences," Ann Halprin recalled. "One said 'death and love,' another 'scared and strong.' People stayed and talked for a long time. Though they had come as strangers, they found themselves communicating on a very deep and intimate level. It was, as it was intended to be, a collective experience."

But was it theater? Dance? Was it a truth lab? A meditation? A sensory awareness session? If pressed, Ann Halprin will say that it was an art experience because, to her, an art experience requires the presence of ritual, "an act of transformation that involves mutual recognition between the acted

250

upon and the actor." But definitions become irrelevant as boundaries break down between forms.

"Atonement" was part of a series of events called "Myths" that grew partly out of reaction to one of the Workshop's major productions, "Parades and Changes," when it toured the country and Europe the previous year. Ann Halprin saw the piece as significant because of the way it brought together strong artists from different media—composers Morton Sobotnik and Folke Rabe, lightman Patric Hickey, sculptor Charles Ross, painter Jo Lander, Mrs. Halprin and her dancers.

"It was a grand experiment that took us three years to evolve," she told me. "We all became interdependent. Soon Morton was choreographing, the dancers began to make sounds, everything became mixed up." In the process, the group began to use nudity. "It wasn't meant to be a shocker," Ann Halprin said. "It just grew out of the natural use of certain materials we were working with." But when the work was done in New York, nudity was what brought the big reaction—including a warrant for Mrs. Halprin's arrest.

After that, Ann Halprin reflected that she had paid too little attention to the state of the audience. "Myths" became a way to explore relationships with it. On another evening, "Totem," people again entered together from the studio next door. This time everyone chose one of some fifty chairs scattered through the room, around several dancers who were already in position—a boy and a girl chained together to a couch, a veiled woman on a dentist's chair, a girl in a white turn-of-the-century dress standing on a toy chair and holding a peppermint-striped pole rising from it; a tall man, in whiteface, dressed completely in black, with morning suit and top hat, sitting rigid on a chair that wore black shoes on its front legs.

Sitting down near these figures, the audience was led through a sensory awareness session by Ann Halprin, exploring their relationship with their chairs. Later as the dancers began to improvise with their chairs and each other, some of the audience moved up next to the performers and joined in. At the end of the evening, all chairs and other sitting furniture was piled into a huge pyre and everyone danced around it.

What would emerge for Ann Halprin and her group from these events was uncertain—it was likely to be many things —but it was also, in one sense, irrelevant. For in this highly experimental company, there are no divisions between experiment and finished work as, in "Myths," there was none between performers and audience.

"I think what is unique about our company is that there is no separation between the training, rehearsing and performance," Ann Halprin said. "It's all one creative experience. Every moment in training and rehearsal is a moment of discovery." Every work evolves in performance and is never done the same way twice. "What makes the truly contemporary artists different is that everything is indeterminate, all compositions have openings, there are many possibilities, allowing each individual to enter in his own way, self-determining his art experience. Everything is process."

If she sounds like Perls, an Eastern mystic or an acid head, that is not surprising, for Ann Halprin's work is very much in the stream of the turned-on view of life. Her dancers have regular sessions with Perls, in fact, and are trained more in awareness than in techniques.

"Craftsmanship is in the process rather than the product," she said. "You cannot worry about making your body a perfectly trained instrument, in the traditional classical sense. Good movement comes through motivation to move. Training concentrates on developing awareness of the inner mechanism of the body, its relation to the environment, and awareness of the flow of foreground and background in interaction."

One class, for example, dealt with a study, in minute detail, of what it is to be open in every single joint in the body and what feelings relate to it. "In order to work on open movement you have to learn to get your body operating as a total unit so that you don't think about what you're doing but what you do contains the thinking process."

Mrs. Halprin is the wife of Lawrence Halprin, the landscape architect, and comes from a background of modern dance. But the principal influence on her, she says, was Margaret H'Doubler, with whom she studied for five years at the University of Wisconsin. Margaret H'Doubler taught a system of movement based on biological and anatomical approach, showing how certain movements would naturally evolve from others and relating them to the feeling states they evoked. She viewed dance as a creative art experience and stressed its powerful educative values.

"What I call the development of a self-style is just another way of saying what H'Doubler said years ago—that each person is unique and each person's body contains within it a background and sense of value and needs and desires which are unique. She did not call it self-style. I gave it a name to clarify that this is not *my* style."

But then Ann Halprin went on to develop H'Doubler's ideas into an environmental art influenced by Bauhaus concepts. "The Bauhaus approach to architecture was one in which they were dealing with breaking open the whole concept of architecture. The idea that architecture was space created with materials for people blew my mind because what they were doing with architecture was what Margaret H'Doubler was doing for individuals in movement. The two things came together beautifully," she said.

In the early 1950s, she began a group called "The Workshop" (Bauhaus means workshop in German) in Marin County, near San Francisco. Her husband, collaborating with Arch Lauterer, built her an outdoor dance deck at their home by the foot of Mount Tamalpais. "It was the first dance space that was completely free-wheeling and open, with no fixed center," she said. "At first I didn't know where to put myself, where to go. All stages and studios are rectangles or squares. But here there was no right or left, no up or down. It was completely irregular but completely valid for where it was in relation to the land, the trees and the mountains. We were forced to orient ourselves differently and it drew us out from the deck itself into areas that included the stairways and spaces beneath the deck and the woods. The whole idea of a beginning, middle and end had no meaning. You could end walking five miles up the mountain and it still wouldn't be the end. So this began to affect the way I composed."

In "Five-Legged Stool," performed in a theater in San Francisco, the dancers stood on stage looking at the audience and at each other for about ten minutes as a non-beginning. At the non-end, doors that led from the stage into the street were opened and feathers came drifting down over the stage. "The feathers just went on and on and people said, 'Well, has it ended or not?' And then the wind and the street sounds and car lights were brought into the theater in this kind of subtle way so that as people finally decided to leave they weren't really leaving, they were taking the whole thing with them into the night because we had brought the night into the theater," Mrs. Halprin said.

In "Apartment Six," differences between performer as role player and as himself were broken down as Ann Halprin cooked a meal onstage and served it to John Graham, exploring the minutiae of emotional relationships in the process. In "Parades and Changes," she continued—on a huge scale this time—to explore ways to being theater into the life context.

Her husband's work in architecture continued to influence Mrs. Halprin. In the summer of 1966, they teamed in running a four-week workshop for artists and architects called "Experiments in Environment." The twenty-nine dancers and fifteen architects and architectural students roamed beaches, woods and city streets on diverse assignments, listening, looking, and borrowing each others' artistic perspective. In the process they created dance architecture and architectural choreography.

One afternoon they sat for three hours in Union Square, in the heart of San Francisco's downtown, observing the city's comings and goings. At the stroke of three o'clock, they stood up, established eye contact, and moved toward the center of the square where they blew up balloons and released them or gave them away. The event was not done for an audience, yet an audience was involved and naturally followed the group as it walked toward the center.

The group spent quite a bit of time in sharpening sensory awareness. One day they roamed the city in teams of three. One in each team was blindfolded and reported sounds, smells and impressions. Another day they took a silent walk in the country.

They joined in building a city on the beach from driftwood, sand and other stuff lying around. The instructions were that each was to build whatever he pleased, working alone or with others, but that there was to be no communication in the process. At the end of a day, to the amazement of all, they had a city with a plaza, a temple, a tower, houses, a stage and a gate—all the basic ingredients. Everyone had built according to his nature, yet the independent efforts combined in a communal creation.

That kind of harmony between self-expression and communal experience has been Ann Halprin's aim in her work. "To me it's very important that the new freedoms and self-expression be in a social context," she told me, "because this is more pertinent, as I see life situations, than going off on your own trip, by yourself. . . . It is possible to overwhelm an audience with what a performer can do. Then you get comments like, 'Isn't that a feat?' 'Isn't that inventive?' I'm not interested in that."

Ann Halprin's way of thinking has parallels elsewhere. In San Francisco State College's film department, students were led blind-folded to the beach to heighten their awareness of sensory impressions other than visual. At the California College of Arts and Crafts, sculpture students have gone through sessions of exploration in movement, created events with balloons and masks. At the San Francisco Museum of Art, fifteen sculptors and painters presented a two and a half hour collection of edible works, which were consumed—meat loaf tiger, bread busts—by artists and guests together.

The breaking of boundaries has made it hard to say, at times, whether an artist is a musician, a dancer, a painter or something else. In New York, Anthony Cox and h s wife, Yoko Ono, presented "The Stone" at the Judson Church Gallery. It was a bag experience: you got into a black bag that let you look out but did not allow anyone to see you, and spent some time in a paper-walled room while lights went on, dimmed and went out, a tape loop played, and the message "From here to here" was projected on one wall. On'y a fourth of the message was visible on any one day. The music and the message were intended to give an endless feeling. People became part of the environment.

Yoko Ono has been called a painter, writer and composer. Usually she uses the word "works" or "events" to describe what she does. Her concert in Carnegie Recital Hall inc'u ed "a piece for strawberries and violin" in which, according to a music critic, "two dancers stood up and sat down alternately for some ten minutes in silence. Then they sat down to a laden table and ended by breaking all the dishes."

On the sales list of Yoko Ono's works is a "sound tape of snow falling at dawn—25 cents per inch. Types: a. snow of India, b. snow of Kyo, c. snow of AOS." Her events, she has said, are spent mostly in wonderment.

Amazement, celebration and wonderment are characteristic of the art that grows out of a sense of reality as an ever-changing pattern of particles. It reminds of a story told by Joseph Campbell, author of *Hero of a Thousand Faces*, about a Western philosopher who visited a Japanese Shinto monastery, did homage to its beauty, and then said he did not understand the theology. The head monk told him, "We have no theology. We dance."

If a process is fully attended to, the boundaries between life and art become hard to distinguish. Frederick Perls, Charlotte Selver, the Zen student eating a meal in the zendo, Ann Halprin and the girl in hobbit-garb in Golden Gate Park are all engaged in artistic experience.

But while Ann Halprin, Yoko Ono and others talk of light shows beamed from skyscrapers to illuminate entire cities, the new openness and freedom have also led to another polarity, a merger of art and therapy, in which the celebration becomes involuted in a microscopic examination of the psyche.

A. A. Leath and John Graham are talented and accomplished dancers, actors and teachers of movement. Leath, like Ann Halprin, was a student of Margaret H'Doubler's; Graham has a diverse background of study, performance and teaching. Both broke away from Dancers Workshop, after an association of more than a decade, to join Dr. Gene Sagan, an ex-disciple of Perls now practicing therapy without Perls' blessing. Together the two dancers and Sagan founded the Institute for Creative and Artistic Development, one of the more bizarre self-game communities on the West Coast.

There is an understanding among ICAD members that they should have no secrets from each other. Sagan and his wife, Juanita, a teacher who now gives lessons in "creative behavior," Leath and Graham constantly examine and re-examine every moment of the process between them. Therapy sessions are tape-recorded and sometimes taken to a Sagan-trained "integrator" for analysis. Some ICAD members tape-record even domestic quarrels for later examination. When I interviewed Sagan, Leath and Graham, each of them also tape-recorded the interview. Leath suggested I take my tape to an integrator who would help me to understand my experience with him.

As dance teachers, both Graham and Leath are widely admired. Graham is on the faculty of San Francisco State College, Leath teaches privately. But another aspect of their professional work, Graham-Leath Productions, is extremely controversial. A performance I attended was to me an annihilation of intimacy by overexposure. It was openness taken to such an extreme it became suffocation.

The site was the New Orleans House, a bar-restaurant on a wide street in suburban Berkeley devoid of night life. It was an unlikely place and perhaps therefore perfect. Shortly before the beginning of the performance—or had it already begun?—people hunched over tables embracing and caressing each other. A girl in a miniskirt and net stockings hugged a tense woman in a Marimekko dress. A barefoot woman with a flowing purple skirt and long brown hair hugged a chinless young man, then moved to kiss someone at the door. A very tall fellow in a blue and white polka-dot shirt with puff sleeves and white collar and cuffs grabbed hold of A. A. Leath's shoulders, looked into the firm-featured bearded face. His hands slid down to Leath's buttocks and pressed, his head sank, he buried his face in Leath's neck. They stood that way in a doorway while the woman in purple watched and others passed. When they separated, Leath looked unconcerned but the other fellow was flushed. This was a public performance but audience and performers appeared intimately acquainted.

About nine o'clock, John Graham, tall and bony, his sensitive face grimacing in self-mockery, brought out a brightly patterned banner with letters resembling Japanese calligraphy

256

and pasted it to a wall. It read: "The meaning of life is the celebration of it."

Eventually, Leath, Graham and a lovely, radiant young girl named Jani Novak began to clown and then dance. Before long it became apparent that they were improvising on the theme of their rather complex relationship. The performance was a continuation of what existed between them not only in New Orleans House but also outside. Each week they offered a new installment, like a TV serial—except that this was not fiction.

Leath and Jani Novak began a love dance while Graham, who was Miss Novak's fiance, watched from a couch. The movements were intense and beautiful but I felt I was watching a very private scene. They looked a hair's breadth from orgasm when I saw an expression of absorption and pain on Graham's face. What was this I was watching? Two lovers watched by a suffering voyeur? Or were we all voyeurs?

When Jani Novak and Graham later danced together, she glowed with inviting sensuality, he rejected her with gestures that began as caresses and ended in smacks, swats and bites. Soon Miss Novak was in tears. As he held her, his hands tapping on her shoulders told of his discomfort. But as soon as she abandoned the sexual come-on, he relaxed and they cuddled on the couch like two affectionate children.

Almost anything could be performed onstage in the winter of 1967–68. But this was not the performance of something —this was real, these people were themselves, they were not acting roles. They were using their skill as dancers to reveal intimate details about themselves. At one point Leath began a rather regal dance but stopped suddenly, collapsed into fetal position and began to roll on the floor. Graham began to spank him. This, I learned later, was a technique advocated by Gene Sagan. Dancers routinely spanked each other or were spanked by Sagan when someone deemed it necessary for some reason. As the scene ended with Leath whimpering, then rising to dance with a mother figure summoned from the audience, I felt someone should draw a curtain. But there was no curtain or stage. The audience, which was as much a part of the show as the performers, was engrossed in the action. The evening ended in a communal dance, but it left me claustrophobic.

Graham-Leath Productions, like Ann Halprin's work, in some ways resembles the method used by Stanislavsky in training actors for the Moscow Art Theater. However, here there is no play to be performed. Life and theater have merged completely. "In one way there is no end product,"

Graham said, "and in another, the process is the end product."

A key difference between the productions and psychodrama is (besides the talent and skill of the dancers) the fact that "we give more credit to each other for what we do," Graham said. By that he meant, he said, "supporting what the person is—helping him to celebrate what he feels is to be celebrated . . . but celebration is something that people don't allow themselves."

The bothersome quality, which put off many people including me in the New Orleans House, became more apparent in a performance of the More Joy Dancers, another ICAD group, which put on a show in a San Francisco theater one evening. Their cavortings, not benefiting from as much style and grace, seemed a repetitive *ad nauseam* fondling of feelings, a cry of ME! Look at this FEELING I'm having, isn't it beautiful? The hugging and kissing audience of in-groupers seemed to dig it and "gave credit." But I felt even more claustrophobic. There seemed to be a total absence of awareness that a wider world was out there, with riots, dreams and spaceships. The group seemed to be reacting to depersonalization in society by such total destruction of distinctions between public and private that the result was again depersonalization, from over amazement at psychological minutiae.

To the extent that the outward-reaching artistic explorers expanded man's context, these self-celebrators diminished it. Instead of becoming specks, each reflecting the universe, they saw the universe as the speck, it seemed to me. It was again a case of the polarities that arise from LSD: some people return from the trip saying "Thou art God" or "All is God," while others cry, "Look, I am God worshiping myself."

Graham's work with students at San Francisco State College, however, was exciting to watch. During three sessions of a beginning movement class, I saw a man who at first could not make the slightest free movement start to develop a self-style. In the first class he was so tense he ran around shooting imaginary baskets while others tried to relax. He did sit-ups while others tried to go with body sensations; he burst into nervous laughter when asked to focus attention on his toes. By the third class, he actually began a tentative dance improvisation.

A strong self-style, growing out of an inner physical, emotional and intellectual freedom, can help a man remain human in an environment that assaults his mind and senses constantly with powerful stimuli. If he is not to become a manipulated puppet, he must become aware of how his organism works and develop the inner tools to deal with his environment. All the turn-on gurus,—be they mystical, sensory, Gestalt or physical—aim in this direction. Dr. Joe Kamiya, a San Francisco psychologist, is a pioneer in still another aspect of this field. He has found a method to teach people to tune in on their brainwaves and so, to some extent, determine their own moods. His work may be a first step toward control of one's own emotions without drugs, and also may broaden our language of inner experience.

Chapter SEVENTEEN

Joe Kamiya— Your Own Mind Music

IN TALKING about expanding consciousness one invariably comes up against the fact that there are no words with generally accepted meanings to describe many inner states. "Cosmic trip" may mean a lot to an acid head but little or nothing to someone who has had no similar experience. Westerners are only beginning to travel in inner space in sizable numbers and have not yet evolved a language for discoveries that have no exterior referents.

In India, where the unconscious that Freud discovered has been known for two thousand years, Buddhists have classified 151 states of mind, according to Huston Smith, the philosopher. In the West we have only imprecise words like joy, sorrow, bliss, anger, serenity, terror, anxiety. The more subtle differentiations are a vague terrain usually left to poets and philosophers. Most scientists consider subjective experience inaccessible to investigation and confine themselves to recording its outer manifestations, such as heartbeat, pulse rate, pupil dilation, respiration.

Among the few who do deem subjective experience to be scientifically relevant is Dr. Joe Kamiya, a psychologist who is pioneering in inner space research at the Langley-Porter Neuropsychiatric Institute in San Francisco.

With the use of the electroencephalogram (the EEG), he is training people to become aware of their brains' electrical activity, learn to control it to some extent and so become able to alter their states of mind. In the process, he believes he is moving toward a language of inner experience.

"We might someday be able to say, 'you arouse in me two-tenths alpha, one-tenth beta, seven-tenths theta' and be understood exactly," he told me. "We don't know to what extent the waves do reflect the whole range of human experience, but all our evidence indicates that the locus of human experience is the brain. Experience is that publicly unobservable response I have to events within and around me. It is a biochemical, electrical, physiological pattern. To the extent our detecting equipment is sensitive to these we should be able to detect experience. If the criterion is whether I will be able to put myself into your skin and experience what you experience, we can never resolve it. But let's say we have developed this coordinate and I make a map of your subjective space and give you an object to describe. To the extent the description coincides we know more clearly that we experience the same thing."

Such a map with coordinates has been worked out to differentiate subtleties in taste, Kamiya pointed out. Mapping ecstasy will not be as simple—and we may find the word obsolete by the time the map is finished—but he believes it may happen as the work he has begun develops and its technology becomes more precise.

Another objective of his research, however, may not be that distant. He foresees that many people may learn to tune in on their brainwaves and so achieve greater control over their own moods, emotions and thoughts without the use of outside agents like psychedelic drugs, tranquilizers or alcohol.

Joe Kamiya is a rather square man. He is not a psychedelic tripper and has no special interest in hip subjects like Eastern thought or C. G. Jung. But his work has aroused such interest among acid heads and meditators that he is besieged with volunteers who want to serve as subjects in his research. Michael Murphy, the president of Esalen, believes that Kamiya's place in the history of the inner space race would be ensured if he only stopped experimenting long enough to publish the results of his work.

That work began in 1958, when Kamiya was part of a team doing research on sleep at the University of Chicago. In the process, he decided to find out if people could detect their brainwaves. He hoped to learn whether there were any images, emotions or feelings associated with their comings and goings.

Brainwaves are voltages generated by the brain and can be recorded by attaching electrodes to the scalp and hooking them to a voltage meter. The graphic record of the waves is the EEG. It looks like a constantly changing series of wave patterns. One of these patterns is the alpha rhythm, which is present in the waking state, particularly when the eyes are closed, but disappears almost completely in sleep and when a person is looking at something.

Kamiya used operant conditioning, as developed by B. F. Skinner, in his experiments, but with one difference: the stimulus was inside the subject. He hooked volunteers into EEG machinery and asked them to guess, when they heard the bell, whether they were in state A or state B. If alpha rhythm was present when the bell rang, A was the right answer. After every guess, the subjects were told if they were right. Within seven half-hour sessions, eight of eleven subjects could distinguish the two states. Soon Kamiya found that ability to discern the alpha rhythm led to the ability to control it. At his request, the subjects began to turn alpha on or off.

In 1962 Kamiya moved to Langley-Porter and there continued the research. Now, instead of guesses, he began to use a tone that beeped when alpha was on. So the subjects were hearing their own brain music and learning to modulate it. Most people learned to increase or decrease the amount of alpha rhythm within four sessions. But when they were asked how they did it, they seldom could say. Alpha stayed on, some noticed, when they felt peaceful, let their minds rest, focused on their heartbeat or listened to imaginary music. It went off when pictures began to flow before their minds' eyes. Some observed that the alpha state was one of passive alertness. Most preferred to stay in alpha rather than out of it, particularly at high amplitudes.

These comments seemed to indicate some similarity between the alpha state and the meditative state. And indeed, studies of Zen monks had shown a correlation. Akira Kasamatsu and Tomio Hirai at the University of Tokyo found that alpha waves appeared in Zen Buddhist priests and students within fifty seconds of their beginning zazen. The amplitudes increased as meditation progressed, then its frequency decreased. In some priests, there appeared still another stage later—a rhythmical theta wave pattern with alpha background.

Drs. Kasamatsu and Hirai found that the zazen state had

no resemblance to either drowsiness or a hypnotic trance. In drowsiness, alpha tends to slow down; in the trance there is no change in alpha rhythm. In the zazen state, they also found, there was a greater sensitivity to sounds and, paradoxically, a lesser tendency to be distracted by them.

The most interesting finding, however, was that the four stages of EEG changes correlated with the Zen masters' evaluation of the sitters' mental states, and with the number of years spent in Zen training.

After reading the study, Kamiya tried his experiment on people who meditated or practiced yoga. He found they learned faster and achieved a greater range of control. Was it possible, then, that the EEG could be used to train people in zazen? Kamiya balked when a reporter wrote he was training Zen masters. "I'm by no means prepared to say that turning on alpha is all there is to meditation," he said. However, he added, "We may have backed into an area of human activity that we don't know much about in the West but that people in the East have been practicing for centuries."

Some people, he found, learned to turn alpha on and off so well that they were able to continue to do so even without the tone signal. One young man, a student at San Francisco State College, told Kamiya that when he could not concentrate in class he closed his eyes and turned on alpha. In a few minutes, his mind was refreshed.

Two of Kamiya's prize subjects came to him after experiences in altered states of consciousness. One, a man of twenty-seven, had tried many psychedelic drugs. When I asked him how he turned on alpha, he said, "There are certain places you'd rather be than other places and you just head for those places. Once I had this thought—it's black here and if it's black then I have to be the light. As a feeling that's good but as a thought it's bad. I don't know. Whatever I say is an intellectual approximation of what goes on. I don't like to talk about it because if you crystallize it you get identified with the crystallization and it isn't that." Like most of Kamiya's subjects, he found alpha pleasant. He spoke of being "high" on alpha. "Sometimes I'd get so high I wouldn't want to come down. The part that does what it's told tries, but the other doesn't."

A twenty-six year-old woman, a laboratory technician, had not tried psychedelic drugs but had other unusual mind experiences, including telepathy and astral projection, before she came to Kamiya. "When I was fourteen, in a summer camp," she told me, "we were watching a movie in the recreation hall when I had the sensation of *leaving* my body. I rose twenty feet above it and was able to see myself among others. It scared me at first, then I began to do what I call 'mental gymnastics.' I found I was highly receptive telepathically to some people and it seems I started to pick up thoughts. I would answer a thought of theirs as if they were speaking to me. It shocked them."

To turn on alpha, she said, "I imagine my attention sweeping over the head like radar. When I get the beat, that's where I concentrate. I put my attention there and alpha comes out."

Once, Kamiya had her go deeper into alpha instead of turning it on and off. The woman said that within four minutes she had alpha for fifty-seven seconds out of a minute. "My experience was a total absence of structured thought or image," she said. "There was color that wasn't color, like pearly gray sky with blue sifting through behind it. I was in a chair and there was no longer any physical boundary between me and the chair. It was a state in which I felt there was no limit between myself and the universe. It left me with some very interesting side effects. I felt good, rested, and when I walked down the street I felt like I knew everyone. For two or three days I was very happy, going around with a Mona Lisa smile."

If that sounds like the reported effects of transcendental meditation, so does the experience of learning to keep on alpha sound like the process of learning meditation:

"It's almost universal that in the first few trials a naïve subject succeeds only in keeping the tone away," Kamiya told me. "The harder he tries—in the usual way in which we try things—the less successful is he likely to be. At the end of the first hour most subjects will say, 'I know now. It's easy. You just forget about the experiment.' That succeeds in getting him back to the level at which he started. It gets rid of attempts to try in the deliberate, conscious kind of way, with careful planning and remembering what they tried before. Their alpha percentage time increases as they learn to go into kind of a passive vigilance—letting the tone come and be glad when it's there, but not trying to produce it. After a while they discover that certain things tend to make the tone go away, like fretting about the experiment. It seems that high alpha state does not need to be devoid of mental activity, so long as there are no visual images and the activity is not harassed. If they think about their friends, let's say, and just kind of appreciate them, that goes with alpha." In other words, what is involved is akin to grokking.

Naturally I was curious to try out this brain wave turn-on

and volunteered as an experimental subject. One evening, Joe Kamiya hooked me into the electronic machinery in his tiny lab.

He first dabbed salt paste on my forehead, my left earlobe and the back of my head, glued on three electrodes and asked me to sit in a straight chair in a windowless cubicle. Then he plugged the string-like wires dangling from the electrodes into the EEG apparatus, turned off the light and left me, shutting the door behind him. In the other room was a console with a multitude of dials. I was hooked into it as into an airplane's dashboard. And indeed, this was to be a trip. Kamiya's voice came through the intercom:

"First I'll ask you to keep the alpha on during a series of five one-minute trials. Later I'll ask you to keep it off. When it is on, you will hear a tone. Try to keep it going as long as you can. At the end of each trial I'll give you a figure so you can see how you're doing. Try to get a higher figure. The tone will vary in loudness with the amplitude of the alpha wave."

The tone was a soft, pleasant note. It was peaceful to sit there, eyes closed, in the quiet darkness. I felt myself slipping into a meditative state, riding the note as I went in. Weird, that your brainwaves should come out like this, as sounds. In the other room, I knew, Kamiya was reading a lot of zigzags drawn by a needle in red ink on a moving strip of graph paper. Pictures and thoughts flowed inside my mind somewhere below the surface. The tones seemed to be on almost all the time, so that flow was not interfering with alpha, even though it was visual. But occasionally a thought would push to the top of my mind: What am I doing? How am I doing this? Such thoughts were insistent, even if they were brief, and they made something in my head tense. At those moments the tone went off. I would be disoriented for a moment, then sink back into the soft nothingness with flowing pictures below, and hear the tone come back on again.

"Now try to keep the tone off," Kamiya's voice said. I summoned vivid visual images, but they did not drive the sound away. I tried nightmare figures, monsters, horror scenes. Still the tone was there. I began counting to ten, visualizing each number big and fat, letting it pass from background to foreground diagonally before my closed eyes. That worked for a little while, then again I lost control. I tensed deliberately, but the tone kept sounding, like a persistent mosquito. I tried multiplication tables and added columns of numbers. That worked as long as I visualized the numbers very clearly. But I could not make myself visualize that clearly for long, and the tone would burst forth again. Next I visualized writing, slowly tracing letters hard and fat with a heavy pencil. The tone decreased, came more softly and sporadically.

As the trials were repeated, I felt myself going deeper and deeper—not far out, as some people had described it, but deep in. Kamiya gave me a score every once in a while. The numbers grew but I barely heard them. I listened to the tone without focusing on it, as if listening beyond it. It was a pleasurable and sensuous experience to keep on alpha. To keep it off was hard work. When the experiment ended, I was sorry.

During three more sessions, I learned to control the tone to a much greater degree. It stayed on, I discovered, when my mind was somehow between things, floating. It went off with grim, harassed concentration. My scores rose twice above the base-line level which was partly, Kamiya told me, the result of my being a person with a normally high alpha rhythm.

W. Grey Walter, in *The Living Brain,* states that the amount of alpha rhythm may be correlated with different ways of perceiving and thinking. People with persistent alpha tend less toward visual imagery and more toward auditory, kinesthetic and tactile perception. People with no significant alpha rhythm think almost entirely by means of visual imagery. Those whose alpha rhythm is blocked by visual imagery—about two-thirds of people surveyed—would fall between the two categories. Walter suggests that many misunderstandings might be the product of brainwave differences. He speculates that the day may come when alpha types will be considered in the choice of diplomats for delicate negotiations.

Kamiya has made only tentative observations on personality differences associated with degree of alpha but believes that people with a lot of alpha tend to be more open, receptive and gregarious. The degree of alpha varies within an individual also, he has found, depending on his state of mind. Anxiety and agitation seem to cut down on alpha rhythm.

Dr. Barbara Brown, who followed Joe Kamiya's lead in studying brainwave pattern control at Sepulveda Veterans Hospital in California, found that people can also be taught to control their beta and theta rhythms. Her preliminary results show that beta is associated with tension and anxiety, theta with daydreaming and uncertainty, alpha with pleasure and relaxation.

Eventually, turning on alpha might become a way for people to fight subliminal commercials, jet noises, and the tensions generated by urban overcrowding. The research pioneered by Joe Kamiya is another thrust toward inner freedom. "We will learn to cut off the outside world," Kamiya says, "or to make music of what comes in." Turning on alpha might become a part of every child's schooling. Spankings might be administered to those who allow their beta or theta to run on in class.

Kamiya believes that we may progress toward a better, more peaceful world as we learn more about the way the mind works. Therefore, he told me, he is especially enthusiastic about the possibility of "specifying human consciousness by mapping the objective dimensionality of subjective space."

"If we look at a tractor," he explained, "we may agree about the description because it's out there, in front of both of us. But when we look at a person in ecstasy we look into ourselves and postulate what is going on inside him. We get into debates because our specific of the property of ecstasy is so vague."

Kamiya is a pioneer in inner space science. There are others scattered through universities and research establishments in the country who think along similar lines. One place where many of them cluster is the Western Behavioral Sciences Institute, a think tank in pretty La Jolla, California.

Chapter EIGHTEEN

Turned-on Inventors at WBSI

MY FIRST reaction to the place was that it couldn't be serious because everyone was having too good a time. People were too relaxed and pleasant to be working. For surely a job—salaried employment—implied a certain amount of suffering and people who did not suffer while they worked were not really working. It was obvious the minute I walked into the breezy white stucco building that nobody was suffering much here at the Western Behavioral Sciences Institute.

Rosemary Ennis, the director's secretary, was not at her

desk. A man in sandals and bright print sportshirt motioned toward an interior courtyard where I found her sitting under a beach umbrella beside the swimming pool, talking with a salesman. She was a rosy-cheeked sunburned woman who looked about twenty-five. I later learned that she was thirty-six, the mother of five children.

"Staff meeting is in about ten minutes," she said after I had introduced myself. "Come along. It will give you some idea of the place."

I followed her to an adjoining building where a dozen or so casually dressed people sat in a circle on bright pastel canvas chairs and floor cushions. When another dozen or so had drifted in, the meeting began—without formalities, without visible planning, organization or agenda. It seemed more like a casual get-together in a clubhouse, where members tell each other about a week's adventures, then a meeting of an interdisciplinary research and development organization.

The reports that were given seemed of equal interest to all. Everyone, from typists on up, seemed to feel free to make comments. When the meeting ended, I felt that everyone had had his say and knew what was going on in the whole organization that week. This was clearly a highly unusual place.

Later, when I was having lunch on the terrace of a nearby restaurant with the Institute's director, Richard Farson, I learned that WBSI was, in effect, a model working community, an effort at what some turned-on people hope will exist in a future when work and play will be inseparable. Everyone does pretty much what he feels like doing and the total program evolves out of independent enthusiasms that relate to each other because the people relate to each other. The process is somewhat similar to that described by Ann Halprin in her Dancers Workshop, where individual self-expression leads to a collective creation. Members of WBSI staff meet frequently in truth labs and psychodrama sessions and are acquainted with each other as persons, not only as bosses, secretaries, colleagues, or whatever. All this produces an atmosphere of relaxed, enthusiastic busyness and explains the lack of that harassed look associated with people on a job.

WBSI is the turned-on scene's biggest connection with the mainstream of American life, for it builds many ideas now being explored in turn-on centers like Esalen or Morningstar into existing institutions like churches, families and schools. Compared to other "think tanks," like the Rand Corporation, it is tiny. In 1968, its ninth year of existence, its budget was only $750,000 and the staff no more than seventy. But its in-

267

fluence had already been felt because it speaks on vitally important issues.

Its scholars and social inventors are exploring and designing ways to expand personal freedom in a society where advances in physical and social sciences are leading toward ever-greater control. They ask: What makes change happen? How does one learn to live with it creatively and to prepare for it? How can the choice of control be maintained by individuals, so that every man may choose his goals and the means to reach them?

To say just that much about the place, however, is to say little. When it gets down to specifics, WBSI thinking becomes heresy to many academicians. For it advocates a kind of radical social democracy rejecting the notion that experts are best qualified to deal with social and psychological questions. Not at all, the WBSI staff say. In fact, often it's just the opposite. Children learn more from other children than from teachers; poor people may be better qualified to deal with poverty problems than social workers; prisoners know more about crime prevention than criminologists; mental patients are often more helpful to each other than is the psychiatric staff."

"There's too much reliance on an elite that is supposed to fix the world," Farson told me. "Every time you get an elite group they get professionalized and forget about the problem they're trying to fix because they get worried about professional standards and things like that. We believe that people can help each other particularly where they have hangups. Alcoholics Anonymous and Synanon have proved it. Our aim is to bring out the resources of people in any group that has a social problem. Right now about a third of our staff is engaged in a study of the community action programs of the war on poverty in San Diego. It's a three-year study for the Office of Economic Opportunity. That fits in with the theme of our work."

Research is only one part of the Institute's work, however. The rest is mostly model-building and social designing that is either linked with research or is what Farson calls "messing around and seeing what's what." Most of it is all aimed at helping people to help themselves without experts, or at expanding the possibilities of life for those not particularly afflicted with problems.

Much of this work has, in one way or another, involved truth labs or truth lab techniques. Two staff members, Betty Barzon and Lawrence N. Solomon, have developed a set of tape recordings that allow people to run truth labs without a leader. They were tested on clients of the Vocational Rehabilitation Administration and found effective. Bell and Howell is now marketing them as "Encountertapes."

Perhaps even more radical than such truth lab automation has been WBSI's experimentation with truth labs that have no guide at all. They were found to be slower starters than groups with a good leader, but had nevertheless proved beneficial.

In 1965, WBSI put on a thirteen-week show called Human Encounter on local TV. It consisted of half-hour excerpts, with comment, from an actual truth lab. Leaderless groups were organized to meet at the time of the program, Sunday noons. They watched the show and then continued with their own truth lab. WBSI people learned that, as a result of the program, spontaneous truth labs sprang up in churches and bars where regulars got into the habit of tuning in.

William Coulson, a philosopher-psychologist on the staff, has advocated the formation of truth labs within families and had been running one at home, with his wife and seven children, for three years by the time of my visit. The family set aside one dinnertime a week for what they called family meeting. During these meetings all normal house rules were suspended and everyone was invited to speak whatever was on his mind. The Coulsons found that this was a way to enrich their family life and become closer with their children.

"Once my son said—there were tears in his eyes, just talking about this brought tears to his eyes, 'Daddy, you and I are out there playing football and then the little kids come out with a kickball and you go play with them and you don't even ask me.' Now I had done that, but I hadn't been aware of it. That was something he would not have told me unless we had this special occasion when you could talk about anything," Coulson recalled.

"On another occasion the kids had apparently had a premeeting before the family meeting and one of them said, 'We don't like the way you holler at us all the time.' I said, 'What would you rather we do?' And they said, 'Why don't you try spanking?' So I raised my eyebrows and we said we would and we did. And if we hollered they reminded us and we had to agree that we promised we wouldn't. A few days later they called a special meeting—they can do that—and said that wasn't working. So we said, 'All right, what would you like to try next?' You see, this was really great. We didn't have to be perfect parents. We could be experimental and how they feel about it would be a factor, though Jeanne and I always retain the right to decide. They suggested standing in the corner and when that didn't work any better we had a fine system. We kept adjusting. Now we're back to hollering, I think. The point is, there's no perfect way to be a parent but thinking one ought to be perfect is intimidating to a parent. Now we can talk with our kids about the fact that we don't know quite what we're doing but can work it out among us."

At first Coulson thought of the meetings as an opportunity, mainly, for the children to speak up. But he discovered they were helpful to him as well. One evening he told his family, "I am concerned about the fact that I'm gone from home so much. I don't know what to do about it because I've got so much work to do." Nobody came up with a solution to the problem, but once it became explicit, he found, the tension it had been causing disappeared.

Most WBSI staff members believe that groups are most effective when they are built into existing institutions. When they are a special turn-on experience outside of the person's daily environment, they sometimes become disruptive to work and family relationships. It has been observed that truth labs, particularly when attended by strangers without their spouses, have a tendency to cause strain within marriages or even lead to splits.

Perhaps the most interesting and significant work with truth labs was being done, in 1967–68 by Carl Rogers, the best-known member of the Institute's staff, in a Los Angeles school system. Rogers is famous for originating client-centered therapy, which is also known as nondirective or Rogerian therapy. After a long career working with emotionally disturbed and neurotic people, he recently became interested in working with well-functioning individuals and exploring how what he has learned about therapy and human emotions can be applied to expanding the potential of people who have no particular difficulty simply making it in society. He became interested in the potential of truth labs in this area, and in their application in a school setting. (Rogers objects violently to the term "truth lab" because, to him, it suggests forced confessions and interrogations rather than the voluntary dropping of masks. He refers to the labs as encounter groups.)

Rogers advocates that teachers be replaced by "facilitators of learning," that is, turners-on for children. Such facilitators can be developed, he believes, through the groups. A teacher, he says, is a person who imparts fixed knowledge. Teaching makes sense in an unchanging environment. But we live in a world that changes all the time and knowledge becomes obsolete even while it is being learned. Physics this year is not what it was five years ago. Neither is psychology, nor history nor art. The goal of education, therefore, must be to produce people who can learn to go with changes. Schools should develop "individuals who can live in a delicate but ever-changing balance between what is presently known and the flowing, moving, altering problems and facts of the future," he said in a lecture given at Harvard University on April 12, 1966. "In the coming world, the capacity to face the new appropriately is more important than the ability to know and repeat the old," he continued in an article published in the magazine *Educational Leadership* in May 1967.

Therefore, he argued, the student must be transformed into a self-directed learner. For this, teachers must be turned into people who meet three conditions: They must be people being themselves and responding to students as people, instead of hiding behind their roles. They must accept students with "positive regard," seeing them as they are, as intrinsically worthwhile individuals with particular characteristics rather than as *tabulas rasas* to be filled with facts. Also, the teachers must seek to see how things look from the students' points of view, rather than simply judging them right or wrong. Once a teacher meets these conditions, according to Rogers, students become learners. The teacher then needs only to follow the current of children's innate creativeness.

Rogers' philosophy of education grew out of his discoveries in psychotherapy. He found that healthy growth in therapy occurs when the therapist is himself rather than a façade, when he is in contact as himself with the client, experiences "unconditional positive regard" for him, understands the client's frame of reference and communicates to him that understanding. He combined these discoveries with two others: that people who are more normal than neurotic gain the most from truth labs; and that they gain more from truth labs than from individual therapy. With that all in mind, he formulated a plan to transform a school system.

He was well aware that there was no shortage of good ideas for improving education. However, new systems often failed to live up to expectations. What was needed, he saw, was a change not so much in the system as in the attitudes of teachers and administrators. In "A Plan for Self-Directed Change in an Educational System," published in *Educational Leadership* in May 1967, he mapped out a project he wanted to try.

"A way must be found to develop a climate in which the focus is not upon teaching but on the facilitation of self-directed learning," he wrote. "Only thus can we develop the creative individual who is open to all of his experience; aware of it and accepting it, and continually in the process of changing. And only in this way, I believe, can we bring about the creative educational organization, which will also be continually in the process of changing."

His plan involved the use of the truth lab to change the educational climate within an entire school system and to enable teachers to move toward greater freedom in the classroom. "This has to grow out of a personal philosophy and conviction," he told me in an interview. "When teachers tried to do it as a method, it was just as full of flaws as any other scheme."

It was essential, he wrote, that at least one person in a position of power—preferably more than one, and including the chief administrator—would be willing to take part in a truth lab for a week, away from the place of work. Later, groups would be held for teachers, and for an entire class together with the administrator, teacher, supervisor and anyone else relevant, perhaps even the janitor. Later still groups might be held for parents, and some would include students, teachers, administrators and dropouts.

Through these truth labs, Rogers believed, teachers could become persons ready to help students in their natural desire to know, and the classroom would become a constantly changing environment where students would change, learn and grow. "This plan would result in the kind of educational revolution which is needed to bring about confidence in the *process* of learning, the *process* of change, rather than in static knowledge," Rogers wrote. He concluded: *"Any takers?"*

There were takers. Among them were a couple of nuns from the Immaculate Heart School System in Los Angeles. Rogers told them no, he preferred to work with a public school system. Besides, he said, Catholic schools in California were generally not as good as public schools and he wanted to work with good schools to make them still better. But the two nuns kept talking and eventually persuaded him. He was swayed partly by their enthusiasm, the enthusiasm of their leaders, and the fact that the Immaculate Heart system included about eighty schools, from kindergarten level to teachers' college, and offered a broad and integrated setting for the experiment. The fifty Immaculate Heart elementary schools were scattered along the West Coast, in a wide variety of socio-economic neighborhoods.

The sisters were, moreover, an interesting group. They had several times come into conflict with James Francis Cardinal McIntyre, the conservative Los Angeles archbishop, for various innovations. One of their members, Sister Mary Corita, was nationally known for her art events, which she presented in many cities before the era of the happening. They usually involved the creation of an enormous collage of magazine cutouts, box tops, bottle tops, buttons.

Dr. Rogers made a two-year commitment to the sisters and began his program in the summer of 1967 with an $80,000 grant from the Babcock Foundation and a $30,000 gift from Charles Kettering II. He began to put the administrators, teaching nuns and students through truth labs. The sisters began to speak out long-buried emotions and to allow themselves to experience thoughts long submerged in prayer. Soon they were appearing at labs in civvies and Cardinal McIntyre pronounced he never wanted to see a nun in a miniskirt again. They went back to habits, then returned to civvies. By spring 1968, the transformation was in full swing, the Cardinal ordered it stopped, the sisters appealed to the Vatican, and a special commission was appointed by the Pope to find out what was going on in Los Angeles.

Rogers is quite accustomed to causing revolution. He is a legend at the University of Chicago and the University of Wisconsin, for holding classes in which he expected students to take the initiative. At WBSI, where he came despite much more prestigious offers from academic centers, he hopes to do a great deal more. Indirectly, he played an important part in the Institute's founding. That story really began when Rogers met Farson in the late 1940s.

Farson, who (as every reporter who interviews him feels compelled to point out) looks like a young Cary Grant, had planned to be a school psychologist until he flunked practice teaching at the University of California, Los Angeles. This was an occurrence that, years later, still caused him wonderment. "I was sort of the fair-haired boy of the education department," he told me. "I thought I was very good at practice teaching, and the kids did too, I think. But the supervisor and the teacher I worked with did not think so. I fell down on things like forgetting to open the transoms. Or something like this: when a kid was tardy, you were supposed to make a line across a square by his name in the book. If he shows up, then you put a vertical line down to make a "T" out of it. One of the things the teacher I worked with didn't like was that my horizontal mark—for absence—was not high enough in the square so that if the kid came in it would make a nice 'T.' It was that sort of thing that absolutely stunned me. I was an A student in my education courses and my kids got better grades on standard tests than regular teachers' students did. I don't know—it was like a war. I think there were six hundred education students doing practice teaching and I was the only one who failed.

"So that kind of shot me down and I went back to life-guarding, which I had done some time back. Then I read someplace that Carl Rogers was coming to Occidental College to teach a summer session. I don't know what he did, but he really turned me on. He just made me feel like I was okay and had something to contribute. He liked me too and asked me to come and study with him at the University of Chicago."

Farson received a doctorate in psychology from the University of Chicago in 1955, spent two years in the Navy, then set up practice in La Jolla and started a consulting firm with Tom Gordon, one of his former professors at Chicago. In 1958, Gordon and Farson organized a conference on group dynamics that featured Carl Rogers. One of those who attended and also was turned on by Rogers was Paul Lloyd, a physicist and mathematician who had become depressed by academic institutional life, left the California Institute of Technology and was living on a nearby cattle ranch, in near isolation.

As a result of that meeting between Rogers, Farson and Lloyd, Lloyd sold two-thirds of his cattle ranch and provided the seed money to launch WBSI as a center for the study of the group dynamics and inter-personal relations. Then Lloyd began on a new project, the building of a diadic logic, which would take into account the simultaneous existence of opposites.

Some of the first studies the Institute did were of a standard behavioristic model. In one early experiment, having to do with the reduction of tension, a fingerprint device was used to measure sweating. In another, the experimenters wanted to see whether they could turn a withdrawn person into an active participant in a group by giving him positive reinforcement. A group, subjects of the experiment, sat around a table while the experimenters watched through a one-way glass. Those in the group were told that he would see a button light up in front of him when the experimenters thought they were doing well. Each button was visible only to the person concerned. The experimenters gave the most timid soul in the group the most flashes and found—as they had expected to find—that he began to speak up more often.

That study, however, was the last on this sort of model, for it led the WBSI people to a shocking discovery: the way they had designed the experiment blinded them to something unexpected in the results. They learned this later, when someone at Stanford University did a study on a study similar to theirs. For it had turned out that not only did the quantity of that timid person's group participation improve—so did the quality. The experimenters were looking for only one thing and missed something else that happened even though it was apparent to those who were not clued in to their purpose and therefore had no set expectations.

"So you see," Dick Farson said, "you do research in this vein and you get something you don't even understand. I will never do that kind of experiment again personally. We no longer do much lab research where you put people into situations that aren't natural to them. We go where they are, watch them, talk with them, try to create conditions that will evoke their best so we can see that."

Another way Farson describes this approach is that it involves using the goal as the means. "This idea comes from the civil rights movement," he told me. "I used to think that the important thing about the sit-ins was that they showed the power of nonviolence. But they also showed us how to create the future by using the goal as the means. Arthur Waskow of the Institute for Policy Studies pointed this out to me. Instead of using a letter to the editor or a petition to get a Negro into a restaurant, they used the Negro in the restaurant. The hippies did this too. They did not drop out. They invented a new society by putting democratic and religious values first instead of talking about the fact that such a thing should happen. Now I see that sort of thing happening in many places, including here where, instead of making artificial models, we make real ones."

Rogers' program is one such model. Others are less systematic and more in the class of what Farson calls "messing around." All of them, however, are designed to give people a chance to develop their potential in some way and to increase their ability to determine their own future.

"It has often struck me that the science of psychology, as it exists today, could be very useful to a dictator who wanted to use the latest procedures, but would not be very helpful to someone who wanted to make his group or his country more democratic," Carl Rogers told me in an interview. "I don't think that's come about through anyone's intent. I think it's quite largely due to the model of science we've followed. For scientific purposes you're not a person, you're a subject, a statistic with a certain number of traits or responses. The interest is in prediction and control of behavior. Whom does that help? That helps a person who wants to control it."

The WBSI scholars and inventors see man as an aware being capable of choice, with an inner experience that cannot be separated from outward behavior. Together with others in the Human Potentialities Movement, they maintain that man has an inner nature and that, beneath all his activity, is the basic drive to actualize that nature. They seek ways that would help him to do so.

The social designing now practiced, Farson pointed out, is geared toward making people work faster, move more efficiently, buy more readily. But too little planning and designing are being done to evoke the inner nature of man and aid in its fulfillment. "What we need is designs that evoke the best in us," he told me.

"I think we are going to get much more democratic formats for society," he went on. "We have matured as a human race and have come to make new demands and have new expectations. Our survival and security needs have been met and now people are demanding higher order fulfillment. That's what this whole Human Potentialities movement is about. You are capable of much more than you think you are. You are capable of almost anything. That's what our psychological research shows. We know that I can put you into an experimental situation where you will give someone an electric shock that will knock him right off his seat. You'll do it deliberately and with full knowledge of what you're doing. I can put you into a situation where you'll pull a trigger and kill somebody you don't know. On the other hand, I can put you into a situation where you will form an affectionate bond with someone you thought you would never like. We can evoke these things from almost anyone."

The Maharishi Mahesh Yogi put it simply: "It is only necessary to rise to one's own glory." At the Western Behavioral Sciences Institute the message is the same but it comes with all the proper footnotes from people with correct academic credentials. It is therefore much less easily dismissed as naïve.

Chapter NINETEEN

Turning On

IT'S A cocktail party in the midtown office of a successful Manhattan designer, one of those scenes where everyone is busy making it. In the midst of conversations, eyes dart about checking who else is here and talking with whom. There's dancing to rock and roll music in one room. It's tight and jerky, very different from the style at the Avalon and Fillmore in San Francisco where people moved loosely in the music. Here they snap and stretch, bounce and grin, twitch like neon flashes.

A man is standing against the wall, glass in hand, blank-faced. He waits rigidly, not daring to begin. All around him are people, here supposedly to meet one another, but he is as alone as he would be on the corner of Broadway and Forty-second Street. I recall how years ago I sat on the edge of a fountain on the Columbia University campus, thinking that I'd enjoy talking with some of the passersby but never would. Our paths crossed daily but we might as well have been on different continents, so great was the space before the word, the look, the recognition. And yet, wasn't it just a matter of saying the word and meeting the look? And now here is this man, unable to get across that space even at this elaborate affair specifically designed for people to enjoy each others' company.

We go to the bar. A hulking bearded architect starts to banter with my friend Mel Moss, who also has a beard. They're into a conversation quickly but then the bartender hands the architect two drinks and he switches off in the middle of a sentence. As he walks off, to hand the drinks to two women, Mel has ceased to exist for him. Everyone is busy performing here, nobody is looking or listening. They're making it. Making what?

Outside it is snowing and the Christmas lights on the young trees in the tiny waterfall park on East Fifty-third Street light up the tense faces of surprised New Yorkers.

Dinner at Mary's. She's like a bird that flits hither and yon, lighting on subjects gracefully, delicately, then flying off dropping snatches of pretty declarative sentences that are never pursued to their further meaning. The dinner is a performance. It has been prepared with care. There is good soup, roast beef and three kinds of wine. The performance is the serving and eating of this dinner. All conversation is just table decoration. Nobody listens to anyone else. Has it always been like this?

So I'm home again now, freaked and flipped, zonked and tripped out, rolfed and massaged a little way into the turned-on existence. I have bits of yoga to offer friends who suffer from backaches or colds and mantras for those who cannot concentrate. I can recommend a new mind or sensory game and give a trippy massage to people who cannot listen or get frozen at parties. And what else? Something was missing in my life and yet it was there all the time, waiting to be discovered, as happens in all the bibles and fairy stories we've read as children. The son leaves the father's house on a quest. He travels to the ends of the earth and discovers that what he sought was right there all the time.

Yes, but he had to travel to get there for "right there" is everywhere and it only takes the very slightest shift of perspective to see everything the turned-on way—and the very slightest shift to flip yourself off a cliff. You have to move and take risks to find the elusive perspective that lets everything be what it is. You have to move in mind and pelvis and lumbar region, in trains and planes and senses and the brain to blast out of the net that makes the world suffocating. I'm not really back because this is not the place I left, nor am I the person who lived here.

A quick trip across the turn-on scene has, of course, not made me into some kind of a glorious superfreak. But I do understand a little better now how every event is woven in multiple intricate patterns that change with every change of point of view, and how each pattern has its own dynamic that you can choose to follow once you see it. The more patterns we are aware of, the more freedom we have to choose our lives. Let's say you tell me something and I hear two things in your voice—that you love me and that you are afraid. I too love you and am afraid. Now I can answer from my fear to yours or I can answer to love. My reply will determine the direction of our trip. Yours can continue or change it. Love and fear are together and we can choose either as long as we perceive both. And there are many more notes in your voice and mine—many more trips for us—if we can only expand our listening to hear them.

Self-games to help people perceive more subtly and thereby increase their freedom of choice have become so popular now, in mid-1968, that they are an economic commodity. Millions of dollars are spent annually on awareness techniques that promise to enrich the lives of middleclass people grown bored with the pleasures of affluence. There are now more than a dozen turn-on centers in this country and Canada modeled after Esalen. Their directors vie for the best awareness gurus. "I feel like Sol Hurok," the head of one such center told me. "I found this man who has really got something. I wish I could sign him up before someone else gets to him or steals his technique."

Self-game marketers and packagers have appeared. William C. Schutz's book *Joy* sold out on first printing. Its success led the publisher, Grove Press, to place full-page ads in various periodicals. One such ad, on the back of *The New York Review of Books*, described the book as a product containing "insights, exercises and little tricks that can transform the whole feel of life for you." Among these, the ad claimed, were "important exercises to do away with disabling aggression" and "a simple thumb-wrestling exercise that can relieve your agonizing doubts about self-worth." I cannot reconcile this piece of promotion with the complex and subtle way I saw Schutz work that weekend a year ago when he was relatively unknown. The ad told as little about Schutz as *Eye,* a glossy hip youth magazine put out by Hearst Publications, tells about hip youth attitudes. Both are commercial distortions.

However, such mass market phenomena are signs that interest in the turned-on life has spread. In California, where many trends begin that later move across the nation, two ways of life are now clearly visible side by side. It is not at all rare to see a man cross from one to the other. A wealthy man in the construction business gives land and money for a commune of assorted dropouts, including a teacher fired for stating publicly she smoked grass while correcting papers at night. A dentist goes to a workshop of Frederick Perls' at Esalen, returns turned on, grows a beard, begins to look at people as humans rather than dentures, cuts down his appointment schedule and takes up gliding. An accountant at Berkeley, a very proper man who belongs to the right civic committees and sends his children to Catholic schools, suddenly rents a house to a set of hippies and begins to bring home to his alarmed wife long-haired youngsters who need a place for the night. He is not the kind of man to ever do such things, neighbors say. Yet he does them. A police sergeant puffs on a joint in full view of television cameras and announces he can no longer prosecute people for smoking a vegetable. All these people, in their different ways, are opting out of the middle-class status race and choosing an alternate way of life with some different values.

In the East the turned-on attitudes are not as prevalent, but signs of them are appearing in many settings. A college professor told me that many of his younger colleagues are less concerned about making points that would raise them within the academic world than they were a few years ago. Instead, they seek to broaden their present experience. A Wall Street lawyer observed that starting salaries at some of the top firms in the financial district had risen to three times what they were when he took his bar exams ten years ago. The reason, he said, was not inflation. It was the difficulty the firms encountered now in attracting top law school graduates. When he made the round a decade ago, this lawyer said, he was competing with the brightest minds in his class. Now many of the most promising graduates see a job on Wall Street as a form of selling out.

Many young people grew up to find that making a living is easy if you're white, a college graduate and reasonably intelligent. They see more choices than their parents, who struggled through the Depression and World War Two. They care less about making a place for themselves in the prevailing social system and less about possessions.

For middle-class whites, this is a fat country. But the science and technology that created the new freedoms also created much more sophisticated methods for potential control over human beings. The biggest question now is who will do the controlling. We can follow the lead of Richard Farson, Frederick Perls, Carl Rogers, Joe Kamiya and Ann Halprin who would have us become more fully our own instruments. Or we can become instruments manipulated by others. We can follow Mike Murphy's vision of an inner space program to develop men of much greater mental, physical and emotional power and greater freedom to determine their own fate. Or we can allow ourselves to be turned into puppets with replaceable parts. Science and technology can be applied in either direction. Right now it is being used much more toward the latter.

Half a century ago, the idea of a heart transplant would

have seemed as unlikely as Robert Heinlein's description, in *Stranger in a Strange Land,* of a human being able to make people and objects vanish with pure mind power. Half a century from now, will we be more like Heinlein's super-turned on man? Will more people see meaning in the phrase "Thou art God"? Or will we, perhaps, have found ways to use drugs like LSD to turn troops on to the god in napalm?

The house is on a steep hillside in Mill Valley with a view of San Francisco's lights. We stop for a moment to admire the glitter, then ring. The door opens on the stocky silhouette of Maynard Dawson (all the names are fictitious). "Come in, come in, we're waiting for you," he says. "Everyone is here but Benjamin."

We step into the aroma of incense and the sound of recorded sitar. The big living-dining space is covered with Oriental rugs. Copper pendants of elegant antique wall clocks glow in the candlelight. A golden Buddha glows on the white marble mantel. Candles have been placed tastefully atop low furniture, illuminating Chinese carvings, a large bright landscape painting, the faces of five people sitting on the couch, in easy chairs and on tasseled brocade cushions.

"What a beautiful house!" I say.

"It's real adobe," says the hostess. "We were so lucky to find it. The location is perfect." She's on the rug with her back against the couch, a Beardsley drawing in her black and white silk lounging pyjamas, the zebra stripes undulating around her in expensive feline elegance. Her manicured right hand lies relaxed on her drawn-up right knee. She smiles up at us. "I'm so glad you could come. I do hope Benjamin also makes it this evening." We take off our shoes and sit down on cushions. Nearby on the rug, refreshments have been placed on wooden breadboards—big cheeses, small square crackers and wine.

It's Maynard we've come to see, Dr. Maynard Dawson, the scholar-psychiatrist turned mystic through an LSD trip taken for conscientious professional reasons. Since that trip his house has become a gathering place for like-minded people, successful professionals who have turned on but not dropped out and who are continuing to explore the possibilities of psychedelic drugs. Recently they've been taking magic carpet trips at Maynard's—smoking grass and tripping out on the Oriental rugs.

The zebra-striped Mrs. Dawson draws deeply on a thin-stemmed copper pipe and passes it to the man in the easy chair to her left. He inhales, passes it to Maynard and leans toward the hostess.

"Last week I tried woodrose," he says. "It's a death trip. You see yourself in a coffin. Really, almost everyone sees himself in a coffin with woodrose. A weird trip, interesting if you've already had the others. But you have to be sure to take the poison—the strychnine—out. You can buy the pulp with the seeds for three dollars a packet in florists' shops—just say you're a decorator. But be sure to get the strychnine out." The man is a physician, he should know about strychnine.

"A death trip whether you do or don't," says a pleasant-faced dark-bearded man, one of the top real estate men in the Bay area.

"Let me show you something," Maynard says, passing toward the back of the dining space in his sock-clad feet. "I just made this last night."

He returns with another little pipe and passes it to Mel, who lights it and looks up at Maynard. "What is it?"

"Cured lettuce," says Maynard, with a pleased look.

"Lettuce! You must be kidding."

"No, it's true," says his wife. "I didn't believe it either at first but that's what it is. I bought the lettuce myself."

Mel passes the pipe to me. It tastes like marijuana but is very mild. "Grass?" I ask.

"Essence of marijuana. But you see it's lettuce. Do you think that makes it legal?"

The sitar sound is drowned in a burst of laughter.

"Oh, Maynard, you would think of something like that," says a plump woman on the couch. The pipe makes the round twice, then the hostess puts it out. Maynard is now sitting on the couch behind his wife, lighting a meerschaum pipe. The smell of good tobacco drifts over and mingles with the incense and grass aroma. We sit quietly a moment. Maynard's velvet shirt of irregularly checkered black and red pattern assumes slightly richer tones. The polished stone pendant on his chest picks up candlelight reflections. The experiment is a success.

"Tell me, Maynard, what is this about a group of people who went off on a mystical quest to Hawaii?" I ask.

"I don't know much about them," he replies. "I met them just before they left. There were about ten of them, some teachers, a couple of artists, I don't know what else. They had started meeting, a bit like we are meeting here, to talk over their experiences. After a while they agreed to leave their jobs for a year and go to Hawaii to seek more understanding and try to integrate their experiences. I had them over one night. I was particularly interested to see what they would say about an experience I had had about a week before on LSD."

"What was the experience?" I ask.

Maynard puffs slowly on the meerschaum and strokes the silk-clad arm his wife has draped across his knees. "I perceived what I can only call a latticework, a vortex-like latticework upon which sort of hangs suspended all of existence. And I was able to perceive that permeating the whole thing was a consciousness so beyond my ability to begin to approach that it was overwhelming. The higher I went the closer I approached it, but I knew that I would have to let go of my whole brain, to die in other words, to reach it. So I wanted to see if my experience paralleled any they had had. It did. When they came in I was sitting in the corner there and they all sat down around me in semicircles waiting to hear what happened. As I spoke some of them smiled and I could see that what was to me a revelation—they had been there. Then they left. I don't know how they did out there."

There's a knock on the door. "That must be Benjamin," Maynard says and goes to open it. A man in his thirties enters, dressed like a rich hippie. He has longish red hair, a small mustache, granny glasses, black boots that look tailor-made and an expensive well-styled leather suit. With him is a wispy girl in a microskirt with sleek short hair around a delicate face that is as pretty, still and vacant as a water lily. Benjamin is one of the top psychedelic drug dealers in the area. "We've got some stuff here," says Maynard. Cool King Ben. "Man, we're stoned," he says, "on cocoa leaves."

"That's cool, man, but we're okay."

"We were just talking about that group that went to Hawaii," Maynard tells him. "You know more than I do about them, Benjamin, why don't you tell them. Your wife and kids went on that, didn't they?"

"Yes, they did," he says, sitting down cross-legged next to the cheeseboard. "I think each individual in the community has a different idea of what the community is going to do. Even if they get it on the verbal level nobody can know what the other one is thinking because in the first place there is an interpretation between the thought and the verbalized structure and then there's another gap when the listener interprets what he thinks you are trying to say. You dig what I mean? Like it's all words. It has to shift beyond the nonverbal level."

He's stoned all right. He rattles on, very fast, tripping out on communication and semantics, veering off into what he sees as the great drug revolution. "Things are happening man, and it's all behind acid, which is now in the hands of some righteous dudes who believe they're on a god trip and that this is really a great chemical and it's probably the Host. Man, I was at the Alan Watts lectures years ago and I was trying to understand what this cat was talking about and then the first damn trip it was Zen, yin–yang, shit, you name it, you know. The Bible, the Koran, really hairy. I would go up on a Zen trip and I'd get on top of it and say, 'that's very similar to' and I'd start up another one. And one time I opened my eyes and everything was in these funny yin–yang symbols and boy, if you don't think that hung me up for a while, wow. Speed of light, wow, that was a trip, speed of sound. Sure is a funny world. I'm glad I woke up to it. I just worry about the others out there, some of them sure put out a lot of static, wow. . . . Wait a minute, let's go a round of that cocoa leaf."

Maynard, I know, thinks highly of Benjamin. He thinks Benjamin knows a lot of mystical things he has not yet come upon. But there's something in the way the dealer is talking, some kind of flippancy, that bothers me. I look at Maynard and see that he seems a little uneasy. I ask Maynard if he'd mind telling how he happened to take his first acid trip. He seems glad to oblige.

"I was interested in it because of some theoretical considerations about five years ago," he begins, filling another meerschaum. "It wasn't illegal then and I planned an experiment with chicks. Then I was overseas for a while, in a research center in Sweden, and there the problem presented itself of what laboratory project I should undertake. As luck would have it, there was someone on the staff who had had experience with LSD. So I got together with him and thought up another experiment, which had to do with schizophrenia. In the course of this I reviewed a lot of literature on LSD and heard a lot of subjective reports. Well, the more I heard, the more I knew I hadn't had the experience. We were going to make arrangements to have me take it, but with one thing or another, I put it off. One thing that stopped me was that I was just then engaged in writing something and my colleague at the lab told me of cases where people had taken LSD and suddenly seen that what they were doing was irrelevant and stopped. I didn't want to take that risk right then.

"By the time I got back the wave of hysteria about this had risen and a law was passed that was so restrictive that we could get no more of the drug to continue our research. [The government's policy was to become so restrictive that by mid-1968 only two institutions in the United States had permission from the National Institute of Health to do research on LSD. Yet people continued to take the drug illegally.] I began to see patients again and the thought began nagging that when some of them talked about the subject I did not know what they were talking about. So finally I took it. I was going to dictate some notes and see what I could observe about the effects on myself and afterward I was going to figure out scientifically what was what." Here Maynard is interrupted by laughter.

"Well, I won't go into describing the whole trip," he continues, "but it did not quite work that way. However, I was elated because I recognized what was happening to each of my senses in terms of many experiments that had been done in psychophysics. Toward the end I began to perceive planes, levels in all directions of universality. Then I realized that no matter through how many planes I looked, if there were a God I wasn't about to find Him because He'd be beyond the farthest one I'd see.

"After that I did not touch LSD again for months because I had so much to do. I had to jot down ideas. I had to check back through reams of literature. I began to look at certain mystical literature which had seemed like a lot of gibberish to me before. Suddenly I understood that somebody else had been there or further and that it wasn't gibberish, that they were just using inadequate words to describe something. The words got across to someone who had been there too. I had been interested in mystical literature as a young man but I had discarded it as bunk.

"Eventually I took another trip and this time I saw the continuity and a certain sense of immortality in life. I also knew that I'd have to die to really make the final leap to the supreme consciousness. Now, knowing that all these things I once thought meaningless and haphazard in life were not, I'm satisfied."

Now Benjamin says, his voice quick and jumpy after Maynard's slow reflective talk, "On each of these trips you were alone, right? If there were other people there, you were the only one who took acid, right?" Maynard nods.

"Well, let's say you concentrate on a piece of cheese and it disappears, okay? Fine. Okay. But let's say there are four people in the room and three of them concentrate on the fourth and the fourth begins to fade off into a kaleidoscope of space. If the three people buy the illusion and the fourth one feels he's drifting off into nothingness, there's no way of disproving it. When you get to that speed, see, the phenomena-proof relationship gets higher. It gets freakier. What you need to do now is trip with other people."

Maynard has been listening intently but a look of distress has appeared on his face. There is something in Benjamin's tone and approach that lacks respect for Maynard's religious experience.

"There are tricks of moving within," says Benjamin. "The answers are all within so the external circuitry has to be shut down. There are ways of triggering your mind. If you lower the sound in the room, with the sound vibrations being the guide, in other words, the hi-fi set would structure the room and it would become part of you because hearing is within. But it's also without. So then you lower the light level to where it will give you more of a floating thing. Two blinking lights on either side of you will keep everything in movement. With the music as a guide you can find that you can almost totally turn yourself inside."

Benjamin keeps talking and Maynard looks ever more distressed. For Benjamin is speaking like a technician who knows that if you push a certain button you get a certain result. LSD is stripped of mystery and fitted in with American technical know-how. Benjamin can package it and sell it on the mystical experience market. But Maynard is the Judeo-Christian scholar and seeker. Hearing Benjamin talk, he begins to question what until this moment had been the most important experience in his life. Could it be that Maynard had merely invented something he had badly wanted? Was his satori a delusion?

I remember what my acid guru said: "It's all in you." According to Humphrey Osmond, I've read, LSD produces a model psychosis from which "much or little can be learned, depending on the skill, intelligence, adroitness, daring and imagination of the model user." Like the splitting of the atom, the discovery of psychedelic drugs by the contemporary West has unlocked the potential for fantastic growth and equally fantastic destruction. We can now either expand our vision of what constitutes freedom or we can go toward a superperfected totalitarianism that will extend into every citizen's mind, body and emotions. The future we invent will either be one where people will grow up more like Heinlein's man from Mars—or it will be the nightmare future described by George Orwell in *1984*.

The difference between Benjamin and Maynard's viewpoint is similar to that which pits behaviorists against the Human Potentialities movement, users of tranquilizers against self-realization seekers. We have been going Benjamin's way for a

286

long time. But on Maynard's side is the power of unfulfilled yearning for something missing, a yearning which became so visible in the delight staid middle-class people experienced in the velvet-garbed beaded hippies and the songs of the Beatles.

Summer of 1968 is one of those moments when the bright and the dark are seen vividly together as the same thing. Congressmen are considering anticrime bills and housewives are learning to shoot in anticipation of racial violence. Martin Luther King, Jr., who said "I have a dream," is dead. The Poor People's March on Washington, which King had planned to lead, is camped in the mud at the foot of the Lincoln Memorial. It is a pathetic last gesture toward that dream, a final effort to use King's gentle ways of achieving justice. Behind the shantytown put up by the marchers looms the image of the Black Panthers, who say, "We have a dream —but we also have guns." The black revolution is splitting the country and spreading fear. Yet this ominous darkness is at the same time an affirmation of justice and a statement of faith in man's potential. The wrongs that created the Panthers and the riots have existed for a long time. But now they are recognized, in full anger, as wrongs that must somehow be avenged or righted.

Another revolution is underway in the universities where students have begun to demand the right to participate in their own education. On the surface their revolt might not look like the outgrowth of smoking marijuana but it is, at least partly. The basic viewpoint of the campus rebels is much the same as the viewpoint of those who form rock groups and call them Mandala, Clear Light, and the Moving Violation. They have all listened to a turned-on sound full of mystery and wealth and forbidden mind-blowing; they have all realized that any system is temporary and must change with the moment.

The world is transformed when one becomes aware of many strands in an ever-changing multiple pattern that makes up the moment. Psychedelic drugs have made the experience of transcendence available to the average Westerner. But with this experience comes the awareness of a conflict. The vision of oneself as a speck in a vast pattern had to be reconciled somehow with a sense of the importance of self. My friend David Johnson, who has been around the world and read more mystics than I ever heard of, couldn't make this reconciliation until one day he understood something that seemed to him the answer. "The infinite moment of intuitive perception can be interpreted either negatively or positively," he told me. "It is either an escape or an entrance, either self-extinction or rebirth. It is self-extinction for those who live only for the experience. For those who use it as a beginning it is rebirth." Seen that way, the freaked-out heads on Big Sur and in Morningstar Ranch, who have beautiful insights but never build anything on them, are engaged in self-extinction. So, perhaps, is Benjamin. But for some of the turned-on artists and gurus the same experience has been the base of a new life.

"If the doors of perception were cleansed every thing would appear to man as it is, infinite," wrote Blake. "For man has closed himself up, till he sees all things through narrow chinks of his cavern."

"It is only necessary to rise to one's own glory," said the Maharishi Mahesh Yogi, who still makes sense, even though he may no longer be the chief guru of the Western world. The glory is there and available with only the slightest shift of perspective. A shift the other way can turn us ninety degrees to everything else and send us back to some soul pool, or world pool, to start all over again. Nils' house is balanced on a cliff's edge, at the mercy of a building inspector. Lou Gottlieb is still the hip Don Quixote of Morningstar Ranch. What would happen if everyone realized that every point is the center of the universe? The country is flying toward its polarities. What will happen when the pendulum reverses and the opposites become one? Will they collide and explode? Will we all become Buddhas or will we blow ourselves up? In either case, there is only this moment, never to be repeated.